The Gardener's Guide
to Growing
SALVIAS

The Gardener's Guide to Growing
SALVIAS

John Sutton

DAVID & CHARLES
Newton Abbot

TIMBER PRESS
Portland, Oregon

For Deidre, my wife

PICTURE CREDITS

Karl Adamson pages 5, 9, 28-9, 38-9, 47, 54-5, 59, 66-7, 74-5, 86-7, 96-7, 114-15, 126-27, 146-47, 151, 152, 153, 154, 156; Marie O'Hara pages 3, 18, 20, 26, 44; John Sutton pages 24, 34, 68, 105, 142; all other photographs by Justyn Willsmore.

NOTE Throughout the book the time of year is given as a season to make the reference applicable to readers all over the world. In the northern hemisphere the seasons may be translated into months as follows:

Early winter	December	*Early spring*	March	*Early summer*	June	*Early autumn*	September
Midwinter	January	*Mid-spring*	April	*Midsummer*	July	*Mid-autumn*	October
Late winter	February	*Late spring*	May	*Late summer*	August	*Late autumn*	November

First published in the UK in 1999 by David & Charles Publishers, Brunel House, Newton Abbot, Devon
ISBN 0 7153 0803 3

First published in North America in 1999 by Timber Press Inc., 133 SW Second Avenue, Suite 450, Portland, Oregon 97204, USA
ISBN 0-88192-474-1

A catalog record of this book is available from the Library of Congress

Designed by Chris and Jane Lanaway
Printed in Italy by Lego SpA

page 1   *S. chamaedryoides* (p.94) forms mats of foliage above which the deep violet-blue flowers are held on slender stems.
page 2   The rose-pink flowers of *S.* × *sylvestris* 'Rose Queen' (p.62) are perfectly complemented by red calyces.
page 3   *S. viridis* (p.57) provides a bright backdrop to this bold planting, which includes polygonum and nepeta.

CONTENTS

INTRODUCTION

Which genus has the blues of gentians and delphiniums, the reds of geraniums, and can also provide pinks, yellows and whites? Which has leaf and flower textures to rival the finest velvets and habit varying from the smallest rock-garden plant to woody shrubs several metres high? Add to that a wide variety of leaf form and colour, diversity of leaf scent and valuable culinary and medicinal uses, and it cannot be unreasonable to expect that every British garden should be well stocked with plants belonging to the genus *Salvia*.

That this situation is not yet the case is due to the fact that a wide knowledge of the genus is still confined to a small, though fast growing, number of dedicated enthusiasts. It is also true that garden centres and most nurseries stock the merest handful of species. Yet the passion for salvias unites keen gardeners and nurserymen all over the world, from Britain to New Zealand, from France to California.

This book casts a spotlight on the diversity of *Salvia* species, and it will take any reader little time to realize than an enthusiasm for salvias can embrace the equivalent of three or four other genera. *Salvia* – one of the largest genera in the plant kingdom – boasts shrubs, as unalike as *S. officinalis* and *S. microphylla*, herbaceous perennials of extraordinarily varying appearance and stature, and some outstanding groundcover plants. There are also – as even the least interested gardener will know – members of the genus that perform outstandingly as bedding plants. Most readers will probably share my feeling that the ubiquitous scarlet

S. splendens is much overbred and overused, but salvias suitable for bedding plants also include *S. coccinea* and *S. farinacea*, both offering entirely different visual experiences.

Owners of greenhouses or conservatories can exploit to the full the fact that the genus has a range of species that are of real distinction as container plants: some of these are gloriously in flower through the most dreary period of the year, after the frosts have struck down most late-summer flowers and autumn colour has passed away into memory. By being able to grow plants under cover – even just one or two specimens of a range of species – the British gardener can have salvias in flower every month of the year.

Some individual species are outstanding for the length of their flowering periods. Perhaps the Mexican shrub *S. microphylla* is the most worthy of mention here: six months of flower each year is not unusual for it if planted at the foot of a wall with a southerly aspect.

Not a few species are grown mainly or solely for their foliage, and some of these look highly attractive for even longer than six months of the year. Deservedly among the most widely grown of salvias, *S. officinalis* Purpurascens Group warrants a mention here. There are, though, many other species, herbaceous as well as shrubby, which have fine foliage contributing handsomely over many months to the garden's symphony of texture and colour.

FLOWERS

Mention of colour must take us back to the flowers. The genus is extraordinarily rich in reds and blues. Pure intense red flowers are a feature found in species after species, and there is something particularly

S. pratensis Haematodes Group (p.64), which was introduced from Greece, is the most widely-grown form of the species.

visually exciting about them when foiled against green foliage. S. *elegans* 'Scarlet Pineapple' (syn. S. *rutilans*) is an autumnal glory in this category, while S. *coccinea* and S. *fulgens* are outstanding in summer. For warmer climates than Britain, S. *blepharophylla* must rank among the most attention-holding of all groundcover plants.

For blues, the colour of the flowers of S. *patens* provokes comparison with gentians, and there is no shortage elsewhere in the genus of blues of a purity and intensity that push the powers of written description to its limit and beyond. I have been spellbound by S. *chamaedryoides* in Somerset, and delighted by S. *cacaliifolia* and S. *guaranitica*, among numerous others, in my own garden.

The subject of salvia flowers ought not to be left without mention of their virtues in the flower vase. Although I have never seen inflorescences of any of

S. *fulgens* (top left) and S. *coccinea* (bottom right) contribute to this striking summer display in the hot-coloured border of a Worcester garden.

the numerous species of the genus offered for sale as fresh cut flowers in a florists, many do last well in water. For those gardeners who like to bring some of the pleasures of the garden into the home in this way, I commend the genus *Salvia*.

SCENT

Although salvia flowers are highly attractive to bees, it is true that most have little scent compared with, say, the rose or the sweet pea. In a wider sense the genus is, of course, renowned for its fragrances, which are mostly associated with its foliage. Many of these are delightful and alone justify the growing of the species concerned: S. *elegans* 'Scarlet Pineapple' (pineapple sage) is among the best-known in this context, while *S. dorisiana* offers a different, but no less pleasing, aroma. Be warned, however, that there are some fine species that have markedly disagreeable odours; these are much better positioned where accidental contact with them will not occur.

These are the exceptions, though, and the attractive scent and delightful texture of the leaves of many salvias should attract anyone who sets out to provide plants for the particular enjoyment of blind and partially sighted people. For texture, *S. argentea* is best known; *S. canariensis* and *S. verticillata* also have foliage that is a sensuous pleasure to handle.

Just exactly when mankind first began to enjoy salvias for their scent, flowers and foliage, it is quite impossible for us to know. Indeed it is very likely that the evolutionary ancestors of *Homo sapiens* had an appreciation of them. The first records of the genus are to be found in the architectural and literary legacy of the Mediterranean pre-Christian cradle of Western civilization. These give the earliest indications of how valued a few members of the genus were in the alleviation of injuries and ills. Some have a time-honoured place in the history of human diet, too, and sage's use as a culinary herb survives to this day.

Although it is unlikely that many people will read this book primarily because of the historic role of the genus in medicine and in the kitchen, it is only right that we should be reminded of the first interest of mankind in the plant kingdom which surrounded and sustained him. In a world of space exploration and information technology, it is not amiss to remember that by it we are surrounded and, ultimately, sustained still.

A NOTE ABOUT THIS BOOK

Although there are about 900 species of salvia worldwide, it is not surprising that not all are worthwhile for growing in gardens. Many will not survive winter outdoors in cooler climates such as that of the British Isles. For these, greenhouse conditions are needed to maintain them from one growing season to the next. The book features the 90 species and their cultivars that I consider to be the most garden-worthy in Britain; they should all do well in most gardens given a little care.

Almost half the species described are hardy; the remainder will flourish outdoors under suitable conditions in summer. They are also the species most widely available in Britain.

The species are divided into four chapters: annuals (p.47), hardy herbaceous perennials (p.59), half hardy herbaceous perennials (p.81), and shrubs (p.109), each beginning with a list of the species it contains.

Within each chapter the species are organized into groups, featuring the species of major significance first rather than being in alphabetical order.

DESCRIPTIONS

The descriptions of the individual species include information on habit, plant size at maturity, the stems, foliage, inflorescence and flowers. Botanical terms are kept to a minimum, but those I have used are defined in the glossary on p.151.

I have tried to avoid going into needless detail. For this reason, most leaf descriptions omit mention of petioles (leaf stalks) even though the leaves do have stalks, unless otherwise stated, and the shapes of the bases and tips of leaf-blades are not generally included. The lengths of leaves given are for the leaf-blade only. Bracts and calyces are not generally described. Similarly, the particulars of inflorescences have often been presented in simplified form. (Anyone specially interested in more detailed botanical descriptions of almost all the salvia species dealt with here should consult the Royal Horticultural Society's *New Dictionary of Gardening* or *European Garden Flora*, Vol. 6.)

Where a species or cultivar has an Award of Garden Merit from the Royal Horticultural Society, this is shown by the letters AGM after its name. If the award was made as a result of the large comparative trial of the genus at the RHS gardens at Wisley in 1995–96, then the year of the award – 1996 – is also given; 27 salvias were awarded AGMs in the trial. Awards made in previous years are indicated by the letters AGM alone; most were made by agreement within the appropriate committee of the RHS, and such agreements are reached on the basis of members' accumulated experience of the garden performance of the plant over a period of years.

1
BOTANY

*S*alvia is one of the largest of all plant genera, approaching a thousand species in all. Among the few that outdo it numerically are *Acacia* with about 1200 species, *Solanum* with about 1400, and *Euphorbia* with around 2000.

The plant family to which *Salvia* belongs is Labiatae, the mint family, for which a more modern alternative name, Lamiaceae, is also used. The genus *Salvia* accounts for about one sixth of all the species in the family. Among other genera of garden value are *Ajuga* (bugle), *Glechoma* (ground ivy), *Lamium* (deadnettle), *Monarda* (bergamot), *Nepeta* (catmint), *Perovskia*, *Stachys* and *Teucrium*. There are also many of our best-known aromatic herbs in the family, notably *Hyssopus* (hyssop), *Lavandula* (lavender), *Mentha* (mint), *Origanum* (marjoram), *Rosmarinus* (rosemary), *Satureja* (savory) and *Thymus* (thyme).

The Labiatae family is partially characterized by flowers in which all the petals are fused into a 2-lipped corolla. The flowers exhibit bilateral symmetry (see illustration below), meaning that it is only possible to cut them into precisely identical halves by making the cut in one particular position. The opposite to this type of symmetry is radial, where any vertical cut that passes through the centre of the flower will result in identical halves, as in a rose or tulip, for example.

Although other plant families also have bilaterally symmetrical flowers – Leguminosae, the pea family, being one such – Labiatae are distinguished from them by a number of other features, such as square stems, opposite leaves (opposing pairs at each stem joint) and the ovary being positioned above the corolla and calyx and developing into a 4-lobed fruit with one seed in each lobe.

LEFT *S.* × *sylvestris* 'Viola Klose' is the dwarfest of the widely-grown cultivars of this species.

BELOW A section of a typical salvia flower showing its structure, and a selection of stamens showing the elongation in the connective that is characteristic of the genus.

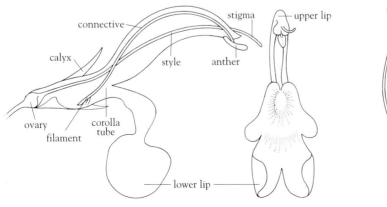
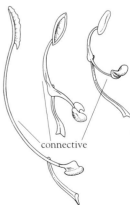

STEM CROSS SECTION

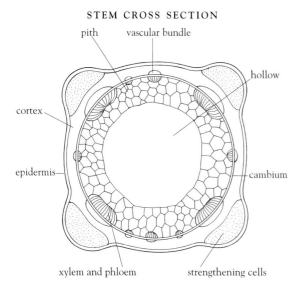

A cross-section of a salvia stem showing the square construction with its strengthened corners.

The square cross section of the stem is a feature shared with only a few other families such as Scrophulariaceae, the foxglove family, which includes genera such as *Antirrhinum*, *Hebe*, *Nemesia* and *Verbascum*. The reason for the otherwise universal round stems in higher plants is their superior strength and flexibility. The square stem shape is, as a matter of engineering, inherently less strong, but in practice each of the four corners is powerfully strengthened by a zone of thick-walled cells (see illustration above).

Features that differentiate the Labiatae from Scrophulariaceae are the inflorescences, described a little later, the widespread presence of glands containing oils, which are generally aromatic, and the presence – in almost all genera – of four stamens in each flower: *Salvia* happens to be one of the few genera in this family with only two stamens. Although in the flowers of many *Salvia* species there are also two staminodes (stamen-like structures), these are sterile and often quite rudimentary, as though, in its evolution, the genus has advanced beyond the need for four stamens.

The number of stamens distinguishes *Salvia* from almost all other genera in the family. The only other well-known members sharing this feature are *Monarda* (bergamot) and *Rosmarinus* (rosemary). The stamens of *Salvia* differ from these two in that the connective –

the part in a stamen that connects the lobes of the anther at the point of attachment to the filament – is characteristically elongated (see illustration p.11).

Salvia species are native to all continents of the world. Well over half of them are American, and nearly a third – not far from 300 – are found in the wild in Mexico. Most of the Mexican species are endemic (not found elsewhere). The second largest concentration of species is found around the Mediterranean and includes the common sage, *S. officinalis*, and Greek sage, *S. fruticosa*. Other species are native to the Indian sub-continent, especially in the southern foothills of the Himalayas, while yet further east more are native to China and Japan. There are two British natives – *S. pratensis* and *S. verbenaca*.

PLANT HABIT

The genus *Salvia* predominantly contains shrubs and herbaceous perennials, with only a small number of true annual species, and no trees or climbers. The dividing line between the shrubs and herbaceous perennials is blurred in many species.

A shrub is defined as a woody plant that produces multiple stems from its base, but – unlike a tree – has no trunk. Species such as *S. officinalis* and *S. microphylla* are obvious examples. A herbaceous perennial, on the other hand, lacks woody parts and has no persistent stems: its growth above ground commonly dies down altogether during the winter, while its survival from one growing season to the next is assured by an underground rootstock or by rhizomes (as in *S. uliginosa*), or, in a few species, by tuberous roots (as in *S. patens* and *S. reptans*). In some herbaceous species foliage may persist over the winter.

The separation between shrub and herbaceous perennial is far from hard and fast in many salvias. Some shrubby species are able to survive frost severe enough to kill their woody stems down to ground level, and renew their growth by putting up fresh shoots from at or just below ground level. Beth Chatto records precisely this happening repeatedly with *S. microphylla* 'Kew Red' (formerly *S. grahamii*) in her Essex garden, located in a part of southern England with comparatively severe winters. To quote her, it 'always sprouted larger than ever from the stock'.

S. officinalis cultivars are sometimes treated virtually as herbaceous perennials by cutting all growth back to ground level in spring, once new basal shoots are in evidence. When cultivated in environments much cooler than those to which they are native, many species that are naturally shrubby accommodate themselves to autumn frosts by adopting the lifestyle of the herbaceous perennial. *S. involucrata* is perhaps the best example, since this Mexican shrub commonly overwinters in favoured garden situations in southern England, although all its growth above ground succumbs to frost.

Correspondingly, there are many species which form woody-based stems but are only cultivated in Britain as herbaceous perennials. In their native environments, and in countries with climates more similar to their homeland, these species survive over winter from one growing season to the next and behave as shrubs. The best-known example is probably *S. leucantha*, which is a familiar shrub in Mediterranean countries.

No true biennial species are described in this book (biennials flower for the first and only time in the year after sowing and then invariably die), however, there are a number of short-lived herbaceous perennials that may sometimes behave as biennials, and their survival from year to year is not predictable, even in the same garden environment.

Predisposing factors leading to the death of the plant after its first flowering include dry soil, low availability of soil nitrogen and, probably, high temperatures. The removal of inflorescences as soon as flowering comes to an end is a traditional prescription encouraging a perennial rather than a biennial life span. Commonsense suggests that this would be effective, but it is not a totally reliable method.

INFLORESCENCES AND FLOWERS

The typical salvia flower is shown on p.11; specific examples are illustrated on the right. The most obvious differences between species are in size, colour and shape. Colour is not a subject which justifies space here: the genus as a whole embraces reds and pinks, almost all shades of blue, white and, in a few species, yellow. Size is likewise an obvious matter, with extremes represented by, for example, *S. verticillata* and *S. patens*.

Differences in flower shape and appearance arise in numbers of ways, and add to the pleasures of seeing and growing more species.

FLOWER SHAPES

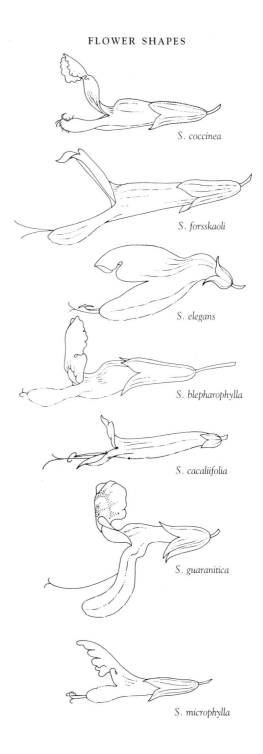

S. coccinea

S. forsskaoli

S. elegans

S. blepharophylla

S. cacaliifolia

S. guaranitica

S. microphylla

Flowers of a variety of species showing a wide variation in overall shape and the different angles of the lips.

A PAIR OF THREE-FLOWERED CYMES

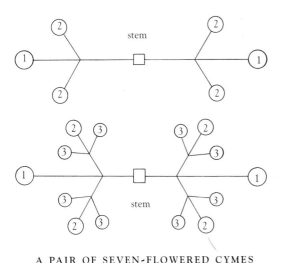

A PAIR OF SEVEN-FLOWERED CYMES

Simple diagrams of the development of false whorls. The numbers show the order in which the flowers normally open.

The upper lip of the corolla may be straight, being simply a continuation of the upper half of the tube, as in S. coccinea, S. blepharophylla and S. splendens. Alternatively, it may be nearly at a right-angle to it, sharply raised, as in many species including S. forsskaolii and S. sclarea. It is often hooded, a feature seen in S. patens and S. sclarea. The upper lip is usually shorter than the lower one, which has three lobes of which the two lateral ones are often widely flared, as in S. candelabrum and S. microphylla. Sometimes, however, it is narrow, rather as a continuation in size of the lower part of the corolla tube, as in S. splendens.

Salvias are good bee plants. Butterflies also often find flowers of some species attractive because of the nectar supply, but it seems that they rarely pollinate the flowers they visit. In their native habitats hummingbirds are important pollinators for some species, such as S. mexicana and S. regla. In North America hummingbird sage is a common name for S. spathacea.

The most common form of inflorescence for salvia is the raceme. In everyday parlance the term spike is more often used, but there is a botanical difference between this and a raceme. Although they are both of indefinite length and commence flowering at the base,

working up to the tip of the inflorescence, they differ in that on a spike the flowers are stalkless (sessile), while on a raceme they are stalked. The stalks of salvia flowers are often very short, but are seldom completely absent. The inflorescences of delphiniums, lupins and many Primula species, such as P. bulleyana, are well-known examples of racemes.

Salvias and other members of the Labiatae have their flowers in whorls, several arising from the same point on the stem of the inflorescence, rather than singly. The whorls may be close together, as in S. uliginosa, or quite widely separated, as in S. spathacea. In a few cases the simplest possible pattern occurs, with a single flower arising only on opposite sides of the stem. This results in a 2-flowered whorl, occurring in such species as S. patens and S. oppositiflora.

If there are more than two flowers in each whorl, their arrangement is not usually a simple one, in which all flowers develop simultaneously. The flowers are instead in a verticillaster, a false whorl (see diagram). On opposite sides of the principal axis of the inflorescence a pair of very small subsidiary inflorescences arise; each comprises a short stem terminated by a flower bud. From this short stem, between its base and the terminal flower bud, a further pair of stems arises, each also terminated by a secondary flower bud. The two opposite subsidiary inflorescences form a 6-flowered verticillaster in which the primary buds that terminate the original two stems open simultaneously and before the secondary buds on the subsequently developed pairs of stems. If you look carefully at the inflorescence of S. splendens, the common scarlet sage, this is the sequence of flowering you will find taking place. The simplest version of what is described botanically as a cyme is where each subsidiary inflorescence bears three flowers.

In many species this arrangement may repeat itself, with each subsidiary stem producing not only its own terminal secondary flower bud, but also a further pair of stems, each of which also bears a terminal (tertiary) flower bud. Where this occurs, each cyme comprises seven flowers (one primary, two secondary and four tertiary). The pair of cymes (or the verticillaster) arising from the same point on the main inflorescence axis together comprise 14 flowers. These many-flowered cymes are often not perfectly regular, and the number of flowers can be between six and fourteen.

If the diagram (p.14) and the account above seem hard to understand, the inflorescences of *S. candelabrum* or *S. interrupta* are very good ones to look at, because in these species each flower in the cyme is borne on a long stem, well clear of the inflorescence axis. Hence the pattern of development of a cyme is easy to see. In most species the cymes are intensely compressed, with the flower stalks usually very short.

BRACTS

Bracts are notable features of the inflorescences of many species. These are leaf-like organs that sheath the whorls of flower buds in the earlier stages of their development. In some species they are very conspicuous: among the best-known examples are *S. sclarea* (clary) and *S. viridis* (syn. *S. horminum*) in which the bracts are a major attraction.

FLOWERING

The flowering of many species is largely controlled by day-length, as is indeed very common in plants that flower naturally in autumn, such as Michaelmas daisies and greenhouse chrysanthemum cultivars. The plants concerned are unable to commence forming flower buds until the day-length falls below a certain number of hours. This is why many of the Mexican species only begin to flower in Britain when the first frosts of autumn are due within a very short time. The actual number of hours is unknown for most species, and varies from one species to another. Once that threshold of declining day-length has been crossed, the actual period of time before the flowers themselves begin to open will also vary according to species as well as to conditions. This variation accounts for some species beginning to flower impossibly late for successful outdoor culture in most gardens in Britain, for example *S. elegans* 'Scarlet Pineapple' (widely known as *S. rutilans*), *S. gesneriiflora* and *S. madrensis*. Others, though still reacting to day-length in the same basic way, do begin to flower sufficiently early in the autumn to make them well worthwhile growing, with perhaps six or eight weeks' flowering on average before frost terminates the display. Examples include *S. spathacea* and *S. splendens* 'Van Houttei'.

If you propagate half hardy and tender salvia species by taking cuttings late in summer, and overwinter the resulting young plants in a greenhouse, it is a common experience to have some display of flowers at the end of the winter and in spring. This is because, in the protective environment of the greenhouse, the flower buds have developed in late winter, at a time when day-length is still relatively short. Flowering on these plants does not continue into the summer because the increasing day-lengths of spring eventually make it impossible for the plants to develop more flower buds. Their growth then becomes entirely vegetative until the shorter daylight hours of late summer enable them to recommence flower initiation.

S. splendens when originally brought into cultivation commenced flowering only in early autumn, as its variety 'Van Houttei' still does. Nearly all of the bedding varieties of *S. splendens* that we know today are the result of a long process of selection of seed-raised plants that were less affected by day-length. The eventual outcome has been what are termed 'day-length neutral' varieties, meaning that they are able to develop flower buds and flower in days of any length. Before such varieties existed, some American commercial growers, who produced salvias in pots for sale, artificially shortened the day-lengths in which their plants grew, to induce earlier flowering. This was achieved with screens of black cloth, drawn into place early each evening and not removed until well after sunrise the following day. Just as most cultivars of *S. splendens* no longer respond to day-length in the same way as the original species, similar variability can also occur in other salvias. For example, there is a selection of the notoriously late-flowering *S. azurea* that flowers from early summer onwards in the USA. In the species *S. guaranitica*, deservedly popular in Britain, the cultivar 'Blue Enigma' is much earlier flowering than the more vigorous 'Black and Blue'.

HAIRS AND AROMATIC OILS

Most salvia species are more or less hairy, and many are very hairy indeed: *S. argentea*, *S. aethiopis* and *S. sclarea* are a few examples among many. Among the functions of plant hairs is the reduction of water loss from non-woody tissues above ground. The hairiness of many salvias accords with their natural habitats, which are characteristically dry for substantial periods during the annual growth cycle.

In many salvia species, a proportion of the hairs is glandular: some of their cells are modified to secrete and store volatile oils, and it is these that impart marked aromas to the plant. The term 'volatile' in this context means of low boiling point. When leaves are rubbed, or even gently brushed against, some of the hairs are ruptured and the contents of the oil-bearing cells are released.

One function of this characteristic is to make the plant unattractive to grazing animals. Sue Templeton, the Australian National Collection holder (see p.145), has observed that rabbits seem to find salvias unattractive. Many leaf-eating and sap-sucking insects are also repelled by some of the constituents of volatile oils. The antifungal and antibacterial activity of other constituents may protect the leaf and stem tissues.

The glandular hairs develop from apparently normal cells in the epidermis of leaf or stem, just as do ordinary non-glandular ones. Both types of hair have a number of stalk cells, but whereas ordinary hairs terminate in a single elongated cell, glandular hairs terminate in a rounded head. The synthesis and storing of the chemically complex volatile oils, which vary in composition and quantity from species to species, take place in these heads. In the larger hairs, an oil-filled space is found between the cuticle and the cells of the head. These oil-filled glands, protected by the thick wax-coated cuticle, survive drying and freezing with very little loss of their contents.

DIVIDING THE GENUS
SUBGENERA, SECTIONS AND SUBSECTIONS
George Bentham (1800–84), the great nineteenth-century botanist, devoted many years of his life to studying and classifying the Labiatae. During this time he produced what is still the only global account of the family, *Labiatarum Genera et Species* (Genera and Species of Labiatae), which was published in parts between 1832 and 1836. He considered the family:

'one of the most natural and distinctly marked of all. The opposite leaves, monopetalous corolla, 2 or 4 stamina, and the free 4-lobed ovarium are characters so easily observed, and so constantly accompanying the general habit of the whole series, that from the time of Linnaeus to the present day but two or three genera have been improperly associated with, or separated from, it.'

Content as he was about the integrity of Labiatae as a plant family, he had other views about its largest genus, *Salvia*. A modern definition of a genus is 'a number of species united by a common suite of distinctive characters'. This leaves open the question of when it is more appropriate to recognize each of two or more groups of species as a separate genus, sharing more closely their distinctive characters, and when it is more appropriate to recognize only one large group which embraces wider differences. Many enthusiastic gardeners are interested in – or at any rate aware of – such debates among botanists. Most of them will realize that the first policy is followed by botanists who are known as 'splitters', and the second by 'lumpers'.

Even by the time of Bentham, 'lumpers' had been at work on the salvias. Sixty years previously, Philip Miller, in the eighth and last edition of his *Gardeners' and Florists' Dictionary* (1768), describes what is now *Salvia* under three generic names. Fifteen species are given under *Sclarea*, five under *Horminum* and twelve under *Salvia* itself. Miller, obviously in spirit a splitter, at least for *Salvia*, wrote:

'according to his [Linnaeus's] system these [genera] may be joined together, but as there is a difference in the lips of the flowers, I have chosen to keep the three genera distinct, because they have always been known by their different titles both in gardens and shops.'

To return to George Bentham in the early nineteenth century, his deeply thoughtful words on the concept of a genus are still well worth noting:

'A genus, therefore, has seldom any real existence in nature as a positively determined group, and must rather be considered as a mere contrivance for assisting us in comparing and studying the enormous multitude of species, which, without arrangement, our minds could not embrace.'

This philosophic context stated, he went on to state that

'all [plant] characters taken from the organic structure of the parts of the fructification [inflorescence, flowers, fruit and seeds] have been considered generic.

'I have, however, made some exceptions: *Salvia*, for instance, according to the above rules, ought to have formed five or six genera, but I have considered that in this case the advantage in point of mere uniformity (for the natural grouping remains the same), would be more than counterbalanced by the necessity of changing more than two hundred names.'

Bentham's 'two hundred' should be seen in the context of the number of *Salvia* species known at the time of his writing, which was 291.

Confronted with what was even then a massive genus, he proceeded to divide it into formally described sections, on the basis of differences in the corolla, the calyces and the structure of the stamens. Bentham proposed and named 14 sections, the names of almost all of them ending with the syllable 'sphace', which is the classical Greek word for 'sage'. Examples include section 'Eusphace', in which he classed S. officinalis, S. fruticosa, S. lavandulifolia and S. interrupta; section 'Drymosphace' with S. glutinosa, S. nubicola and S. hians; and section 'Aethiopis' with S. aethiopis, S. argentea and S. sclarea. In section 'Calosphace' were placed exclusively American native species, already so numerous and so diverse in detail that Bentham further divided it into seven subsections.

Bentham had a very long and productive working life, and 40 years after his 'Labiatarum', he reduced the number of sections by two (to twelve) in his *Genera Plantarum* (1876). This great botanical masterwork, of which Sir Joseph Hooker was co-author, was the crowning glory of his working life, and is to this day a major reference work. The twelve *Salvia* sections were grouped into four subgenera, two of Old World species, *Salvia* and *Sclarea*, one of New World species, *Calosphace*, and finally subgenus *Leonia*, containing species from both the Old World and the New.

Botanists in the last hundred years have largely not endorsed the work of Bentham, or of those who developed his concepts later in the nineteenth century, in grouping *Salvia* species into subgenera and sections. Ian Hedge of the Royal Botanic Gardens, Edinburgh has criticized many of these as essentially artificial. However, among the small number of botanists who have studied *Salvia* classification seriously, there does seem to be agreement that the subgenus *Calosphace* is a distinct, natural grouping. Even so, the American botanist Carl Epling, who in the 1930s reclassified the species placed in *Calosphace*, criticized Bentham's seven subsections within it as 'rather vague' and 'arbitrary'. Epling's views carry great weight scientifically since his studies of the American species of the genus were profound and extensive. His formal descriptions of over four hundred of these are a botanical labour quite unmatched in the history of the genus.

In this huge genus numerous groups of closely related species can be identified, although in many cases the size of the group is very small. There is also a large number of species which simply defy rational grouping with others, and stand in isolation in any attempt at classification within the genus. An illustration of this is a study of the 59 species in Africa by Ian Hedge, published in 1974. His conclusion was to divide them into 23 informal species-groups, of which a number contained only one species.

NAMING THE SPECIES – SYNONYMS AND ALZIAR'S 'CATALOGUE'

The correct and clear naming of species is obviously in everyone's interests, and unfortunately the genus *Salvia* has more than its fair share of confusion: since 1940 S. officinalis, common sage, known and cultivated over thousands of years, has been scientifically described under six other scientific names; S. microphylla and S. sclarea, clary, also known and cultivated over a very long period, have likewise, in relatively recent times, been graced with five and six names respectively; and S. forsskaolii has been incorrectly called S. bifida, S. bithynica, S. bulgarica, S. longipetiolata and S. pontica; later chapters detail further name 'problems'.

So every salvia enthusiast should be aware of the monumental work of Professor Gabriel Alziar, director of the botanic garden of Nice, France. Over many years he has scanned the literature of botanical classification in order to reduce the confusion of names applied to so many *Salvia* species.

Professor Alziar published his findings in a French scientific journal under the title *Catalogue Synonymique des Salvia du Monde* (World Catalogue of Salvia Synonyms). He found that claims for over two thousand distinct species and subspecies could be reduced to under 700. With few exceptions I have used Professor Alziar's 'Catalogue' as the best available authority.

2

A HISTORY OF
SALVIAS UNTIL 1945

Almost all that we know about the genus *Salvia* before the eighteenth century has come down to us because of belief in the medicinal virtues of *S. officinalis* (common sage) and *S. fruticosa* (Greek sage). That belief was not unfounded in fact, since modern biochemical studies have established that some of the constituent compounds in the volatile oils that are characteristic of many members of the genus do indeed have antibacterial activity.

The use of the foliage in compresses for the treatment of wounds and injuries is recorded by a number of writers in ancient Greece and Rome, and their authority was widely respected by practitioners of medicine in Europe and the Middle East up to the nineteenth century. Those who wrote of sage and its medicinal properties, and whose writings have survived, are Theophrastus (c372–287BC), Pliny the Elder (AD23–79) and – most importantly – the Sicilian Dioscorides who wrote *De Materia Medica* in about AD64. His account of over 500 plants became the principal source in Europe of information on herbs and their uses until Elizabethan times.

Older than the written records, by over a thousand years, is the identifiable representation of *S. fruticosa* (Greek sage) on a fresco at Knossos, Crete, which has been dated at about 1400BC. This is another indication of the respect in which *Salvia* was held for its medicinal properties in the days of classical Greece.

The Latin name *Salvia*, was first used by Pliny and is directly derived from the verb *salvere*, to heal. And heal – or at least assist in healing – sage almost certainly would have done in appropriate cases: claims for its

properties other than healing, for example as an aid for conception or for 'bringing down the courses of women' or 'the treatment of epilepsy' are very much open to question.

It can quite safely be assumed that the Romans brought sage to Britain (AD43–410), and we have one piece of evidence that it was known and valued in Anglo-Saxon times. The Benedictine monk Aelfric (cAD955–1010) was a major literary figure of his day, writing in both Latin and Anglo-Saxon. In AD995 he compiled a list of over 200 trees and herbs, among them sage, in his *Colloquy (Nominum Herbarum)*. The monastic tradition of cultivation and use of herbs about which Aelfric wrote must date even further back. A ninth-century plan for the ideal monastery and its associated gardens shows the medicinal (or physic) garden in the form of a square comprising 16 beds, one for each herb included, one of which is sage.

THE HERBALL OR GENERALL
HISTORIE OF PLANTES

Around the beginning of the sixteenth century, sage was included in the 'Fromond List', in a cookery book, the property of Thomas Fromond, of Carshalton in Surrey. The 'List' comprises 138 'herbys necessary for a garden'. About 25 years later, sage was mentioned in *Bancke's Herbal* (AD1525), the first to be printed in English. The first enumeration and description of a number of *Salvia* species came in 1597 with the publication of the most famous of British herbals: *The Herball or Generall Historie of Plantes* by John Gerard. This work is a masterpiece for the grace of its language and the quality of its illustrations. However, much of its content was obtained, without acknowledgement, from an original work by Dodoens, a Belgian botanist.

Among the finest blues in the plant kingdom, *S. patens* is seen here with its cultivar 'White Trophy' and *S. viridis*.

In the herbal, Gerard described nine sages, four under that name and five under clary. One of the species is S. *officinalis*, and Gerard was clearly familiar with variegated forms, for he wrote 'We have in our gardens a kind of Sage, the leaves whereof are reddish, part of these red leaves are striped with white, other mixed with white, green and red, even as nature list to plaie with such plants.'

The two British native species, S. *pratensis* and S. *verbenaca* are also described, the former as mountain sage and the latter as 'Wilde Clarie or *Oculus Christi*'. The name in Latin is in recognition of the use of the seeds in removing foreign objects from the eye. Common clary, S. *sclarea*, clearly created just the same disagreeable olfactory impression in the sixteenth century as today, for Gerard stated that 'The whole herbe yieldeth forth a ranke and strong smell that stuffeth the head'. The other species described include S. *glutinosa* (*Iovis colus*, Jupiter's distaff), S. *indica* and S. *viridis* (syn. S. *horminum*, annual clary). The final two cannot be identified with complete certainty, though one is very probably S. *fruticosa*.

GARDENERS' AND FLORISTS' DICTIONARY

Our next major source of information, coming almost 150 years later, was the renowned horticulturist and botanist Philip Miller (1691–1771), whose great *Gardeners' and Florists' Dictionary* was first published in 1743 and saw eight editions in his lifetime. From 1722 to 1770 Miller was 'curator' (gardener) of the Chelsea Physic Garden, which was founded in 1673 by the Worshipful Society of Apothecaries of London. He had a passion for the introduction of new species to Britain and for the spreading of knowledge about them. He was a man for his time, as seeds and even plants of species previously unknown in Europe were then beginning to flood in, both from the New World and from Africa and the Far East.

In 1768 Miller recorded a doubling of the number of plants cultivated in England since the first edition of his dictionary 25 years previously. He communicated regularly over many years with the curators of the great

A late summer display in a raised bed with harmonious colours and contrasting forms in the bracts of S. *viridis* and the inflorescences of the verbena and the sedum.

botanic gardens in Leiden, south of Amsterdam, receiving them at Chelsea and visiting them in return, and they frequently exchanged new acquisitions. In the eighteenth century the Netherlands was still a great mercantile power, with many sailing ships plying the great trading routes to and from India and the East Indies via the Cape of Good Hope. New seeds and plants were sought-after cargo in both Holland and Britain. Thus it came about that among the salvia species Miller described in his dictionary are almost certainly S. africana-lutea (syn. S. aurea), from the Cape of Good Hope, and S. aurita, native to an area of South Africa that is a little east of the Cape. Any uncertainty is due to the changing of the way species were named.

Miller knew Carolus Linnaeus, the Swedish founding father of the modern system for naming plants, and became convinced that his system was superior to older ways of naming. In the last edition of his dictionary he adopted some of Linnaeus's names. In most cases we can be confident about which species Miller writes: some specific epithets are exactly those in use today.

Like Gerard, Miller described some salvia species under the separate heading of clary, Sclarea. Yet others are dealt with under a third generic name Horminum. In addition to those described by Gerard, and the two African species already mentioned, we can be certain that he included S. argentea, S. aethiopis, S. broussonettii, S. cretica, S. dominica, S. interrupta, S. lavandulifolia, S. mexicana, S. napifolia, S. patens and S. verticillata. In all he laid claim to 32 species, though the true total may have been a little smaller.

GENERA ET SPECIES LABIATARUM

By the nineteenth century the species known in Britain had become much more numerous. George Bentham, in his Genera et Species Labiatarum (Genera and Species of Labiatae; 1832–36), lists 291 salvia species. How many of these were in cultivation in Britain it is impossible to be certain, though the great majority were probably not. Nevertheless, the 1837 catalogue of John Cree of Addlestone Nursery, Chertsey offered 31 species, including S. azurea, S. chamaedryoides, S. fulgens, S. involucrata, S. leucantha, S. lyrata, S. napifolia, S. verticillata and S. microphylla (which was listed as S. grahamii Benth.). John Cree's catalogue, priced at three shillings – a very large sum for those days – was clearly catering for a clientele that

rejoiced in the pursuit of both botany and horticulture. Its cover tells its readers that the contents include numerous synonyms and references to figures in the leading botanical periodicals.

ENCYCLOPAEDIA OF PLANTS

After Miller's death, and 39 years after the last edition (in his lifetime) of his dictionary, a much enlarged edition was prepared under a new title, The Gardeners' and Botanists' Dictionary. Following its publication in 1807 there was then a lapse of almost 80 years before the next comparable reference work for gardeners was published. However, among the more comprehensive books for gardeners that were published during this period was Loudon's extremely popular Encyclopaedia of Plants (1822), which, like Miller's dictionary, went through a number of editions. The last, in 1834, listed 94 salvia species.

Loudon followed George Bentham in including in Salvia some species formerly separated in the genera Horminum and Sclarea. Among his species was S. splendens, which was introduced to Britain in 1822. Of the then best-known species, S. officinalis, Loudon wrote 'formerly of great repute in medicine [it has been] discarded from our pharmacopiae, but still used by self-practitioners and herb doctors'.

SEED CATALOGUES

Seed catalogues of the second half of the nineteenth century begin to show the emergence of some of the species that are still important to us as bedding plants today. By 1867 the London firm E. G. Henderson and Sons, by then already well-established and a Royal Warrant holder, listed nine species. These included S. coccinea and S. roemeriana (both recommended in the catalogue for bedding purposes), S. patens and – 'for the greenhouse only' – S. splendens. Among thirteen species, Henderson's 1881 catalogue, has, as a novelty, S. farinacea.

The enthusiasm for dwarfer versions of S. splendens (the height of which was given by Loudon as 3ft/90cm) is not new. S. splendens was offered by Henderson's in 1881 as three items: the species itself, S. splendens compacta and S. splendens compacta alba.

Sutton and Sons, then of Reading, was founded in 1806 and is, of course, still with us, unlike its nineteenth-century competitor, Henderson's. In its 1871 catalogue, Suttons listed *S. coccinea* and a dwarf form *S. coccinea pumila*, as well as *S. patens* and *S. roemeriana*. Two hardy herbaceous species, *S. argentea* and *S. barrelieri*, were also offered.

ILLUSTRATED DICTIONARY OF GARDENING AND THE ENGLISH FLOWER GARDEN

Two major horticultural publishing events occurred in the 1880s: Nicholson's *Illustrated Dictionary of Gardening*, the direct successor to Miller's great dictionary, was published in parts between 1884 and 1888, while the first edition of *The English Flower Garden* by William Robinson made its appearance in 1883. In the dictionary 71 *Salvia* species are described. The genus is especially singled out for its autumn- and winter-flowering greenhouse plants, with *S. azurea*, *S. cacaliifolia*, *S. involucrata*, *S. rutilans* (*S. elegans* 'Scarlet Pineapple') and *S. splendens* particularly commended. For spring-flowering under glass 'amongst the best' then available were *S. fulgens*, *S. gesneriiflora* and *S. heerii* (under its synonym *S. boliviana*). For use as a bedding plant, only one species is specifically mentioned: *S. patens*. It is described as 'one of the most distinct and beautiful of deep blue-flowered plants in cultivation'.

The English Flower Garden by William Robinson was to see 15 editions in the author's lifetime, the last in 1933. It reached a mass market of urban and suburban gardeners, and had a profound influence on them.

Robinson was an admirer of *Salvia*, writing that 'the Mexican species are among the best ornaments of the conservatory and greenhouse during the autumn and winter months, and others are exceedingly effective in our beds and borders during the summer'. The species for which he reserved special praise are *S. hians*, 'the finest of the hardy sorts', *S. patens* and *S. roemeriana*.

By the eleventh edition, in 1909, the number of species Robinson described had almost doubled, to 40. *S. splendens* receives much attention. 'For glowing colour in early autumn there is nothing to come near masses of *S. splendens* – much improved in its newer forms' and 'the most showy and useful of the family' are among his commendations. What had changed in the 26 years since the first edition was the introduction of 'good early-flowering varieties [of *S. splendens*] which come fairly true from seed.... These garden forms have all come by careful selection within the last few

years...[and] are vastly superior to the original plant, which, besides being of ungainly habit, has few and small flowers...'.

The dozen varieties of *S. splendens* he lists have all long since passed into history, but their successors, dwarfer still and even more early-flowering, are with us in countless millions worldwide. Perhaps the most famous cultivars of this species were 'Bonfire', and the rather dwarfer and earlier-flowering 'Blaze of Fire', introduced in 1939. 'Bonfire' has followed Robinson's varieties of 1909 into history, but 'Blaze of Fire' is still being catalogued, its long-established name ensuring enough demand to justify its continued retention.

The last edition of *The English Flower Garden* in William Robinson's lifetime was published in 1933. Rather strangely, the 40 species of 1909 had shrunk to just 13. It would be interesting to know why there had been such a cull, which included *S. argentea* and *S. involucrata*. Perhaps the genus began to seem less exciting to British gardeners because, by 1900, the stream of introductions of new *Salvia* species to British horticulture had slowed to an intermittent trickle.

None of the few salvia additions to our garden flora in the first four decades of the twentieth century were in the front rank of importance, though *S. flava* var. *megalantha* (syn. *S. bulleyana*), introduced in 1912, is arguably the best, in British conditions, of the few yellow-flowered species. *S. blepharophylla*, a 1930 introduction, is a Mexican species of distinction, but is unlikely to attain wide popularity in countries as cool as Britain, this side of a great deal of climatic change.

Looking at seed and nursery catalogues of the 1920s and 1930s gives the impression that rather few species would have been seen in gardens. The famous Loddon Gardens nurseries of Thomas Carlile at Twyford, Buckinghamshire, catalogued just three species among the '1001 best plants of 1925'. These were *S. sclarea* 'Turkestaniana', *S. uliginosa* and *S. nemorosa* (listed as *S. virgata nemorosa*). *S. glutinosa* and *S. pratensis* were widely available from other nurseries as were the shrubby species *S. greggii*, *S. microphylla* and Graham's sage (now called *S. microphylla* 'Kew Red').

The next major change to those salvias that *were* in British horticulture occurred after the end of the Second World War when a German nurseryman, Ernst Pagels, made his mark with species at the opposite end of the hardiness spectrum to *S. splendens* (see p.25).

3

PEOPLE, PLANTS
AND SOCIETIES

Salvias since the Second World War

The Second World War brought the development in gardening for pleasure more or less to a halt over most of the globe. The scope of activity in nurseries and seed companies in many of the combatant nations was controlled: fruit and vegetable production became absolute priorities, and in the British Isles maintenance of stock of ornamental plants was only on a scale to ensure the survival of species and varieties. In gardens everywhere space previously devoted to flowering plants was turned over to food production.

While most of the continental European countries were closer than Britain to national self-sufficiency in food, it was over their homelands that the closing stages of the war were fought. Nurseries, parks and gardens suffered damage and neglect both then and, in many cases, for a prolonged period after the end of the war.

The comparative absence of *S. splendens* from the gardens and parks of a war-torn Europe was, of course, soon put right. By comparison with its principal rival as a red-flowered bedding plant, the zonal pelargonium, the salvia was an inexpensive plant to produce. Severely restricted domestic and municipal budgets needed to take good notice of the cost of plants, and one fairly cheaply raised from seed compared well with pelargoniums (at that time always propagated by cuttings taken months before eventual planting out late in the following spring). In Eastern Europe red flowers were politically correct; there *S. splendens* was planted widely in municipal bedding schemes and other public open spaces.

After the end of the war, the first substantial new development that was significant for British gardeners came, strangely enough, from Germany. Ernst Pagels, a young nurseryman of unusual talents and great dedication, was beginning to make his way in life as a selector and breeder of herbaceous perennials. In 1954, from his nursery in Leer, Ostfriesland, which he opened in 1949, Pagels made the first of his salvia introductions. This was the cultivar 'Ostfriesland', which rapidly received widespread recognition as an outstanding hardy garden plant. Almost 50 years after its introduction, it remains among the most popular of hardy herbaceous perennials.

From the same nursery, later in the 1950s and 1960s, followed other fine cultivars of *S. nemorosa* and its hybrid species *S. × sylvestris*, among them 'Blauhügel', 'Amethyst' and 'Tänzerin'. As they were cultivars of easily-grown species that were already well known in Britain, Ernst Pagels' introductions rapidly received recognition. They were also popular in other west European countries with comparable climates. The four cultivars mentioned above all received the Award of Garden Merit (AGM) in the Royal Horticultural Society's trial of the genus in 1996.

Undoubtedly, these salvias would have become very popular garden plants in any event, but the context in which the use of herbaceous perennials was to develop in Britain saw two notable developments in the 1950s. In Norfolk Alan Bloom changed the course of his business in order to specialize in the propagation for sale of the herbaceous perennials that he had formerly used to produce cut flowers for the wholesale market. A man of energy and vision, he also pioneered the concept of island beds as an informal, pleasing and adaptable set-

S. misella, here thriving in the early summer in Provence in France, is a pretty species that deserves trial in cooler areas.

ting for their culture. The rectangular borders that had been the traditional home of herbaceous perennials in the garden began to lose ground, and in their classic form, as a pair separated by a wide grass walk, are now little seen in private gardens. Alan Bloom practised what he preached in The Dell, the large garden he developed and opened to the public, adjacent to his nursery at Bressingham. There, customers and other visitors were able to see – and remain able to see – the success of his ideas. Although not set up to provide a display area for any particular genus, it is a notable garden for the number of hardy herbaceous salvia species to be seen there.

THE HARDY PLANT SOCIETY

Alan Bloom was the prime mover in the founding in 1957 of one of Britain's most successful national gardening associations, the Hardy Plant Society (HPS). Although in a sense it was simply one more organization for enthusiastic amateur gardeners with a special interest, it was unusual in its dedication to a very large group of diverse plants. In this it differed sharply from those groups already well established and dedicated to a single genus, such as the Royal National Rose Society. In 1975 the Nottingham group of the Society took a remarkable initiative, which was to have far-reaching consequences for gardening enthusiasts and for the nursery trade and would eventually impinge on the availability of huge numbers of species and cultivars, including those of salvias: it published The Hardy Plant Finder, a successful attempt to make it very much easier for gardeners specifically interested in herbaceous perennials to find out which nurseries stocked which plants.

The first edition of this manual was a modest affair of 47 pages, but the venture was judged a success, and a second edition followed three years later. The third, greatly expanded, edition came in 1982. The burden of assembling and collating information, which fell on unpaid volunteers, had by that stage become very considerable. The continuation of the increasing effort required was clearly a worrying problem for the future.

Fortunately the success of the The Hardy Plant Finder had attracted much attention. Publishers could see the possibility of a profitable annual publication, and so The Plant Finder as it became known, came into being in 1987, its range broadened by the inclusion of trees, shrubs and, in subsequent editions, aquatics and rock garden and conservatory plants. In 1996 it received the endorsement of the RHS and is now known as The RHS Plant Finder.

Salvia has experienced a rapid burgeoning of species available in this country since the 1970s: the first edition of The Hardy Plant Finder (1975) listed just eight species, while 12 years later the first edition of its successor, The Plant Finder, listed 52, the sixth edition had 92, and the twelfth, published in 1998, a total of 168.

Without The Plant Finder we can be sure that this growth would have been much slower. Enthusiasts for the genus would have had a much more limited awareness of the availability of new introductions. Nurseries would have been much more sparing in obtaining them because of the reduced prospect of selling enough to make it worthwhile.

THE NATIONAL TRUST

The National Trust was founded in 1895 to preserve permanently places of historic interest or natural beauty for the nation to enjoy. It was not until 1948 that the National Trust took possession of a property which had gardens that were recognized as a feature of

major importance and significance in their own right. This property was Hidcote Manor in Gloucestershire.

Hidcote was just the first of many other such properties. The National Trust recognized its additional role as a guardian of some of Britain's finest gardens by the appointment of its first gardens adviser, Graham Stuart Thomas. His enthusiasm and guidance ensured that the organization increasingly attracted members and visitors whose interests were strongly horticultural. This trend was reinforced by the explosion of private car ownership from the mid-1950s onwards, and thus many Trust properties became the focus of people who wanted to see plants and to widen their knowledge of them.

POWIS CASTLE

Salvia species and cultivars, especially the hardy herbaceous perennials and shrubs, were and are widely present in National Trust garden plantings. A few National Trust properties have also had a special place in raising visitors' awareness of the half hardy and tender species. Coleton Fishacre in South Devon is one, but it is Powis Castle in mid-Wales which deserves special mention.

S. patens 'Cambridge Blue' (p.56) is a lovely pale blue version of this large-flowered species.

Not only did the former head gardener Jimmy Hancock grow species like *S. guaranitica*, *S. involucrata* and *S. patens* with conspicuous success, but by doing so he also showed that it was unnecessary to have a garden in a climatically privileged area in order to cultivate these fine plants successfully. Granted the terraced borders on the very steep south-facing slope below the castle have their own micro-climate; they are, nevertheless, on the same latitude as Birmingham and Peterborough. It could perfectly truthfully be said that many private gardens are, likewise, privileged because of the shelter given by house, wall, hedge and fence, and most of their owners do appreciate the fact that their gardening opportunities are greatly enhanced in consequence.

S. viridis (p.57) occurs in several different bract colours, three of which are shown in the mixture here.

PLATE I

SALVIA INFLORESCENCES AND FOLIAGE

S. canariensis

S. lyrata

S. azurea

S. sinaloensis

S. broussonettii

S. argentea

S. lyrata

S. africana-lutea

All specimens are shown at approximately life size

THE NATIONAL GARDENS SCHEME

The numbers of gardeners visiting gardens country-wide have been greatly swollen by the success of the National Gardens Scheme, widely identified by its yellow-covered annual guidebook *Gardens of England and Wales Open for Charity*. Many gardening enthusiasts who would not otherwise have considered opening their gardens to the public have done so under the scheme, and salvia enthusiasts have, of course, been among them. In my own home county, Worcestershire, the gardens of Terry Dagley, and of Tony Poulton and the late Brian Stenlake are salvia-rich examples.

THE ROYAL HORTICULTURAL SOCIETY

A national organization that must have a place in any account of the progress in public esteem of the salvia is, of course, the Royal Horticultural Society. Wisley has always been among the better gardens to visit to see a wide range of salvia species and cultivars. Additionally, it has been, for many years, world-famous as a site of rigorous comparative trialling. Until recently, a very few salvia species have featured in these from time to time: for example, cultivars of *S. splendens* were trialled in 1956, 1967, 1974, 1981 and 1994, *S. patens* in 1971, 1981 and 1994, and *S. farinacea* cultivars in 1971 and 1981. Outstandingly the greatest coup struck by the RHS for the genus as a whole has been the comparative trial in 1995–96, embracing all salvias except the bedders. No fewer than 236 entries were received, embracing 88 species. A remarkable total of 27 AGMs were given. A number of nomenclatural problems were resolved, at least one species – *S. spathacea* – scarcely known previously in the British Isles was brought to public attention by being among the AGM winners, and the trial became a virtual shop-window for a large number of other little-known species.

WRITERS

ALAN BLOOM

Writers about salvias have obviously had their part to play in raising awareness of their garden possibilities. Alan Bloom has already been mentioned in connection with his influences on the use and popularity of herbaceous perennials, and for his role in the foundation of the HPS. No book on herbaceous perennials could possibly exclude the genus and it received considerable coverage in his first book on gardening *Hardy Perennials*, published in 1956. This brought him wide attention among gardeners for his knowledge and enthusiasm for herbaceous perennials, and for his ideas on using them to best effect in the garden. An article by him on hardy salvias was published in the July 1980 issue of the Royal Horticultural Society's monthly magazine *The Garden*.

BETH CHATTO

Beth Chatto is one of the today's most respected gardeners, plantswomen and nurserywomen. As was the case with Alan Bloom, it was her first book – *The Dry Garden* (1978) – which drew attention to her exceptional plant knowledge and her innovative ideas on garden design and planting. In this she described 'the aromatic, drought-resisting [salvia] species from the Mediterranean regions' as 'invaluable in the dry, sunny garden'. The popularity of two salvias at least would certainly have benefited from the praise in her book, given clearly on the basis of affection and long experience: these were *S. argentea* and *S. microphylla* 'Kew Red' (then known as *S. microphylla* var. *neurepia*).

BERYL DAVIES

Both Alan Bloom and Beth Chatto founded nurseries in addition to their activities as writers. Beryl Davies was and has remained an amateur horticulturist. She nevertheless finds herself in select company as being one of very few indeed to write anything about the genus exceeding the length of a magazine article, or a relatively short section in a book about a much wider range of plants.

A lifelong gardening enthusiast and one of the longest-standing members of the HPS, her career in teaching brought her to Cornwall. There she played a very active voluntary role in establishing and maintaining the Probus Demonstration Garden. She also fell under the spell of the genus *Salvia*, her interest initially fired by her success, in her own garden, with the lovely *S. uliginosa*. As her collection widened, and her interest and curiosity deepened, she found herself confronted by a great dearth of published information on all but a comparative handful of species. At the time, the HPS was beginning to publish a series of specialized guidebooks and the idea of a booklet by her on salvias met an enthusiastic response.

The task proved lengthy and difficult, but she eventually succeeded in writing an informative account of 50 species, almost half of them half hardy or tender, and 22 of which were illustrated by line drawings made from specimens either grown in her own garden or at the Probus Garden near Truro. At the time, there were no publications in print specifically on the genus. The only major contemporary comprehensive source of information was James Compton's contribution on salvias to *The New RHS Dictionary of Gardening*.

Unfortunately the intended publication of her completed booklet by the HPS was delayed and eventually Beryl Davies decided, in the interests of seeing the booklet being made available more promptly, to withdraw it from the Society. It was, instead, published as the second in another series, the Probus Gardens Handbooks, in 1996. However, by then the first of Christine Yeo's booklets had been published (in 1995).

Beryl Davies' booklet has had some adverse criticism by at least one reviewer, particularly for some specific errors of naming. Nevertheless, it remains a very valuable source of information and observation, clearly well based on first-hand experience. The difficulties she confronted in gathering information were quite formidable at the time: her achievement in the circumstances was remarkable. Had she set out to write it three years later the two booklets by Christine Yeo, and the subsequent book on the genus by the American gardener Betsy Clebsch, would have provided her with a mine of information.

Christine Yeo

As the holder of the largest of the three National Collections of the genus and vendor of by far the widest range of salvia species in the country, Devon nurserywoman Christine Yeo was particularly sharply aware of a need for a comprehensive publication on the genus. The larger her own collection grew, and the more species she was able to offer for sale, the more the requests for information came from her customers.

Her response was to write two handbooks, both including colour photographs of most of the species described. To this day, these remain the publications dealing with by far the largest number of species, outdoing both *The New RHS Dictionary of Gardening* and *A Book of Salvias* by the American Betsy Clebsch. She is a contributor to this book.

BOTANISTS
James Compton

Dr James Compton could very well also appear under the previous heading as a writer, since he has contributed notably to literature on the genus. As already mentioned, he was responsible for the salvia entry in *The New RHS Dictionary of Gardening*, published in 1992. He is likewise the author of the salvia entry in the *European Garden Flora* (in preparation at the time of writing). Additionally, he has contributed on Mexican salvias both to *The Garden* and *The Plantsman*, magazines published by the RHS.

A former student of the Royal Botanic Gardens Kew, James Compton entertained no doubts from his teens onwards that the worlds of botany and horticulture were to be the focus of his working life. His interest in the genus salvia originated even before his days at Kew, with the confused nomenclature of Graham's sage, now *S. microphylla* 'Kew Red', particularly engaging his attention. Coincidentally, this is the same salvia which was the starting point of Christine Yeo's enthusiasm for the genus, as she herself relates on p.140 of this book.

After graduating from Kew having been awarded its prestigious diploma, James Compton was fortunate in his first employment. He worked at the famous Chelsea Physic Garden, becoming supervisor after five years as deputy. This post presented him with exceptional opportunities to choose new plants to add to the Garden's rich collections.

Botanic gardens worldwide have collaborated with one another since the eighteenth century, exchanging lists of seeds available on request. During James Compton's time, over 800 such lists arrived annually at the Chelsea Physic Garden. The genus salvia was chosen as one for particular attention, and the number of species burgeoned, with major contributions from Kew, the Logan Botanic Garden in Scotland, the Jardin Thuret in Antibes, and the Hanbury Botanic Garden at La Mortola on the Italian Riviera.

During his years at Chelsea, James Compton was a frequent visitor to Turkey on plant-collecting missions. At the end of 11 years of working at the Physic Garden, he went to China as a member of a team of collectors which brought back to the British Isles *S. campanulata*, *S. dolichantha*, *S. przewalskii* and the two closely related, and often confused, species *S. flava* and *S. bulleyana*.

Of his numerous contributions to the knowledge of both the botany and culture of the genus, those arising from Dr Compton's 1991 trip to Mexico have attracted most attention. From this visit, both S. × jamensis and S. darcyi were identified and described for the first time, and both have proved themselves as notable additions to the garden flora. Since then many cultivars of S. × jamensis have been raised: no fewer than 11 are listed in the 1998–99 'Plant Finder', and one – 'Los Lirios' – holds the AGM.

Now recognized as a leading authority on the salvia species native to Mexico, James Compton was asked by the editor of The Plantsman to write an account of those of greatest garden value for the magazine. This article, Mexican Salvias in Cultivation, covering 24 species, was published in 1994. The experience of preparing such a detailed description, which required the clarification of some long-existing confusion in nomenclature, convinced him that his professional future should be as a botanist rather than a horticulturist. The practical result of his decision was a period of three years researching the taxonomy of two genera of the Ranunculaceae (buttercup) family, Cimicifuga and Actaea, at the University of Reading. Following the

award of a Doctorate of Philosophy for this work, he is now a Post-Doctoral Fellow of the University and is currently working on relationships between genera in Ranunculaceae.

His interest in salvias continues, and living evidence of his enthusiasm is, of course, very notable at the Chelsea Physic Garden. It is also apparent in the salvia-rich gardens of Cannington College, near Bridgwater, in Somerset. A succession of diploma students from the college spent part of their course gaining experience at Chelsea during his time there, and a considerable number of cuttings and young plants were given to the college for establishment in their walled gardens, which are open to the public.

Dr Compton has also left his mark in another, apparently unlikely, location. This is the fine, extensive gardens of Newby Hall, a seventeenth-century house (open to the public) near Ripon in North Yorkshire. Because of its northerly location, the gardens would not appear to be a particularly natural hunting ground for salvia enthusiasts. In fact, the genus is very well represented there, and currently includes such species as S. leucantha, S. darcyi, S. guaranitica, S. greggii, S. patens 'Cambridge Blue' and 'Oxford Blue', and the S. microphylla cultivars 'Newby Hall' and 'Pink Blush'. The reason is that Newby Hall is the home of James Compton's parents, and over a prolonged period he has introduced salvias to its fine gardens, where his own enthusiasm for the genus has infected both his parents and the head gardener, Chris Jakeman.

DR RAY HARLEY AND IAN HEDGE
In Britain, two other botanists have played a significant role in the recent history of Salvia as a British garden plant.

Dr Ray Harley has specialized in the family Labiatae at the Royal Botanic Gardens Kew since 1968. His interest in salvias has concentrated on the South American species, especially from Colombia. Ray Harley and James Compton share optimism for the prospects of still further species being successfully introduced to British gardens from the New World. Dr Harley is confident in particular that some of the species native to the Andean area, and as yet unknown

S. greggii × lycioides (p.120) has attractive reddish-purple flowers and purple calyces.

in cultivation in Britain, may well prove rewarding when they are put to the test.

At the Royal Botanic Gardens Edinburgh, Ian Hedge has maintained a strong interest in the genus over a long period. He has specialized in Old World species and contributed entries on the genus in the published floras of both Europe and south-west Asia.

His influence is plain to see at the Logan Botanic Gardens in south-west Scotland, an annexe of Edinburgh's botanic gardens. This garden was private property until acquired as a specialized garden of the Royal Botanic Gardens Edinburgh, in 1969. Despite its northerly location, Logan is certainly a garden for the salvia enthusiast, the diversity of species there in late summer being one of its outstanding features.

BREEDERS OF BEDDERS

Proper respect must be paid to the professional plant breeders who have done so much to transform the garden characteristics of the three species of salvia best known as 'bedders'. Not everyone likes the modern cultivars of S. *splendens*, but that they are popular is beyond doubt. Most of the efforts of the breeders concerned – almost all of them employed by American and West European seed companies – have concentrated on ever-dwarfer, ever earlier-flowering scarlet cultivars.

The large improvements to cultivars of other colours deserves full recognition also. These were, by general agreement, less satisfactory in garden performance than their scarlet-flowered counterparts in the past, but the modern series 'Salsa' and 'Sizzler' now include a wide range of colours.

The garden potential of S. *farinacea* has been considerably widened during the last 25 years by the introduction of comparatively dwarf, bushy cultivars. Despite many derogatory remarks by gardening writers about the obsession modern breeders of bedding plants have with dwarfness, it would be hard to maintain that S. *farinacea*, in its natural state reaching up to 1.25m (4ft) tall at maturity, is necessarily to be preferred to its modern cultivars, which are almost all well under half that height.

About S. *coccinea* the same comments can be made. The bedding varieties 'Lady in Red' and 'Coral Nymph' are fine garden plants, no less valuable in their place than, say, the extremely vigorous 'Pseudococcinea' which grows to twice their height.

S. *darcyi* (p.101), found growing in the wild in 1991, has won many admirers.

The seed companies now involved in salvias for bedding are keenly competitive. They have, however, co-operated to form the organization 'Fleuroselect', the members of which account for 85 percent of flower seed production worldwide. The rigorous trialling system of this organization has enabled an objective consensus to emerge, identifying the new cultivars that are distinctively different from those already introduced, and are of outstanding worth over a range of conditions. To be awarded a Fleuroselect Gold Medal, or a Quality Mark, a new introduction must perform well on trial sites hosted by the member companies in Japan, the USA and western Europe. Fleuroselect gave its first awards in 1973. These have been sparingly bestowed, but as a genus *Salvia* has done well. Its award-winning cultivars at the time of writing are S. *coccinea* 'Coral Nymph' and 'Lady in Red', S. *farinacea* 'Strata', 'Cirrus' and 'Victoria', and S. *splendens* 'Sizzler Orchid' and 'Sizzler Salmon Bicolor'.

4

CULTIVATION

Common requirements

Salvia is a large genus of diverse species, varying in character, hardiness and cultural requirements. Despite this diversity, many of the requirements for cultivation can be applied generally. This chapter covers general needs: what applies only to one group of species is dealt with in the relevant individual chapter.

There are few gardens in which a wide range of species cannot be successfully grown in the open. In the British Isles, the greatest limitations in practice are that some Mediterranean and Asian species, and most of those native to America, are too tender to be grown in outdoor beds and borders in northern England and Scotland. But even there, many can be grown successfully in containers on a sheltered patio or close to a wall with a sunny aspect.

PREPARATION FOR PLANTING

Most salvia species will thrive in most soils, and gratifyingly for owners of clay soils some of the most attractive species – S. *guaranitica* and S. *cacaliifolia*, for example – do particularly well in them because of their water-retaining properties. On the other hand, many of the species are native to limestone areas so if you have dry, fast-draining, stony and alkaline soil and sometimes feel disagreeably limited in what you can grow, you will not be short of choice within the genus.

Where soils are in need of improvement, it makes sense to add organic matter. Improvements in soil aeration, root penetration and moisture-holding capacity can be achieved with composted bark fibre, leaf mould, mature garden compost, spent mushroom compost,

S. *amplexicaulis* (p.63) is a fine, free-flowering hardy perennial that deserves to be more widely cultivated.

and peat, to name some of the more common materials. Perlite, although not organic, markedly improves the workability of clay soils, albeit expensively.

DRAINAGE

Good drainage is generally desirable: without it, there is a greater risk of the less hardy herbaceous perennials dying in the winter. On soils lying wet for prolonged periods slug and snail attack is more likely to be a cause of loss among many species, especially those forming rosettes of foliage at ground level, such as S. *argentea* and S. *forsskaolii*. In gardens where the soil is inherently wet and slow draining in the winter months, the best places outdoors for most salvia species are a raised bed or a container.

Salvia species of Mediterranean origin generally do well in less fertile, comparatively dry soils. The best-known example in this group is common sage, S. *officinalis*, although it is also capable of thriving in heavier, moister soils, if drainage is reasonably good. Other species sharing the same geographic origin and soil preference are S. *aethiopis*, S. *argentea*, S. *barrelieri*, S. *candelabrum*, S. *forsskaolii*, S. *fruticosa*, S. *heldreichiana*, S. *interrupta*, S. *jurisicii*, S. *lavandulifolia*, S. *taraxacifolia*, and the annual S. *viridis*.

FEED

Nitrogen-rich soils encourage shoot and foliage growth at the expense of flowering. However welcome this may be for leafy garden occupants, such as lettuce and Brussels sprouts, it is not at all desirable for most salvia species. So when preparing soils for salvias refrain from adding excess nitrogen. Animal manures and fresh garden compost may be undesirable for this reason.

Forking fertilizers into the soil when preparing for planting is generally good practice, again so long as a large supply of nitrogen is not added. Although all proprietary ready-mixed compound fertilizers contain this nutrient, their two other major components are useful in cultivating salvias. These are phosphorus, which primarily promotes root growth, and potassium, which enhances flowering. So choose a compound fertilizer in which the percentage of nitrogen is substantially lower than that of potassium. A satisfactory application rate on most soils of average fertility is 150 grams per square metre (4 oz per square yard) of a compound containing 10% of potassium oxide (potash).

Rather than using a compound fertilizer, an alternative is to make up your own mixture using nitro-chalk, superphosphate and sulphate of potash in a ratio of 4:3:2 by weight. Apply this at the same rate as above. The benefit of preparing your own mixture is that if you feel, from observing plant growth, that there is already enough nitrogen in the soil, you can omit or reduce the nitro-chalk.

The best time to apply fertilizers is just before planting, but they should be forked well in, not merely scattered on the surface or raked into the top few centimetres: plant nutrients are needed near the roots.

ACID OR ALKALINE?
Although in the wild many salvia species grow in limestone areas, there seems to be no indication that they have any particular adverse reaction to acid soils. Therefore, within the ordinary range of soil acidity and alkalinity, the gardener preparing soil for salvias need take no action. I have no first-hand experience of growing on naturally very acid, peaty soils, but on these liming would be a wise precaution. Ideally, if your garden is on such a soil, buy a soil testing kit – they are quite inexpensive – and apply lime before planting according to the test result and the advice given in the leaflet sold with the kit.

SITE
Nearly all species originate in sunny countries, so even where they thrive in considerable shade in their native habitat, it does not follow that they particularly benefit from this in cultivation: an altogether less powerful sun shines in England than, for example, in Spain or Mexico. On naturally dry soils, though, species such as

S. guaranitica and *S. involucrata* may be all the better for some relief from full sun on hotter days. Many species tolerate some shade, and some do well in quite heavily shaded sites. Two of the most memorable groups of salvias I have ever seen were growing where tree cover meant they were shaded through most of the day – *S. atrocyanea* in London's Chelsea Physic Garden, and *S. concolor* in Abbotsbury Gardens in Dorset. As a general rule, however, salvias grown in the British climate do best in situations exposed to full sun for most of the day. In warmer countries a wider range of species do best with the benefit of some shade, among the better known being *S. blepharophylla*, *S. buchananii*, *S. cacaliifolia*, *S. discolor* and *S. roemeriana*.

Protection from wind is an asset for most plants. Many salvia species are notoriously brittle-stemmed, so windswept gardens are particularly unsuitable for them. Fortunately, the vast majority of established private gardens are reasonably sheltered. Where shelter has to be provided, in the short term nothing is more effective than vertical screens made of the plastic netting sold in garden centres for the purpose. Firm support for the netting is essential, and usually costs more than the netting itself. Nailing to stout wooden posts, each with a generous proportion of its length – about a third – driven into the soil, should ensure that high winds do not blow these over.

Needless to say, where there is a long-term requirement for shelter, planting hedges should be made a very high priority.

PLANTING
Purchased plants are almost invariably pot-grown, as, indeed, are many home-propagated ones. Hardy species may be planted at any time so long as the soil is neither very wet nor frozen. Once autumn has arrived, however, any plants still in their pots are usually best retained in them until early spring. Clearly, young plants of tender species must be kept somewhere safe from damage by the cold until all risks of frosts have passed, at whatever time in spring is appropriate for the area concerned.

As a general rule, divisions of older plants are also best planted in spring. The same holds true for plants of hardy species raised from seed sown the previous year and overwintered in nursery beds. The advantages of planting hardy salvias in spring compared with autumn are discussed in chapter 9 (p.129). Naturally, spring planting is the rule for greenhouse-raised young plants of the large number of species that have little or no resistance to frost.

HOW TO PLANT

Pot-grown salvias should be very thoroughly watered the day prior to planting. Before planting, if they are root-bound, it is well worth breaking up the virtual sheath of roots that forms a kind of cylindrical mat around the compost in the pot. Although some damage is inevitable, root growth out into the surrounding soil is greatly facilitated by such treatment.

It is important to make the planting hole as deep as the pot, and to firm the soil into position around the sides of the rootball. If the soil condition falls short of what you would like, potting compost is ideal for filling in immediately around the rootball. Do not complete planting by pressing on the upper surface of the compost from the pot. As this is already very well settled, nothing positive is achieved, and if you press too hard you will probably break some roots.

SPACING

The spacing generally recommended between plants in a group is around two-thirds of their spread. For example 50–60cm (20–24in) separation is usual for plants, such as S. sclarea, that can be expected to reach a diameter of 80cm (32in) as they flower. This is, of course, no more than a guide for use if you have no previous experience of the plant concerned. Without the certainty of knowing how large and how quickly they will grow, the temptation, where there are sufficient plants, is to set them relatively close together, with the result that some hard-hearted thinning is needed after a year or two or sometimes even in the year of planting. The first time you grow a species native to a much warmer area, err on the generous side in allowing space. This avoids the plants, which are already disadvantaged by cooler conditions, being overwhelmed by the growth of their neighbours.

WATERING AND PROTECTING

Depending on the soil conditions, the time of year and the weather forecast, watering in may be advisable. When in doubt, do water, because there is no substitute for this as a means of bringing newly disturbed soil and roots into intimate contact. Plants from pots are particularly likely to need more than one watering to establish their root systems thoroughly in their new environment. The need for repeated waterings is naturally much greater when plants are set out in late spring, rather than earlier in the year or in autumn.

Quite the cruellest conditions for transplanting are warm, dry and windy. If it is possible for planting to be delayed in such conditions, to await a change to more favourable weather, then this is the best policy. Otherwise, use temporary shade and – if practicable – frequent overhead damping, as well as watering, to relieve the stress on the plant.

AFTERCARE

Once plants have become established, weeding and prompt removal of inflorescences as soon as flowering is over may well be all the attention they will require until the autumn. In the first season after planting into well-prepared soil in beds and borders, no benefit is likely from any kind of feeding. Container-grown plants are another matter, though: see p.45.

Low-growing S. arizonica (p.94) is ideal for a sunny border.

PLATE II

NATURALLY SHRUBBY, HALF HARDY SALVIAS

S. aurita

S. interrupta

S. keerlii

S. chamaedryoides

S. canariensis

S. leucantha

All specimens are shown at approximately ⅔ life size

For gardeners on drier types of soil, one practice of particular value is the application of a mulch around the plants very soon after planting. This cuts down the loss of water by evaporation from the exposed soil surface. There is also the well-known and well-appreciated supplementary benefit, the repression of weed seed germination. Suitable mulching materials include garden compost, composted bark and bark chippings. Some of their useful effect is lost if they are applied when the soil is already dry, and if necessary a soaking watering should immediately precede the mulching operation.

In autumn, herbaceous perennial species that are to remain in position for a further year should have their stems cut down at or just above ground level and removed. The time to do this is when flowering is at an end and the foliage is beginning to senesce. Along with the stems also remove dead basal foliage and weeds, all of which if left in place help to create a dangerously slug-friendly environment.

Species of uncertain hardiness are more likely to survive the winter if their roots and subterranean shoot buds are given some protection from freezing. Covering the crowns of the plants to a depth of 8cm (3in) or more with a dry mulch material, such as chipped bark, undoubtedly reduces the penetration of frost into the ground. Alternatives to bark include straw (rather unsightly and inclined to blow around everywhere), dry bracken (if you have a convenient local source) and fallen leaves. Spreading slug pellets before laying down the mulch material is a wise precaution.

Shielding plant species of uncertain hardiness from rain as well as from low temperatures will further improve their chances of survival: wet, cold soil is a much worse enemy to salvia roots and buds than dry, cold soil. Unfortunately, there is no way of doing this without introducing some kind of visually unattractive shelter, but if this is acceptable you could try using a large cloche or even a simple piece of, say, corrugated PVC or plywood supported on bricks to run rainwater off the salvia site.

No more attention is likely to be needed until spring approaches. Keep a watch for the very first signs of shoot growth, applying slug pellets again if there is a risk of damage from slugs and snails. At this time a fertilizer application is likely to benefit established plants, particularly those on fast-draining, poorer soils where

'Salsa Purple' (p.49) is among the more subtle and less commonly grown of the many S. *splendens* cultivars.

most nutrients are rapidly leached away by winter rainfall. An application of half the rate suggested for initial soil preparation is adequate, and it is best made in late winter to give reasonable opportunity for rain to dissolve it and transport the nutrients into the plants' rooting zone. The greater the number of years the plants have been in place, the more they are likely to benefit from this annual feed.

PESTS AND DISEASES

If your salvias are growing outdoors in the garden, you may well never feel any compelling need to spray them for the control of any of the small numbers of pests or diseases that commonly affect them.

In the open, perhaps the most likely problems are aphids (greenfly) and powdery mildew. However, by no means all species are equally susceptible. S. *splendens*, for example, is more severely affected by aphid attack than the great majority of other species, while S. *nemorosa*, S. *officinalis* and S. *verticillata* are among those particularly subject to powdery mildew.

In greenhouse conditions, some salvias are susceptible to severe attack not only by aphids, but also by whitefly and red spider mite. These three pests flourish from spring to autumn in the vast majority of greenhouses, infesting most plants grown in them. Because of the higher temperatures that prevail in greenhouses and the consequent rapid build-up of pest numbers, active control measures are essential if plants are not to be very seriously damaged.

Noone likes spraying or fumigation, but in greenhouses one or both usually become practical necessities at times. For those gardeners who avoid synthetic chemical products, there are alternatives. Insecticidal soap solution, specially formulated for horticultural use, is one. If sprayed repeatedly at short intervals, it can be effective in preventing pest populations reaching damaging proportions. Pyrethrum and rotenone (derris) are plant-derived insecticides, and hence natural products. Biological control (the releasing of parasites or predators of the pests into the greenhouse) has become increasingly popular, although it is not always easy to achieve satisfactory control.

Aphids mainly infest the growing shoots and youngest leaves, and large numbers of them will cause distortion and seriously checked growth. They are notoriously damaging to young plants of S. *splendens*.

If spraying becomes necessary, insecticidal soap solutions can be used successfully. More immediate results are obtained from spraying an insecticide containing pirimiphos-methyl, which is also effective against capsid bugs, leafhoppers, glasshouse red spider mite and glasshouse whitefly. Among many alternatives are dimethoate, which will also control capsids and leafhoppers, and permethrin, which is also suitable for combating leafhoppers and glasshouse whitefly. Insecticides containing pirimicarb, which is described scientifically as a specific aphicide, are effective against aphids only; they cause no harm to the many species of beneficial insects that prey on aphids and other pests. An organic alternative is pyrethrum.

Capsid bugs These are also sap-sucking pests, generally not commencing activity until late spring. Misshapen young leaves, punctured by small holes, are symptomatic of the damage caused by their feeding. Among many other host plants, caryopteris, chrysanthemums and dahlias are often particularly affected.

Insecticides containing dimethoate, pirimiphos-methyl and fenitrothion will all give control, though most gardeners accept the damage without resorting to any of this chemical armoury.

Glasshouse red spider mite Also known as two-spotted spider mite, this is troublesome in greenhouses in summer. It may also severely damage outdoor plants in favoured positions, such as close to a wall with a sunny aspect. The mites are very small, yellowish-green and scarcely visible to the naked eye. They feed as sap-suckers on the undersides of younger foliage. First symptoms are a very fine mottling of the leaves, but in a heavy infestation entire leaves may dry up, and a very fine webbing develop around the shoot tips. Attacks are most severe in dry atmospheric conditions.

Spraying with insecticidal soap solutions or with an insecticide containing malathion, pirimiphos-methyl, bifenthrin or rotenone (derris) will give some measure of control. Repeated applications are essential because none of these effectively destroys all stages in the life-cycle of the pest. There is a biological control agent, for use in greenhouses only. This is the predator *Phytoseiulus persimilis*, a South American mite with a voracious appetite for the pest. The predator should be introduced as soon as the first red spider mites are seen.

Glasshouse whitefly A nuisance in greenhouses but seldom causing notable trouble outdoors, glasshouse whitefly is yet another sap-sucking pest. It is a very well known affliction of tomatoes and fuchsias, but many *Salvia* species appear not to be attractive to it. Its feeding causes reduced growth, and the sugar-rich excreta of the pest drops onto the upper surfaces of the leaves below. This sticky material, called honeydew, encourages sooty moulds, which in bad infestations turn the leaves quite black. Resistance to insecticides is common but, as a rule, useful control is obtained with pirimiphos-methyl (as spray or fumigant), or with sprays of permethrin, bifenthrin, insecticidal soap or pyrethrum. As with glasshouse red spider mite, repeated applications are needed to eliminate the pest.

The parasitic wasp, *Encarsia formosa*, can reduce whitefly populations to acceptably low levels. It is well worth a trial by anyone who maintains a greenhouse in year-round use.

Leafhoppers Close relatives of aphids, leafhoppers are, once again, sap-sucking insects. Of the numerous species of the pest, the chrysanthemum and glasshouse leafhoppers are those particularly likely to trouble salvias. They live on the undersides of the leaves, the adults being very prompt to jump off when they are disturbed. The symptoms of their attack are a coarse, pale yellow mottling of the leaves when viewed from above: rose enthusiasts are likely to be very familiar with the appearance of infested leaves. A near-relative to the salvia genus, the Jerusalem Sage, *Phlomis fruticosa*, is also very susceptible. *S. officinalis* and closely related species are quite susceptible but many gardeners will not feel spraying is necessary. All the insecticides mentioned for aphid control, with the exception of pirimicarb, are effective against this pest.

Slugs and snails These are universal pests, a problem to salvias as well as much else. Most at risk are young plants of tender species being overwintered in frames or on the floor of a greenhouse. They may also cause serious harm to young shoot growth developing late in winter, especially under a protective mulch.

Good practices in reducing damage include destroying weeds and eliminating the pests' preferred resting and hiding places: decaying leaves and stems, large clods of soil, stones and litter of all descriptions provide moist, shaded sanctuaries for them. Slug pellets, scattered thinly, may also have a role to play: metaldehyde is the active ingredient. They are poisonous to cats and dogs. Dead and dying snails may be eaten by birds and other natural predators, and although they are unlikely to die as a result, the effects of this pesticide in the natural food chain is a cause of concern.

Other, more environmentally friendly means of slug and snail control include aluminium sulphate for application onto the soil surface and adhesive copper barriers for containers. Biological control is yet another possibility: supplies are now available of a microscopic nematode worm which is a lethal feeder on slugs. The nematodes are watered onto the soil. The treatment is fairly expensive and, unfortunately, works less well on clayey soils than on lighter ones.

And if all else fails – in my own extremely heavily slug and snail infested garden, a great improvement has resulted from regular collection of the pests, dropping them in a bucket of salted water in which they die

S. verticillata 'Purple Rain' (p.79) is especially attractive where it can spill over onto the path or lawn.

instantly; a pinch of salt dropped carefully on each one will achieve the same result. The time to achieve the greatest harvest is just after rain especially in the evening. Another good move is the installation of a garden pond, which will attract frogs and toads – the natural enemies of slugs and snails.

Grey mould (botrytis) In the greenhouse there is a winter counterpart to the terrible spring and summer trio of aphids, spider mite and whitefly. This is the ubiquitous grey mould disease *Botrytis cinerea*. A parasite of dead, dying and damaged plant tissues, it is most troublesome where humidity is high, as of course it needs to be during the rooting of leafy cuttings; this is the stage at which the disease is most likely to be of concern to the salvia enthusiast.

and frequent picking over of plants in greenhouse and frame while cuttings are being rooted and plants over-wintered is the best bet for containing the disease. A need for fungicidal dusting is usually a sign that there has been less than due diligence in this matter!

Powdery mildew Most gardeners know of powdery mildew on roses, apples and Michaelmas daisies, and it is quite conspicuous when it attacks. Upper leaf surfaces become coated with the white, powdery growth of the fungus. A humid atmosphere and dry roots are predisposing factors to infection.

The species most often affected include S. *lavandulifolia*, S. *nemorosa*, S. *officinalis*, S. × *superba*, S. × *sylvestris* and S. *verticillata*. The disease can be quite disfiguring in summer and autumn. A sharp eye for its onset, and prompt removal of infected leaves and shoots, will often be control enough. Watering – although not generally required or even particularly beneficial for these species – may help where infection has been observed and seems likely to become a problem. Put the water on the soil, not the stems and leaves.

If, despite all, it seems that chemical intervention is justified, you can use a fungicidal dust containing carbendazim, mancozeb, or sulphur, or you can spray with one containing triforine with bupirimate.

Seedling diseases A number of common fungi can kill seedlings during and shortly after germination. They are more prevalent in greenhouses than in the open, and are best known in causing damping-off disease, where seedlings collapse and die due to infection at or just above compost level. Salvias seem to be less susceptible to this than many other greenhouse-raised subjects, such as antirrhinum, lobelia and zinnia.

Where losses occur nevertheless, they are mostly because of dirty water, dirty pots or seed compost that has been used before. Overwatering and overcrowded seedlings exacerbate problems with these fungi. Water at this stage of a plant's life should always be from the tap, not a water-butt or – worst of all – a storage tank in the greenhouse.

To arrest losses that are already occurring, remove infected seedlings, water with the fungicide Cheshunt Compound, and otherwise reduce watering to the necessary minimum. (Incidentally, the fungicide is named after a small town in Hertfordshire.)

Grey mould is a serious and widespread problem against which spraying is usually a last resort. Good hygiene, avoidance of high humidity except where absolutely essential, and keeping stems and leaves dry, are the best shots in the gardener's war against botrytis. What good hygiene means in practice is the prompt and frequent removal of dead and dying foliage, flowers and, if necessary, entire plants. Where accidental breakage occurs, cut back to undamaged growth just above a node (leaf joint): stubs of stem or leaf-stalk usually die back in due course and are sometimes points of entry for the fungus.

Electric heating creates a better greenhouse environment in terms of humidity than paraffin or gas, because unfortunately water vapour is a combustion product of both the latter. Ventilation whenever the temperatures permit helps to keep humidity down.

If, despite all, a fungicide is required, you can dust with one containing carbendazim. For salvias, meticulous

GROWING SALVIAS
IN CONTAINERS

Plants in containers often differ in behaviour from those grown in the open ground. They are seldom so tall, however well watered and fed, and this is much more often an advantage than a defect. Better yet, they tend to flower earlier and more freely. The reasons for this are not fully understood, but an indirect result of restricting the volume of growing medium available for the roots appears to be a change in the carbon and nitrogen levels in the plants: root restriction results in relatively high ratios of carbon to nitrogen. Simply put, where the ratio of carbon is high, the development of flowers is favoured and where it is low, vegetative growth predominates over flowering. I have had container-grown specimens of *S. semiatrata* in flower continuously from early summer whereas border-grown plants in a friend's garden, in the same year, were not in flower until early autumn.

S. roemeriana (p.57) is an excellent salvia for growing in a container.

Container growing should have a special appeal for gardeners in cooler areas for whom the outdoor success of many tender species would be very doubtful. Even in relatively favoured areas, the flower display of some fine species is usually short-lived as they commence flowering very late in summer and the days of their glory are almost invariably terminated prematurely by the first killing frosts of the autumn. Among those affected are *S. azurea*, *S. elegans* 'Scarlet Pineapple' (syn. *S. rutilans*), *S. gesneriiflora* and *S. leucantha*, all of which only give of their best outdoors in exceptionally favoured locations. For the gardener with greenhouse or conservatory space available, plants of these species can continue to give pleasure until very late in the year, and even into the beginning of the next. To achieve this, they should be grown in containers outside in the summer, and moved indoors in early to mid-autumn.

There are other tender species that, in a favourable location, usually begin flowering early enough to have justified their keep before the first frosts. However, in return for the same cultural treatment described above, most of these, too, will deliver a handsome bonus in the form of autumn flowering. They include *S. cacaliifolia*, *S. elegans*, *S. involucrata* and *S. semiatrata*. There are two fine herbaceous species which usually flower in late winter and spring, as well as in late summer and autumn: these are the vividly red *S. fulgens* and *S. gesneriiflora*.

In British climatic conditions, *S. blepharophylla*, *S. buchananii* and *S. roemeriana* are usually seen to best advantage as container plants. Because of its very pendent flowers *S. discolor* needs to be at or above eye-level. A hanging basket is the obvious answer. The shrubs *S. microphylla*, *S. greggii* and *S. × jamensis*, are hardy enough to be grown permanently outdoors in sheltered sites in many gardens in southern Britain. In less hospitable circumstances, it is very worthwhile treating them as long-term container plants. They can be stood out in late spring, to flower from early summer on. Moving them into a greenhouse just before the first frost will prolong the display.

The choice of hardy salvias rather than the tender ones as container plants is unusual. It may nevertheless be worth considering *S. argentea*, *S. pratensis* Haematodes Group, *S. × sylvestris*, *S. verticillata* 'Purple Rain' and the cultivars of *S. officinalis*, *S. × superba* and *S. × sylvestris*, all of which can be successful. Apart from the *S. officinalis* cultivars with variegated and golden foliage, these are all perfectly hardy; there is no need for them to be brought into the greenhouse or conservatory at any time.

CULTIVATION

For best effect, plants should be grown in containers in small groups – usually three – rather than as individuals. Stronger growing species grown in threes will need a container at least equivalent in size to a pot of 27-30cm (11-12in) diameter. The corresponding minimum container size for three plants of smaller species such as S. *buchananii* and S. *roemeriana* would be 23-25cm (9-10in).

For taller growing species, use clay rather than plastic containers, to reduce the risk of plants being blown over in windy conditions. If you must use plastic, choose pots that are shallow in relation to their diameter, rather than a traditional 'plant pot' shape.

Herbaceous species grown in containers are generally best propagated annually because their appearance

A SELECTION OF SALVIAS FOR CONTAINERS

S. *argentea*	S. *fulgens*	S. *officinalis*
S. *azurea*	S. *fruticosa*	S. *oppositiflora*
S. *blepharophylla*	S. *greggii*	S. *patens*
S. *buchananii*	S. *gesneriiflora*	S. *pratensis*
S. *cacaliifolia*	S. *greggii* ×	Haematodes
S. *coccinea*	*lycioides*	Group
S. *discolor*	S. *involucrata*	S. *reptans*
S. *dorisiana*	S. × *jamensis*	S. *roemeriana*
S. *elegans*	S. *juriscii*	S. *semiatrata*
S. *elegans* 'Scarlet	S. *leucantha*	S. *sinaloensis*
Pineapple' (syn.	S. *lycioides*	S. *splendens*
S. *rutilans*)	S. *microphylla*	S. × *superba*
S. *farinacea*	S. *multicaulis*	S. × *sylvestris*

in their second and subsequent years is usually less attractive than in their first. Some of these – for example S. *elegans*, S. *fulgens*, S. *gesneriiflora*, S. *involucrata* and S. *leucantha* – may be better grown from cuttings taken in the spring, rather than in late summer of the previous year, which is normal for their cultivation in borders and beds. The delayed start to their vegetative growth does not cause a delay in the time at which they commence flowering, but does result in relatively dwarf plants – an aesthetic advantage for larger species grown in containers.

As with growing any kind of plant in a container, an absolute essential for success is sufficiently frequent watering. To increase the capacity of the compost to hold water, it is worth mixing a water-retaining gel into it before use.

Feeding will also be required; only limited amounts of nutrients can be incorporated in the compost without risk of damage to roots, and nutrient losses because of drainage are inevitable. Regular liquid feeding is ideal, but the use of dry fertilizer scattered thinly over the compost surface and well watered in is a convenient alternative. So is the use of proprietary fertilizer sticks inserted into the compost according to instructions. A feed substantially richer in potash than nitrogen is required: tomato fertilizer is very appropriate.

Pinching out the growing points of plants of some naturally taller-growing species will help to prevent their making excessive height. S. *elegans* 'Scarlet Pineapple' (syn. S. *rutilans*) is a case in point. Pinching out can be done repeatedly, but should cease before late summer.

Container-grown plants can be kept in greenhouse conditions throughout their lives. However, the quality of leaf and stem growth is usually better if they spend the months of high summer outdoors, and the colour of red flowers is brighter and deeper because the warmer conditions indoors produce a fading effect on the pigments concerned. Summer pest problems are usually much less pressing in the open, too.

For any container plants being overwintered, an assured minimum temperature of 5°C (40°F) is quite sufficient. Many species will in fact tolerate mere frost exclusion, and some will also survive some exposure to freezing conditions in a totally unheated greenhouse. After all, they will experience less frost there than outdoors, as well as benefiting from shelter from both wind and rain.

The principal risk of plant loss in the cool, dark conditions of winter is from overwatering rather than cold, and in young plants, foliage that is damp over long periods may become infected by botrytis (see p.42). In both cases, the remedies are obvious: when in doubt, don't water, and do use ventilation, as well as heating, to avoid the sort of humid air conditions that encourage water vapour to condense on leaf surfaces.

5

ANNUALS

Only one of the six salvias featured in this chapter is a true annual – S. viridis. In horticultural terms, though, all are normally grown as annuals, and, in practice, just S. patens is sometimes treated as a perennial.

Pride of place in terms of popularity goes without question to S. splendens. This is almost universally known to the general public, as well as to gardeners, and in the conception of the great majority is salvia, virtually to the exclusion of all other species in the genus.

The four other perennial species which, like S. splendens, are also cultivated as half hardy annuals are S. farinacea, now gradually achieving the recognition of its attractiveness that is its proper due, S. coccinea, S. patens and S. roemeriana. Of these, only S. patens is likely to overwinter successfully in the open in Britain, and all four are ordinarily grown just like S. splendens – sowing in a greenhouse early in the year and planting out once frost risk has passed.

S. farinacea 'Strata' (p.51) produces flowers with deep blue corollas that contrast strikingly with the silver calyces and stems. In Britain it was Bedding Plant of the Year in 1997.

S. coccinea, S. farinacea, S. patens , S. roemeriana and S. splendens do best in comparatively fertile, moisture-retentive soils and none are at their happiest in light, poor, fast-draining soils. To grow them in this type of soil, improve its moisture retention properties as much as possible during preparation for planting by addition of organic matter.

Plants of all of these species are usually stopped – the growing points removed – while still in their early growth stages, at a height of about 10cm (4in). This helps to promote their natural branching habit.

All of them will respond well to watering during spells of dry weather. S. splendens is very susceptible to aphid attack, which causes young leaves to curl over in a disfiguring fashion, so the plants are worth including in any spraying against this pest that you may be doing primarily for other purposes – of roses, for example. Deadheading is certainly worth doing for these species; S. splendens responds especially well.

S. viridis (syn. S. horminum) is the only species in the genus that lends itself to traditional hardy annual treatment in the British climate. This can be, and usually is, sown where it is to flower; it is thinned, and kept weed-free, but otherwise may be left to its own devices with a good prospect of a very happy outcome. It is a true annual and does best when in a sunny spot on poor, dry soil.

SALVIA SPLENDENS
Sello ex Roemer & Schultes (1822), Scarlet sage
A native of Brazil, S. splendens was introduced to European horticulture early in the nineteenth century. Now grown as a bedding plant almost worldwide, especially throughout Europe and the Americas, it is nearly

always raised from seed and treated as an annual. *Splendens* means 'shining' or 'brilliant'.

The species is a tender herbaceous perennial with woody stem bases and, in the wild, usually attains a height of around 1m (3ft). It has very little resistance to frost, and overwinters in the open only where frosts are unusual and slight. During the nineteenth century it was mainly grown in northern Europe and North America as a greenhouse plant for its display of flowers in autumn and winter. As with the variety 'Van 'Houttei', flowering did not commence until very late in the summer. From the dwarfer-growing variety 'Bruantii' (now, I think, lost to cultivation), the forerunners of modern bedding varieties emerged early in the twentieth century. These were characterized both by dwarfness and the fact that they flowered much earlier in the season.

The growth habit is naturally erect and the plant is more or less hairless. The dark green leaves are ovate and up to 7 by 5cm (3 by 2in). The leaf margins are dentate or crenate, and the tips are pointed. The flowers are borne in whorls of 2–6, usually close together in terminal spike-like racemes up to 20cm (8in) long. The colour effect is given jointly by the bracts, calyces and corollas, all of which are scarlet in the species. The bracts may be over 1cm (½in) long. At first they conceal the flower buds, but they fall as the flowers open. The wide calyces are around 2cm (¾in) long. The corolla is up to 5cm (2in) long, the tube being notably deep in relation to its width. The hooded upper lip is a straight continuation of the tube, while the flared lower lip is the shorter of the two. Flowering commences in early to midsummer.

S. splendens Salsa Series has a wide colour range as shown here. The flower display is sustained for months so long as plants are kept adequately supplied with moisture.

Cultivation

In its strident shades of red, *S. splendens* features in municipal bedding schemes almost everywhere, in parks, squares and shopping precincts. It is now even seen on roundabouts, where the display is ideal for providing a visual jolt to any motorist whose attention to his duty of unfailing observation is beginning to flag. Plants in their millions are sold to amateur gardeners, too, and surely they have little competition in the plant world for anyone looking for a veritable shout of red in the garden. *S. splendens* can be overwhelming, particularly in a small garden where its brightness can destroy the opportunity to appreciate any other plant

life. Nevertheless, red cultivars of *S. splendens* will doubtless continue to meet a huge demand. And it would be very wrong to claim that it should never have a place in the garden of a self-respecting plantsman, as when planted in association with other plants, say *Petunia* 'Mirage White', *Senecio cineraria* (syn. *Cineraria maritima*) 'Silver Dust' or *Tanacetum ptarmiciflorum* (syn. *Pyrethrum ptarmiciflorum*) to balance its strident tones, it can be very effective.

In the past the performance of *S. splendens* varieties with flower colours other than red has been relatively poor. This has been rectified in variety series such as 'Salsa' and 'Sizzler', where there are now salmon- and

of foliage. In frost-free countries, such as Madeira, *S. splendens* is valued mainly for its winter flowers. In such places, the plants that are grown much more closely resemble the original species, and their intensely coloured flower spikes can be appreciated individually because the foliage is not obscured. Tastes vary, and those gardeners who feel that the original appeal of *S. splendens* has been too radically changed, would get the response from the breeders that their efforts have been widely appreciated, as evidenced by the massive popularity of the current products of their work.

S. splendens is best in full sun, and benefits markedly from watering in dry weather and regular deadheading. Where plants suffer from prolonged shortage of water, flowering will end prematurely. The young plants are very susceptible to aphid attack, which can be easily controlled by insecticides. Propagation of the cultivars is almost invariably by seed, sown in a greenhouse in late winter, although it is quite possible to take cuttings in late summer, and overwinter them in a cool greenhouse.

Cultivars

Numerous cultivars are available, and new ones are introduced frequently. Those with purple and white flowers share with the traditionally coloured scarlet cultivars the specific feature of having bracts, calyces and corollas all of the same colour. The bicoloured cultivars have white corollas, with calyces and bracts of another colour.

Among the best red varieties are **'Blaze of Fire'** (syn. 'Fireball'), height 30–40cm (12–16in), **'Red Riches'** AGM, height 30–40cm (12–16in), and **'Vanguard'** AGM, height 25cm (10in). **'Carabinière'**, height 30cm (12in), is a later-flowering variety, retaining some of the natural response of the species to day-length in initiating its flower spikes.

'Orange Zest' is orange-red, height 30cm (12in). **Phoenix Series** is red, white, pinks, purple, and 25–30cm (10–12in) high. **Salsa Series** and **Sizzler Series** (see pp.74-5) are similar to one another and to Phoenix Series, but differ from the latter in including salmon-pink and scarlet bicolours, both of which are white-flowered with coloured calyces and bracts.

'Van Houttei' is very different from the bedding varieties. It is dealt with separately as a half hardy perennial (see p.101).

rose-pinks, purple, burgundy, white and bicolour combinations, all fully comparable in growth habit, freedom of flowering and length of flowering period with their scarlet counterparts. Some of these colours and colour combinations have an appeal of a very different character from the red varieties. I very much like the salmon bicolours for their visual softness of touch.

The results of decades of intense breeding effort have also been to reduce heights of currently popular cultivars down to as little as 25cm (10in) in some cases, with a spread similar to the height. Because of selection for the production of as many spikes with as large flowers as possible, the foliage almost disappears from view during the prolonged flowering period. An aesthetic objection to these plants must be that the vivid colours of inflorescences lack foiling by a visible background

S. *farinacea* 'Cirrus' has all-white corollas and calyces and contrasts well with red- or blue-flowered bedding plants.

SALVIA FARINACEA
Bentham (1837), Mealy sage

Among so many salvia species that deserve to be seen very much more often in gardens than they are, S. *farinacea* seems likely to make more progress in the popularity stakes than most in the early years of the third millennium. Three cultivars hold the AGM. A more recently introduced fourth – 'Strata' – was chosen as Bedding Plant of the Year for 1997 by the British Bedding and Pot Plant Association. With such a weight of informed opinion and commercially inspired publicity now behind this species, surely the conservatism of much of the gardening public will gradually crumble to give it the welcome it deserves.

The species is native to Mexico and the bordering states of the USA, Texas and New Mexico, and became a popular garden plant in North America in the second half of the nineteenth century. It is a herbaceous perennial and authorities differ quite widely as to its hardiness when wintered outdoors. This is probably because little experience has been accumulated. However, it grows readily and speedily from seed and is probably best regarded as a half hardy annual for all practical purposes.

The species itself is seldom grown, and is a much larger plant than the widely available modern cultivars. It can grow to around 1m (3ft) in height with a spread of 60cm (24in). The stems, usually branched, are erect and densely hairy. The closely spaced leaves are glossy, mid- to dark green and up to 8cm (3in) long. They are mostly several times as long as they are broad, being ovate-lanceolate to linear-lanceolate.

The densely packed but slender inflorescences are 15–30cm (6–12in) long, with the flowers in whorls of 8–16. The greyish-white calyces, which are around 1cm (½in) long, are a conspicuously attractive feature. They are densely hairy, giving the floury appearance for which the plant is named (*farinacea* means 'floury'). The corolla, also hairy, is about 1.5cm (½in) long and may be blue, violet or purple. The short lower lip is relatively broad at its bottom end.

Cultivation

The most widely grown of the other three salvia species used for formal bedding, S. *farinacea* is as cool in its visual effect as red S. *splendens* is hot. The colour range available embraces white, blue and silver. There is a refinement in its growth habit and flower display, too.

Thanks to its harmonious character, *S. farinacea* is an admirable gap filler near the front edges of beds and borders of herbaceous perennials and shrubs. In recent years it has been used for the purpose in the classic pair of perennial borders in the RHS Gardens at Wisley with indisputably pleasing effect. Successful associations in beds and less formal plantings include those of the varieties 'Victoria' with *Cosmos* 'Sonata White' or *Zinnia angustifolia* 'Tropical Snow', and 'Strata' with *Verbena speciosa* 'Imagination'.

Flowering commences 3½–4 months after sowing, and is continued freely until the autumn.

S. farinacea is a species of easy culture, though it will do best in full sun. It is a valuable filler among herbaceous and mixed plantings and will do very well as a container subject. Propagation may be by cuttings taken in summer and overwintered in a greenhouse, although, in practice, the plants are almost universally raised from seed, which should be sown in heated greenhouse conditions in late winter or early spring.

Cultivars

In all the cultivars now available the inflorescences are held well above the foliage. Plant spread is usually about 25cm (10in).

'**Cirrus**' is white flowered with white calyces and greenish-white inflorescence stems. Height 40cm (16in). '**White Victory**' AGM is also all white – stems, calyces and corollas alike. Height 35cm (14in). '**Blue Victory**' AGM has dark violet-blue stems, calyces and corollas. Height 35cm (14in).

'**Victoria**' AGM has purple-blue stems, calyces and corollas. Height 50cm (20in). '**Rhea**' is closely similar to 'Victoria' but is more compact. Height 35cm (14in).

'**Strata**' has silvery-grey stems and calyces, with the deep clear blue corollas providing a striking contrast. Height 40cm (16in). Awarded a 'Fleuroselect' Gold Medal, this was also chosen in Britain as the Bedding Plant of the Year for 1997.

SALVIA COCCINEA
Jussieu ex Murray (1778), Tropical sage

S. coccinea is found growing wild or naturalized over a large area of South and Central America and in the West Indies but, like so many salvia species, is thought to be Mexican in origin. In cultivation for over two

The popular cultivar *S. farinacea* 'Victoria' is valuable as a bedding plant or as a gap filler in herbaceous borders.

centuries, listed in the catalogues of major British mail-order seed companies, and honoured by major trials awards, this species is still little seen in gardens. It is a true perennial, but one that is easily raised from seed as a half hardy annual. And, as with *S. splendens*, this is almost invariably the method of propagation chosen, and the plant is rarely treated other than as an annual, except in completely frost-free climates. Although not at all hardy, in exceptionally favoured situations in southern England it may sometimes overwinter successfully in the open with the aid of a protective mulch.

The species reaches a height of around 1m (3ft) and although fairly upright in habit, the hairy stems branch freely so that the spread of the plant is usually well over

half its height. The dark green hairy leaves are up to 6cm (2½in) long and are grey underneath. They vary from ovate to triangular, usually with pointed tips. Their margins are crenate-serrate.

Coccinea means 'scarlet', and the flowers are, indeed, usually red in the species. They are borne in whorls of 3–6 on branched racemes that are up to 30cm (12in) long. Individual flowers are 2–2.5cm (¾–1in) long, with the lower lip much longer than the straight upper one. The calyces are green or purple tinged. The stamens are exserted.

Cultivation

This, the third 'bedder' in the genus, very fully makes up in subtle appeal what it lacks in up-front impact. Like S. splendens, its flowers are in the hot colour range, but the effect they create is entirely different because of their smaller size and less dense presentation on the inflorescence, and of their foiling by dark-coloured calyces and the dark green of foliage, stem and buds yet to open. The difference is accentuated by the growth habit – upright rather than spreading. It is not a plant for mass effect but can be very pleasing spaced out in a carpet of ageratums or a gazania variety like 'Cream Beauty'.

S. coccinea does best in full sunshine and on a fertile soil. It responds well to being watered freely in prolonged dry weather. The species is among the more brittle-stemmed in the genus, so avoid growing in relatively unsheltered situations. Flowering commences in midsummer, from plants sown in early spring in a warm greenhouse, and continues until ended by the first frosts of autumn.

Cultivars

Cultivars differ from the species in height and flower colour. Those described below come true from seed. It is also possible to take cuttings in late summer and overwinter them in a greenhouse.

'Pseudococcinea' AGM 1996, formerly regarded as a subspecies but now only as a cultivar, is characterized by the large number of flowers in each whorl, and by its particular vigour: it may reach 1.2m (4ft). It is a rather more hairy plant than the species. Those who saw

An outstanding cultivar with a long flowering season,
S. coccinea 'Lady in Red' is easily grown from seed.

plants at the Wisley trial in full flower are unlikely to forget them, fantastically spectacular visual firecrackers that they were.

'Lady in Red' AGM 1996, Fleuroselect Gold Medal 1992, also has bright scarlet flowers. Height does not usually exceed 50cm (20in). **'Coral Nymph'** (syn. 'Cherry Blossom') tends to be slightly taller – up to 60cm (24in) high. The corolla tube and upper lip are very pale pink, the lower lip a deep coral-pink. This cultivar also has a Fleuroselect Gold Medal.

'Lactea' and **'Snow Nymph'** are white-flowered, with calyces untinged by darker coloration.

'Coral Nymph' and 'Lady in Red' were bred with a view to their use in summer bedding, and they are outstanding among the taller plants for this purpose. They can also be used to create striking displays when grown in large patio tubs.

Salvia patens AGM
Cavanilles (1799), Gentian sage

'Undoubtedly one of the glories of the genus…with huge royal blue flowers hardy surpassed by any [other] in intensity of colour,' wrote Dr James Compton, a leading contemporary authority on the salvias of Mexico, to which S. patens is native.

The species is 'doubtless, the most brilliant in cultivation, being surpassed by none and equalled by few other [garden] flowers'. From these words, written over a century earlier, there is no mistaking the enthusiasm, either, of William Robinson in his classic book *The English Flower Garden*.

Widespread in cultivation by the mid-nineteenth century, S. patens has remained one of the handful of salvia species that are widely known to British gardening enthusiasts. It is not far from hardiness over much of the milder parts of southern England and Wales. On well-drained soil in these areas, it is commonly treated almost as a hardy perennial, overwintering outdoors aided only by an autumnal mulch for frost protection.

In Britain, mature plants may be up to 75cm (30in) tall although in favoured conditions in warmer countries they can achieve twice that height. The spread of well-grown specimens is around three-quarters of their height. The stems are erect but branching, and are sticky to the touch. The numerous leaves, often rather pale green, may be quite large, and exceptionally reach 20cm (8in) in length. The shape is usually triangular or

PLATE III

SALVIAS GROWN AS ANNUALS

S. coccinea 'Lady in Red'

S. coccinea 'Coral Nymph'

S. farinacea 'Cirrus'

All specimens are shown at approximately life size

S. farinacea 'Victoria'

S. viridis

S. farinacea 'Strata'

hastate (spearhead-shaped), though sometimes more nearly ovate. They are mostly quite long stalked, and are slightly hairy above and more so below. Margins of the leaves are toothed, sometimes sharply (serrate) but otherwise they are crenate (round-toothed).

The large royal-blue flowers are borne in pairs, widely spaced on inflorescences up to 40cm (16in) long. The flowers in each pair are on opposite sides of the inflorescence stem, and each pair is set at a right-angle to the ones above and below. The result is four rows of flowers up the length of the inflorescence, one on each of the four faces of the square stem. Individual flowers are commonly over 5cm (2in) long, with a broad, relatively short tube and a large, hooded upper lip. At a wide angle to this is the lower lip, also large, which has two spreading lobes (*patens* means 'open', and refers to the angle between the upper and lower lips). There is a pair of narrow bracts at each whorl; these persist after the flowers have fallen.

S. patens often overwinters outdoors in southern England.

Cultivation

Striking though its flowers are for their size and intense colour, too few open at one time on a single plant to give the visual impact that is associated with bedding plants: *S. patens* is seen at its best in mixed plantings.

The plant performs best in sun on fertile soil, and will benefit from watering in dry weather. It tolerates some shade, and may even flower all the better for it in particularly warm summers. The flowering period commences in midsummer from plants raised by early spring sowing in a greenhouse. An earlier start may occur when plants are vegetatively propagated.

Propagation is most commonly from seed. An alternative method is to exploit a feature of the species, unusual in the genus, of forming tuberous roots. These are of the same botanical character as those of dahlias and can be stored over winter in exactly the same way, being replanted each year in spring. Once frost has destroyed the top growth in autumn, they should be lifted and allowed to just dry, after the removal of adhering soil, and then stored in a box, surrounded with sand, peat or perlite. Whichever material is chosen, it should be just very slightly damp, to ensure the tubers do not dehydrate. The container should be kept in a frost-proof place until late winter when the tubers can be potted up and grown on in a warm greenhouse. It is quite possible to multiply stock by splitting up the

tubers before potting. This entails cutting the woody base of the stem lengthwise into 3–4 pieces. You will need a very sharp knife, and the operation is easier if you recruit someone to hold the tuber cluster while you cut. Make sure some tubers are attached to each group of shoot buds.

Cuttings root easily and can also be used as a means of propagation. They should be taken in the middle of the summer, in order to allow the young plants time to build up the tuberous roots which will help to ensure successful overwintering. The young plants need frost-free greenhouse conditions.

Cultivars

With due respect to the various cultivars which bear flowers of different colours to the deep blue of the species, that particular colour is so special that my own first choice must fall on *S. patens* itself. As well as the species, the following cultivars are widely available.

'Cambridge Blue' AGM has pale blue flowers. It comes 100 per cent true from seed. **'Chilcombe'** is lilac-flowered and was found in the 1980s in the Dorset garden of John Hubbard, a salvia enthusiast of long standing. The flowers of **'Guanajuato'** are very much larger than the species, up to 8cm (3in) long, and – happily – of the same colour. The plants are rather taller than those of the species. This form is a recent addition to the range, having been found in the wild in 1991 by Compton, d'Arcy and Rix. It comes true from seed. **'White Trophy'** is a white form, widely available.

SALVIA ROEMERIANA (syn. *S. porphyranthera*)
AGM 1996 Scheele (1849)

This species is a native of Texas, Arizona and Mexico. It earned high praise in print in the nineteenth century, and was among the species and cultivars that received the AGM at the RHS trial at Wisley in 1996. Even so, in the intervening hundred-odd years it has remained surprisingly little-known. The surprise must particularly attach to this species, because it comes easily from seed, and is also among the relatively few that approach full size and come into flower within a very short time from sowing. It is able to survive at least a few degrees of frost in well-drained soil, but in practice it is almost always treated as a half hardy annual.

This is a small, compact plant, usually reaching a height, during flowering, of 30cm (12in) in cultivation. On well-grown specimens the dark purple-tinged stems are quite numerous. The leaves are dark greyish-green, and more or less round or cordate. They are only 2–3cm (about 1in) long, with margins notched or sometimes slightly lobed.

It flowers from midsummer to early autumn. The inflorescences, which are 10–20cm (4–8in) long, are displayed well above the foliage. Each whorl comprises only 2 or 4 flowers, but in relation to the size of the plant these are large, up to 3cm (1¼in) in length. Between scarlet and deep cherry-red, their intense colour is complemented by dark calyces. Each individual flower is held in an upright poise, and has a spreading lower lip.

Cultivation

S. roemeriana has been recommended as an edging plant for beds of taller half hardy annuals, but it needs a warm sheltered site to do itself justice. It has a neat habit in its first season from seed and a long flowering period. Most often seen as a pot plant in the majority of British gardens, it is likely to be seen at its best only where grown as such. The fortunate owners of environmentally favoured gardens who have not tried it as a bedding plant should do so.

Propagation is usually from seed, but cuttings can also be rooted readily and used as a means of overwintering the plants. Very fine specimens, which had been propagated vegetatively in this way, were seen in the RHS trial at Wisley in 1995–96.

SALVIA VIRIDIS (syn. *S. horminum*)
Linnaeus (1753), Annual clary

The only true annual described in this book, *S. viridis* is native to much of southern Europe, North Africa and parts of western Asia. It is believed to have been introduced into England by 1596 and was among the species described in Elizabethan times by John Gerard in his *Herball*. The common name clary is now widely used for it, but properly refers to *S. sclarea*.

Used in the past as a culinary herb, it is now grown only for its remarkable coloured bracts which crown the flowering stems. Slightly aromatic, it makes a good cut flower, and may be used dried as well as fresh. It is hardy enough to be sown outdoors in mid-spring, and on well-drained soils in favourable situations self-sown seedlings frequently survive the winter.

It is a hairy plant of very erect habit and up to 60cm (24in) in height, although modern cultivars are usually rather shorter. The stems are usually branched, and bear mid-green, ovate to oblong leaves which are up to 5cm (2in) long with blunt ends and notched margins.

White, lilac or purple flowers are borne in whorls of 4–8 on long racemes. They are small, 1.5cm (½in) long. Both the calyces and the two bracts immediately below the whorl of flowers persist after the fall of the corollas. At the upper end of each inflorescence stem a number of pairs of papery textured, enlarged bracts develop from early summer onwards. They persist until autumn, and, unaccompanied by flowers, are the principal feature of attraction in the species. They are white, pink, blue or purple, sometimes with the veins darker in colour than the rest of the bract.

Seed of separate bract colours is not generally obtainable, which is unfortunate as single colours provide much better possibilities of effective associations with other plants. The most widely available mixture is **'Claryssa'**, a selection for more intense bract coloration and larger bract size.

Cultivation

It thrives on poor, dry soil, and may become rather rampant on those that are more fertile. Propagation is always by seed.

6

HARDY HERBACEOUS PERENNIALS

As befits such a large genus with such a wide geographic spread, many of the herbaceous salvias are truly hardy in the British climate. Nearly all of the hardy species are native to Europe and cooler parts of Asia. Indeed, *Salvia pratensis* and *S. verbenaca* are British natives, and the former is among the species that are relatively commonly grown.

There are two major groups of hardy herbaceous perennial salvias. One of these includes a small number of species – *S. × sylvestris* for one – which are among the best known and most widely grown in the genus, firmly established as reliable garden performers with a distinctive habit. The second group also has many admirers, but one can walk one's dog along many miles of pavement without seeing a single front-garden specimen of, say, *S. argentea*, *S. forsskaolii* or *S. sclarea* – surely these are species that deserve to be more widely known and grown. The third group of hardy perennial salvias consists of those that do not fit into the first two groups.

The hardy herbaceous species are generally tolerant of a wide range of soil types; any marked preferences of individual species are noted below under the individual descriptions.

Protective mulches applied in autumn are unnecessary. As a whole, the plants are sufficiently stiff-stemmed not to need artificial support. The major exceptions are the tallest cultivars of *S. nemorosa*, *S. × superba* and *S. × sylvestris*, such as 'Indigo', 'Lye End' and 'Rose Queen', which may need support, particularly in relatively exposed gardens.

S. nemorosa 'Ostfriesland' (p.61) was the first of Ernst Pagels' introductions. The colour of the persistent calyces adds to the attractions of this deservedly popular cultivar.

CLUMP-FORMING SPECIES

S. amplexicaulis p.63	*S. × sylvestris* p.60
S. nemorosa p.60	*S. virgata* p.62
S. × superba p.60	

ROSETTE-FORMING SPECIES

S. aethiopis p.76	*S. jurisicii* p.73
S. argentea p.76	*S. lyrata* p.77
S. austriaca p.72	*S. moorcroftiana* p.70
S. barrelieri p.71	*S. pratensis* p.64
S. candidissima p.77	*S. przewalskii* p.70
S. canescens p.73	*S. recognita* p.72
S. flava var. *megalantha* p.70	*S. sclarea* p.64
S. forsskaolii p.68	*S. staminea* p.72
S. haematodes –	*S. taraxacifolia* p.73
see *S. pratensis*	*S. transsylvanica* p.72
S. hians p.70	*S. verbenaca* p.71
S. hierosolymitana p.69	

OTHERS

S. glutinosa p.77	*S. napifolia* p.79
S. judaica p.79	*S. nubicola* p.78
S. koyamae p.78	*S. verticillata* p.79

CLUMP-FORMING SPECIES

The first group is characterized by three clump-forming species – *S. nemorosa*, *S. × superba* and *S. × sylvestris*. Once established, these and the others in the group all produce many upright, leafy, branched shoots. The narrow leaves are quite small and the long, dense but slender spikes of small flowers open over a long period.

The three species mentioned above are closely related: S. *nemorosa* is a parent of both the interspecific hybrids. Their flower colours, according to variety, are mainly in the range from blue to violet and purple, and the height of all of them falls between 50cm (20in) and 1.5m (5ft).

This is an invaluable group of plants to position among other herbaceous perennials, especially those of brighter flower colour like yellow or white. The blue colour range is well known for its restful effect on the eye, as it is for creating an illusion of being at a greater distance from the beholder than it actually is. In flower – and the flowering season is long – these salvias also look particularly good against neighbouring plants with fresh, bright green foliage. They can, with advantage, be planted in front of or alongside drifts of perennials that do not flower until late in the summer, such as ox eyes (*Heliopsis*), Japanese anemones (*Anemone japonica*) and Michaelmas daisies (*Aster novi-belgii*).

As a schoolboy experiencing for the first time the fascination of plant life and gardening, I had the good fortune to live quite close to the Royal Horticultural Gardens at Wisley, Surrey, and I became a frequent visitor, travelling there by bicycle. I can still remember the effect of at least one of this particular group of species – S. × *superba*, I believe – for its sheer, deep, almost solemn colour impact. Gardens need such plants, like symphony orchestras need double basses. Without them, uninhibitedly bright-coloured performers, such as gaillardia, coreopsis, hemerocallis and rudbeckia, lose their edge for want of visually soothing plant associations. This group of *Salvia* species comes into its own here, with its very different and harmonizing horticultural charm.

SALVIA NEMOROSA, SALVIA × SUPERBA AGM AND SALVIA × SYLVESTRIS

These three species are too closely related for there to be any sense in dealing with them separately. They are among the most easily grown and reliable hardy herbaceous perennials, and have the distinction of being categorized by Graham Stuart Thomas in his classic book *Perennial Garden Plants* as outstanding for their habit, foliage and flower. Of the two species, one subspecies and 22 cultivars listed in the *RHS Plant Finder* 1998–99, no fewer than nine have the AGM. As a group, these are certainly the best-known salvias in

British gardens after S. *officinalis* (common sage) and the bedding salvia S. *splendens*.

S. *nemorosa* (Linnaeus, 1753) is a native of central Europe and western Asia, and is fully hardy in Britain. The two hybrid species, S. × *superba* and S. × *sylvestris*, both originated in cultivation. They share the hardiness of S. *nemorosa*, unsurprisingly, as it is a parent of S. × *sylvestris* and a grandparent of S. × *superba*. Plants and seeds of S. *nemorosa* and S. × *superba* are readily available, but garden plants are almost always of one or another of the numerous cultivars.

Although first described in 1753, S. *nemorosa* is recorded as having been introduced to Britain over 30 years earlier. It must have been among the very first salvia species cultivated in British gardens. There is a large number of German names among the modern cultivars of this species, and those of S. × *superba* and S. × *sylvestris*. This reflects the major work in selection and breeding undertaken by the dedicated German nurseryman Ernst Pagels in the middle of the twentieth century.

The leaves of all three species are up to 8cm (3in) in length, and are usually about twice as long as they are wide. Their shape is lanceolate, and the colour in most cultivars is mid-green. Basal leaves are either short-stalked or sessile, and stem leaves almost always sessile. The upper leaf surfaces are typically dull and rugose, with those of S. *nemorosa* being matt. Leaf margins are usually finely toothed.

The spike-like inflorescences vary between 10 and 25cm (4–10in) in length according to cultivar. They are densely furnished with small flowers – under 1.5cm (¾in) long – in whorls of up to 6.

All three species have violet flowers, although this colour may vary to shades of purple in many plants of S. *nemorosa* and S. × *superba*. The inflorescences remain in an attractive condition for anything up to two months, in early and mid-summer. If they are promptly removed as this period of flowering comes to an end, a second display usually develops in early autumn.

Cultivation

There is no question that the plants in this group are natural strong candidates for almost any herbaceous bed or border, or for mixed plantings of herbaceous perennials and shrubs. Plants to associate closely with them should be chosen to complement or contrast with their characteristic upright habit and their colours – mainly in the range blue, violet and purple. Among many attractive possibilities for this are the herbaceous perennials *Achillea filipendulina*, *Gypsophila paniculata*, *Hemerocallis lilioasphodelus* (syn. *H. flava*) and *Thalictrum aquilegifolium* 'White Cloud', or *Thalictrum delavayi* 'Album'.

Shrubs that are particularly interesting for juxtaposition with these salvias include a wide range of species and cultivars of cistus and potentilla, *Brachyglottis* 'Sunshine' and *Lupinus arboreus*.

Propagation is most often by division. An alternative method is by cuttings, which should be taken in early spring and will root readily. Raising from seed – which is relatively small – is also easily achieved, but the only cultivar that reliably comes entirely true from seed is

Unlike its cultivars, *S. nemorosa* comes dependably true from seed. It is well worthwhile growing in its own right.

S. × *sylvestris* 'Rose Queen'. If seed is sown early in the year in a heated greenhouse, flowering late in the summer of the same year is often achieved.

Heights given in the lists of cultivars can only be indications, with variations in soil and season having a large influence on actual height achieved.

Cultivars of Salvia nemorosa

Cultivars of *S. nemorosa* include: **'Amethyst'** AGM 1996, bright purplish-violet, 80cm (32in) high, and **'Lubecca'** AGM 1996, which is violet-blue and has pretty pinkish-purple bracts and calyces which persist after the flowers have fallen, adding valuably to the ornamental effect. Height 75cm (30in).

'Ostfriesland' ('East Friesland') AGM 1996 is the most widely seen of all the cultivars in this group. Its violet flowers are complemented by pink to purple bracts. These are attractive after the flowers have dropped. Height 75cm (30in).

'Plumosa' AGM 1996, which is 60cm (24in) high, has a very distinct inflorescence, being quite bulky and about 5cm (2in) in diameter. The flowers themselves are not visible, but a striking dense mass of long-persisting bracts, pinkish-purple in colour, is. I find the effect is a little too top-heavy for my taste, but the Wisley trial judging panel was favourably impressed.

'Porzellan' ('Porcelain') AGM 1996 has blue-tinged, white flowers with yellowish-green calyces. Height 70cm (28in).

S. nemorosa subsp. tesquicola differs from the species in being taller – about 1.2m (4ft) high – and less bushy, with slightly larger pale blue flowers.

CULTIVARS OF SALVIA × SUPERBA

S. × *superba* is believed to be a hybrid between *S.* × *sylvestris* and *S. amplexicaulis*. Other parentages have been suggested, but all the species concerned are quite similar to one another. *S.* × *superba* itself grows to about 1m (3ft) in height and has violet-blue flowers. These are in whorls slightly more widely separated from one another than in *S. nemorosa* and *S.* × *sylvestris*.

'Superba' is a confusingly named cultivar of the species. It differs principally in the colour of the bracts, which are reddish-purple, as against the purple-tinged green bracts of the species.

'Rubin' AGM 1996, is 60cm (24in) high and has

S. × superba 'Superba' (p.61) is a very popular hardy salvia.

bicoloured flowers with pale pink upper lips and pinkish-purple lower ones. The persistent bracts and calyces are both maroon.

CULTIVARS OF SALVIA × SYLVESTRIS

S. × sylvestris is a hybrid between *S. nemorosa* and *S. pratensis*, which is an equally hardy species, though of considerably different growth habit.

'Blauhügel' ('Blue Mount') AGM 1996, has intense violet-blue flowers and is very compact. Height 60cm (24in).

'Blaukönigin' ('Blue Queen') is rich violet. Height 60cm (24in).

'Lye End' bears lavender-blue flowers with dark calyces. The inflorescence is more open than in other cultivars in this group. Height 1.5m (5ft). One of the parents of this tall-growing cultivar may have been *S. pratensis* Haematodes Group rather than the species itself.

'Mainacht' ('May Night') AGM 1996 produces violet flowers with buds and calyces of purplish-black. Conspicuous green bracts subtend the lower whorls of flowers on the inflorescence. Height 60cm (24in).

It is earlier-flowering than the other cultivars, and among the most widely grown. Graham Stuart Thomas has described it as 'gorgeous with *Paeonia officinalis*': it is!

'Rose Queen' is rose-pink with red calyces. It grows to 75cm (30in) high and comes true from seed.

'Tänzerin' ('Dancing Girl') AGM 1996 is violet and 90cm (3ft) tall.

'Viola Klose' has dark green leaves and deep violet flowers. Height 50cm (20in).

SALVIA VIRGATA (syn. *S. regeliana* hort.)
Jacquin (1770)

This species, which is similar to *S. nemorosa*, is not commonly seen in British gardens. It is native to south-eastern Europe and is naturalized in California. Some authorities believe that it is one parent of the hybrid *S. × superba*. Though it is hardy in the British Isles, it may be susceptible to dying out over winter in wet soil conditions.

Some of the plants and seeds sold as *S. regeliana* are in fact *S. virgata*. Other plants sold as *S. regeliana* belong to the species *S. verticillata*.

Plants attain a height of up to 1m (3ft), and have long-stalked basal leaves which are much larger than those of *S. nemorosa*. There are also far fewer stem leaves in *S. virgata* and the whorls of flowers are more widely spaced along the inflorescence axis. The calyces are purple and the flower colour varies from pale lilac to purple. The corolla tube is more or less entirely enclosed by the calyx, but the hooded upper lip is prominent.

Propagation of this species is by seed or cuttings. From an early sowing, some plants will flower in their first summer.

SALVIA AMPLEXICAULIS (syn. *S. villicaulis*)
Lamarck (1791)

Like *S. virgata*, this species is also closely related to *S. nemorosa*, but is a more hairy plant. Again like *S. virgata*, it is thought by some botanists to be a parent of *S. × superba*. It is native to south-eastern Europe and, though not widely grown, makes a fine, free-flowering garden plant.

The stalkless stem leaves clasping the stems give the species its name: *amplexicaulis* means 'stem-clasping'. Whorls of violet-blue flowers are close together to form an almost continuous spike, as in *S. nemorosa*, and the plants reach up to 90cm (3ft) high.

ROSETTE-FORMING SPECIES

The species belonging to the second major group are altogether distinct in habit from those in the first. Almost all of the leaves of each plant arise very close together from ground level. In the first year from seed there is a single rosette of leaves, but after this has produced a flowering stem the plants take on a less symmetrical appearance, each with a number of leaf clusters that individually lack the size and regularity of shape of the first rosette. From each basal leaf cluster, a leafless or nearly leafless flowering stem develops.

Plants of many of these rosette-forming species are relatively short-lived – a very few years only – and some commonly behave as biennials, dying after a single flowering season. In most, the leaves are large, and so different in size and shape to those of salvia species belonging to other groups that it is hard to accept they are all members of the same genus.

The type plant of this group, if there can be one, might well be clary sage (*S. sclarea*). It is almost certainly the member of the group most often seen, usually in the form of its superior variety *turkestanica*. The flowering stems bear few leaves, and those are very small. In spring they virtually erupt from the basal rosette or cluster of leaves, eventually reaching a height of up to 1.2m (4ft). Cutting the first flush of stems down to ground level as soon as flowering is over commonly results in the production of more – repeat flowering, as it is called. Although the other species in this group differ in leaf shape, size and hairiness, in stem height, and in flower size and colour, this is the pattern of development of all the rosette-forming species.

In the garden, placement must take into account that the foliage is almost entirely at ground level and that the decorative effect of these species is during the flowering period, after which most lack in interest.

Two species, *S. argentea* and *S. aethiopis*, are worth a special mention because of the attractiveness of their foliage, which is, indeed, the reason why they are often grown: the flowers are a secondary attraction. The leaves of both are covered with long, silky hairs, turning them silver-grey, and creating a texture that seems to belong more nearly to the animal kingdom than the plant. Constant stroking is nevertheless perhaps best avoided! *S. argentea* makes a most attractive foliage pot plant and is widely grown as such by professional horticulturists for use at spring shows. Neither species tolerates wet soils, and both are more than usually susceptible to the attentions of slugs and snails.

Numbers of the species in this group – notably *S. flava*, *S. forsskaolii* and *S. pratensis* – are happy in a fair amount of shade, and add to garden interest when grown at the front of established shrubs or in the shadow of trees. Almost all the group members are very resistant to cold. Unfortunately, some are not very tolerant of the persistent wet conditions that are so characteristic of winter in the British Isles and the milder parts of northern Europe. This applies particu-

S. argentea (p.76), which has attractive, densely hairy leaves, thrives in well-drained soil and full sun.

larly to species that originate in the wild in rocky, mountainous environments where drainage of excess moisture from the soil occurs rapidly. Silver sage (*S. argentea*) is an example of such a species, and the fact that it thrives in dry stone walls illustrates the point.

SALVIA PRATENSIS
Linnaeus (1753), Meadow clary

The British native flora includes only two salvia species, of which this is one. Also found in the wild over much of continental Europe, *S. pratensis* is much less widespread in Britain than in the past, true native populations now being confined to meadows on limestone soils in southern England from Kent to Gloucestershire, and in Monmouthshire.

Plant height when in flower is up to 1m (3ft), with the few stems often unbranched below the flowering level. The spread of established plants is 50–75cm (20–30in), with the lax inflorescences of 'Indigo' usually spreading more widely.

Nearly all the leaves are formed at the base of the plant, and in the first year of its life they are in a simple rosette. They are dark green, long-stalked, up to 15cm (6in) long and ovate to oblong with a blunt tip. The upper surface is rugose and short-haired, and the margins are crenate or notched. Stem leaves are comparatively few, much reduced in size and often sessile, in which case the overlapping bases of the two leaves of each pair surround the stem.

The inflorescences are freely branched, each branch being up to 45cm (18in) long, with as many as ten whorls of 4–6 flowers. The corolla is up to 3cm (1¼in) long, with a falcate upper lip. Violet is the usual flower colour in the wild, although white and pink also occur. Seedling plants commonly display some variation in colour. The flowering period is primarily early summer, but some flowers will also be produced in later summer if the stems are cut down as the last flowers fade.

Cultivation
Despite being perfectly hardy and of easy culture in British gardens, *S. pratensis* is a short-lived species. Probably 2–3 years is a fair life expectancy: occasionally plants may even behave as biennials. It will thrive in relatively dry soil conditions and it tolerates partial shade happily, though full sun is equally acceptable.

Propagation is almost invariably by seed.

Cultivars
There are a number of varieties and cultivars of *S. pratensis* and these differ in flower colour and size, and in plant height.

Bertolonii Group has deep blue flowers. Height 60cm (24in). **'Dumetorum'** has relatively small, purple flowers on short spikes. Height 75cm (30in). **Haematodes Group** AGM has large, violet-blue flowers with a paler throat. Height 75cm (30in). A variety introduced from Greece, it is probably the most widely grown and showiest form of *S. pratensis*. In the past it has been regarded by some botanists as a separate species. *Haematodes* means 'bloody-veined'.

'Indigo' AGM 1996 has a lax habit, and requires some support for its thin, brittle stems. The long-stalked leaves are larger than those of the species, up to 20cm (8in) in length, but the flowers are smaller and a vivid violet colour. Height 1m (3ft). This cultivar has been authoritatively claimed as a hybrid between *S. pratensis* Haematodes Group and *S. × superba*. ('Indigo Spires' is emphatically not the the same cultivar as 'Indigo': see separate entry p.89, among the half hardy perennials.)

'Tenorei' Also very free-flowering, is notable for the deep blue of the flowers. Height 60cm (24in).

SALVIA SCLAREA
Linnaeus (1753), Clary sage, Vatican sage

This species is native to southern Europe, and southwest and central Asia, and has become naturalized in other parts of Europe and the USA. It is very hardy and will survive a British winter without difficulty.

The history of mankind's use of *S. sclarea* is known to extend at least as far back as the days of Classical Greece. The English name, clary, is thought to be a corruption of 'clear eye': in the past, anyone suffering from a foreign object in their eye had a seed from the plant put into it as well. Around this seed, mucilage rapidly formed, in which the offending item became enveloped and the whole was readily removed. The botanical name, similarly, is derived from the Latin *clarus* meaning clear.

Clary sage has also been used in times past as a flavouring for wines in Germany, rather as wormwood (*Artemisia absinthium*) is used today as the principal flavouring agent in vermouth. Aromatic oils extracted from the plant have also been used in incense, and the common name Vatican sage is in recognition of this. These oils are still used in the preparation of perfume.

Robust and vigorous, achieving a height and spread up to 120 by 80cm (48 by 32in) in the year after sowing, the species' principal attraction is the conspicuous coloured bracts which subtend the whorls of flowers. In hot weather all parts of the plant have a disagreeable odour when touched.

The large grey-green leaves, ovate to oblong, are coarsely hairy. The basal leaves are up to 25cm (10in) long and about half as wide. Their margins are notched or irregularly toothed. Unlike most other species in this group, the stems also have large leaves, some of which are sessile.

The much-branched stems are coarsely hairy like the leaves. They terminate in large inflorescences, also branched, which are narrowly pyramidal in outline. The whorls of 2–6 flowers, each subtended by a pair of large bracts, are clearly separated from one another by the time flowering commences. The bracts persist after flowering is over and are much more eye-catching than the flowers. They are membraneous, up to 3.5 by 2.5cm (1½ by 1in) and pink, mauve or lilac. The flowers are up to 3cm (1¼in) long, with the upper lip arched strongly upwards, and variable in colour, but usually lilac or blue, with the lower lip cream. The basic colour of the flowers is masked by the numerous short white hairs on the corolla. Flowering usually commences in early or midsummer.

var. turkestanica is white-flowered with pink-tinged white bracts. It is a little less vigorous than the species, and the bracts are larger. Its cultivar **'Alba'** has bracts more or less free of any pink tinge.

Cultivation

S. sclarea is easy to grow, doing best in full sun and on freely drained soil. The size and vigour of the plant should not be underestimated: smaller neighbours planted too near are liable to be covered and smothered by the edges of the basal foliage. It is perhaps seen at its best against a background of taller shrubs. Cutting down flowering stems as soon as the later flowers begin to fade encourages the production of more, and discourages the premature death of the plant. For this species, however, a biennial life span is common.

Propagation is usually by seed. Self-seeding occurs if any flowers are left to complete their development.

The fine cultivar *S. pratensis* 'Indigo' is believed to be an interspecific hybrid.

PLATE IV

HARDY SALVIAS

S. forsskaolii

S. verticillata 'Alba'

S. verticillata

All specimens are shown at approximately ⅔ life size

S. glutinosa

S. pratensis
Haematodes Group

S. taraxacifolia

S. hierosolymitana

S. sclarea var. *turkestanica*, here growing on a wall, is a popular plant, regarded by many gardeners as superior to the species.

SALVIA FORSSKAOLII
Linnaeus (1767)

Of the species in this group, *S. forsskaolii*, *S. argentea*, *S. pratensis* and *S. sclarea* are probably quite the most widely grown. A rather less aggressively vigorous plant than *S. sclarea*, this species' fine summer display of distinctive flowers is the reason for its popularity. A native of the far south-east of Europe (Greece and Bulgaria) and of Turkey, it is found growing quite high on mountain slopes and is fully hardy in the British Isles. As with *S. sclarea*, wet soil conditions are far more likely to be the cause of any winter losses than cold.

The species has been in cultivation since 1880, and owes its botanical name and some of the variability of its spelling to the eighteenth-century Finnish plant collector, Peter Forsskål, after whom it is named.

Established plants may reach a spread of 1m (3ft) and, when in flower, an equal height, though plants in poor dry soils in dry seasons may be considerably smaller. The hairy, dark green leaves are mostly basal with relatively long stalks. In size they may be up to 30 by 23cm (12 by 9in), and are usually broadly ovate with serrate or crenate margins. The foliage dies down completely in winter in Britain.

The stems, usually but not always branched, may have a few small leaves below flowering level. Between 4 and 8 flowers are found in each whorl, and these are widely spaced along the inflorescence axis. The flowers are up to 3cm (1¼in) long. Their colour varies from violet-blue to pinkish-magenta, with the centre of the lower lip clearly marked white or yellow. The split upper lip is markedly recurved (bent back) and the long stigma protrudes from it. Flowering takes place from early summer onwards, with some smaller spikes sometimes developing in early autumn.

Cultivation

This species will do best when grown in full sun, but does tolerate some shade. It looks at home in mixed plantings and herbaceous borders. A position allowing the detail of the flowers to be seen should be chosen if possible. Unlike most species in this group, S. *forsskaolii* is long-lived in favourable circumstances.

Propagation is usually by seed. From a very early greenhouse sowing, flowering will occur in the first season. Most gardeners prefer the darker end of the flower colour range: if the opportunity presents itself to collect seed from plants with such flowers it is well worth taking. It is also possible to propagate by division.

SALVIA HIEROSOLYMITANA
Boissier (1853), Jerusalem sage

This is another of the numerous herbaceous species that are of the same basic habit of growth as S. *pratensis* and S. *sclarea* with young plants forming a basal rosette of foliage, while the flowering stems have much smaller leaves and very few of them. Coming from the Middle East, S. *hierosolymitana* might almost be regarded as a southern cousin of S. *forsskaolii,* differing from it only to a very limited extent, and being perhaps less hardy. If that delightful low-growing shrub S. *multicaulis* (p.116), also a Middle Eastern native, overwinters successfully in your garden, S. *hierosolymitana* will probably do so as well.

The large, hairy, long-stalked leaves are similar in size and shape to those of S. *forsskaolii*. The petioles sometimes have a reddish tinge or may even be noticeably red. The branched flowering stems take the plant height to 60–90cm (2–3ft).

The flowers, which are about 3cm (1¼in) long and have hooded upper lips, are borne in widely spaced

S. *forsskaolii* is often long-lived and is widely valued for its attractive flowers with distinctively recurved, split upper lips.

whorls. Flower colour varies in the range from pink to purple. The specimens I have seen were a pretty mauve. Flowering takes place in early summer and again in early autumn if the first stems are removed after they lose attractiveness.

Cultivation

The plants will do well in dry conditions, and tolerate some shade. Propagation is usually by seed: from a greenhouse sowing very early in the year, flowering will occur in the first season.

SALVIA HIANS
Royle (1833)

In *The English Flower Garden* William Robinson rates this species as 'one of the best border salvias' and 'the first of the hardy sorts'. A native of the southern slopes of the Himalayas, *S. hians* is found from Pakistan in the west to Bhutan in the east. Its habitats are forest and open slopes at altitudes of up to 4000m (13,000ft). It is a short-lived perennial, capable of withstanding very low winter temperatures.

Established specimens reach a height and spread of up to 60cm (24in). The hairy, deep green leaves are ovate to lanceolate, and have pointed tips and toothed margins. The leaf-blades may be up to 25cm (10in) long, and the petioles can equal and sometimes exceed them in length. The foliage dies down in winter.

The flowering stems, often branched, are almost leafless and the flowers are borne in widely spaced whorls of 2–6. The flowers are large, up to 4cm (1½in) long, with a relatively wide corolla tube. They are violet-blue, with the lower lip – much larger than the upper – often tipped with white. The calyces are brownish-red, and enhance the colour of the corolla. Flowering takes place from early summer to late.

Recently, seed purportedly of *S. hians*, but in fact of *S. forsskaolii*, has been sold by at least two generally reputable suppliers, and I have also seen plants of the latter species labelled as *S. hians* in gardens open to the public where plant naming is usually authoritative.

Propagation is by seed or division.

SALVIA PRZEWALSKII
Maximowicz (1881)

S. przewalskii is a closely similar species, native to China. It is a larger plant than *S. hians*, being up to 1.5m (5ft) tall and 90cm (3ft) in spread, with leaves rather narrower in relation to their length. The flowers are similar in colour to *S. hians*. Although the two species are commonly confused in the trade, *S. przewalskii* can be distinguished by the unmistakeable scent produced by the inflorescence when bruised.

SALVIA MOORCROFTIANA
Wallich (1830)

Like the better-known *S. hians*, this species is a native of the southern Himalayas. The distribution in the wild is from eastern Afghanistan eastwards to western Nepal. It is a plant of mountain slopes between 1500 and 2800m (5000–9000ft) above sea-level.

As with other species in this subgroup, including *S. hians*, it is not uncommon for plants to behave as biennials, dying after flowering in the year after sowing. Information on its hardiness is conflicting, but as it is not found in the wild at such great altitudes as *S. hians*, *S. moorcroftiana* is probably rather less cold-resistant. In practice, though, winter wet rather than winter cold is more likely to be a cause of loss in British gardens.

The entire plant is hairy. In flower, plants typically reach a height of 75–100cm (2½–3ft) and a spread of around 50cm (20in). The long-stalked leaves are large – up to 25 by 15cm (10 by 6in) – and vary from ovate to lanceolate, elliptic or oblong. They are blunt-ended (*S. hians* has pointed leaves). The upper surfaces are grey-green, the lower ones white and very hairy. The foliage dies down in winter.

There is only one flowering stem in the first flowering year. This develops in early summer; it bears few leaves, and branches freely. The flowers, in widely spaced whorls of 4–10, are very pale lilac-blue and about 2.5cm (1in) in overall length. A pair of pink, green-veined membraneous bracts, up to 1.5cm (½in) long, at the base of each whorl add to the attraction of the flower display, just as they do in *S. sclarea*.

Cultivation

A spot in full sun and freely drained soil are the main cultural requirements of *S. moorcroftiana*. Prompt removal of the flowering stems once the last flowers begin to fade will reduce the chance of the plant dying in the aftermath of setting seed. Propagation is by seed.

SALVIA FLAVA VAR. MEGALANTHA
(syn. *S. bulleyana*)
Forrest ex Diels (1912)

In *Salvia* this species is unusual in having mainly yellow flowers. A hardy species, native to Yunnan in southwest China, it was introduced by the plant collector George Forrest in 1912. The synonym *S. bulleyana*, by which the species is more widely known, is in honour of Forrest's sponsor Arthur Bulley, a cotton magnate whose fine garden at Ness on the Wirral Peninsula is now the University of Liverpool Botanic Gardens.

At maturity, plants typically have a height and spread of around 60cm (24in), though they may be larger in very favourable conditions. The mostly basal leaves are bright green and ovate to deltoid-ovate. The margins are regularly crenate, and the leaf surface rather puckered. The foliage dies down completely in winter, reflecting the winter temperatures of Yunnan.

The flowering stems are usually unbranched and leafless, with the upper ends often drooping slightly in an elegant fashion. These bear well spaced whorls of two flowers only. Each flower is up to 3cm (1¼in) long, and is usually a muted deep yellow with a contrasting deep maroon or purple spot on the lower lip. As with many species, there is some variability in flower colour, some plants having flowers that are almost all purple. Flowering commences in summer.

Cultivation

This is a plant of some distinction, and a natural complement to inherently showier neighbours. It is the most attractive of the yellow-flowered salvia species that can be depended upon to flower freely in the British Isles. It is happy in some shade, but does not do well during prolonged shortages of soil moisture and is rather attractive to slugs and snails. Some support is needed for the sprawling flower stems.

Propagation is by seed or division.

SALVIA BARRELIERI (syn. *S. bicolor*)
Etlinger (1777)

This herbaceous species is very much in the style of *S. pratensis* and *S. sclarea* and – like them – is a short-lived perennial which very often dies after its first flowering season. Despite being native to south-west Spain and North Africa it is quite hardy.

The young plants form a basal rosette of hairy, long-stalked, large leaves, up to 25cm (10in) in length. These have interestingly lobed or coarsely toothed margins. Long, slender, usually unbranched racemes of violet flowers, produced from early summer onwards, take the height of the plant up to around 1m (3ft). The flowers are about 3cm (1¼in) long, with a strongly hooded upper lip. The lower lip is paler in colour and on some plants is white (hence the synonym *S. bicolor*).

Cultivation

S. barrelieri is usually propagated by seed. If given an early start by sowing in a heated greenhouse, it will flower in the late summer of the year of sowing.

SALVIA VERBENACA
(syn. *S. horminoides* Pourret)
Linnaeus (1753), Wild clary, Vervain

This species is found growing wild over much of southern and eastern Britain. It is one of only two British native salvias (*S. pratensis* is the other). It is otherwise found in the wild not only over much of Europe and western Asia, where it is thought to be truly native, but also naturalized in parts of Africa, North America and Australia. It is very hardy and seeds itself freely.

The value of its seeds for removing foreign objects from the eye has been claimed in the past, just as for those of clary sage (*S. sclarea*, p.65). The seeds of both species rapidly develop a thick coat of mucilage once wet. It has been known under the common name vervain, but this is usually applied to *Verbena officinalis*.

S. verbenaca is a robust, vigorous and aromatic herbaceous perennial; the erect flowering stems reach a height of 50–75cm (20–30in). The dark green leaves are ovate to oblong, up to 10cm (4in) long and 7cm (3in) wide, and are long-stalked with wavy edges that are notched or irregularly dentate. The upper surface is rugose and has glandular hairs.

The flowering stems, usually branched, have few leaves, and these are small and stalkless. The inflorescences bear up to ten whorls of flowers, each whorl most commonly having six flowers. The flowers are small, usually only about 1.5cm (just over ½in) long, and vary from lavender to purple. Flowering extends from midsummer to early autumn.

S. verbenaca subsp. *clandestina* is native to the Channel Islands. It is smaller and narrower leaved than the species, but has longer, deeper-coloured flowers. At the time of writing, this plant is catalogued by at least one nursery in France, but by none in the British Isles.

Cultivation

S. verbenaca is one of the few salvia species that are suitable for naturalizing in the British Isles, particularly on sandy or gravelly soils. Otherwise, it is unlikely to appeal as much as many others that are equally hardy and which have a better floral display or more attractive foliage, or both.

It is easily raised from seed. From a sowing early in the year, in a heated greenhouse, it may be had in flower in the same year. Plants are often short-lived, but self-seeding usually ensures continuity of presence.

SALVIA RECOGNITA
Fischer & Meyer (1854)

Pinnate leaves easily distinguish this hardy Turkish species from most other perennials of similar general habit. This leaf form is found in a few other salvias, most notably in *S. jurisicii* (p.73) and the shrubby *S. interrupta* (p.113). *S. recognita* tends to be short-lived, although in favourable circumstances it will perpetuate itself by self-seeding.

In flower, the plant reaches a height of up to 1m (3ft) or even more, and the basal foliage will form a clump 50–60cm (20–24in) across. The pinnate leaves, in overall length up to 30cm (12in), comprise a large terminal leaflet and one or two pairs of much smaller lateral leaflets. The leaflets are ovate to lanceolate, grey-green and covered with long hairs. Few leaves are borne on the branched stems, which are also hairy.

The upper half of each stem bears many widely spaced whorls of flowers. These are lilac-pink, 4–6 in each whorl, and are up to 4cm (1½in) long. They are held in a rather upright poise which displays the lower lip and throat of the flower to advantage. The hooded upper lip is a straight continuation of the corolla tube. The flowering period is quite long, from early summer to early autumn.

Cultivation

This species will do best on well-drained soil in a reasonably sunny position.

Propagation is by seed. As with some other species in this group, germination may be poor, or worse, without a period of chilling of the seed while it is moist.

SALVIA TRANSSYLVANICA
Schur (1853)

This species is native over a wide area in central and southern Russia, spilling over its border with Rumania into the Transylvanian Alps. Unsurprisingly, given its origins, *S. transsylvanica* is very hardy in well-drained soil and its growth dies down altogether in winter. Though well-known botanically since the nineteenth century, it is only in recent years that the species has begun to attract the attention it deserves. Seed is now available in garden centres nationwide.

Established plants may attain a spread of up to 1m (3ft) and can produce flowering stems of an equal length. These have a natural tendency to sprawl, so

plant height when in flower is usually around 60cm (24in). The base of the plant is formed by numerous large, handsome, deep green leaves. These are long-stalked, hairy, ovate, and are up to 20 by 12cm (8 by 5in). Their margins are crenate, and their upper surfaces are attractively patterned by their venation. Smaller leaves grow on the lower portions of the stems.

The first inflorescences are produced in early summer, and flowering may continue until autumn. They are large and freely branched, with the whorls of 3–6 flowers densely borne on long, spike-like racemes. The deep violet flowers are up to 3cm (1¼in) long and have hooded upper lips.

Cultivation

Propagation is by seed or by division. From a greenhouse sowing early in the year, flowering may take place in the same growing season.

SALVIA AUSTRIACA
Jacquin (1774)

This very hardy species, native to central and eastern Europe, is among the very few yellow-flowered species that are comparatively commonly cultivated. It has a rather disagreeable odour if handled.

Plants reach about 1m (3ft) high in flower, and the basal rosette of foliage is usually at least 60cm (2ft) across. The dark green leaves can reach up to 30cm (12in) long. They are ovate with markedly rugose upper surfaces and irregularly notched margins.

The unbranched flowering stems, produced in summer, have few leaves and bear flowers in whorls of up to nine. Held in an upward poise, these are a very pale creamy yellow and have markedly exserted stamens.

Cultivation

S. austriaca does best in a sunny position on freely drained soil but is easy to cultivate. Stems and foliage die down completely in winter. Propagation is by division or – more usually – by seed.

SALVIA STAMINEA
Bentham (1836)

Closely related to *S. austriaca*, and in most respects very similar, this hardy species has a more southerly distribution in the wild: Turkey, Iran and the Caucasus.

A major point of difference is the white flowers, of

which there are fewer in each whorl. The plant is also rather smaller, the often branched flowering stems reaching about 75cm (30in) high. The leaves are shorter, ovate to lanceolate and regular in outline, although the margins are coarsely toothed.

It is easy to cultivate and dies down in winter.

SALVIA TARAXACIFOLIA
Hooker (1872)
This species, a Moroccan native, is possibly the least hardy in this group and one of the smallest in stature. When in flower it may stand up to 60cm (24in) tall, while the rosette of basal foliage is only about 30cm (12in) across.

Taraxacum is the genus to which dandelions belong, and this species was given its name due to the shape of its small leaves. Unlike those of the dandelion, however, these are stalked and both surfaces are hairy. The upper surfaces of the younger leaves are silvery because of the white hairs, while the undersides of all the leaves are white. The narrow leaf-blades are up to 8cm (3in) long, with stalks not much less in length. The leaves are wavy-edged and usually have a basal pair of lobes forming part of the single leaf-blade.

The pink flowers, large in relation to the plant, are produced in well-spaced whorls, usually of six flowers, on erect unbranched racemes. Flowering takes place from midsummer onwards.

Cultivation
Easily succumbing to prolonged winter wet, *S. taraxacifolia* is most at home on a raised bed, in a sunny spot in a rock garden or in a container in an alpine house.

Propagation is usually by seed, although division is also possible. If sowing is done in a heated greenhouse early in the year, plants will flower towards the end of the summer.

SALVIA CANESCENS
(possibly *S. daghestanica*) Meyer (1831)
This small Caucasian native does best in the same conditions as *S. taraxacifolia*, but is quite capable of surviving fairly low temperatures.

In flower in late spring and early summer, plants that produce a good show of inflorescences look stunning.

The grey-green leaves, about 5cm (2in) long, die down in winter. Forming a dense basal clump that can

eventually reach 30cm (12in) in diameter, they are oblong to lanceolate, with notched margins, and covered with short white hairs.

The violet flowers, large in relation to the size of the plant, are borne in widely spaced whorls of 4–6 on unbranched leafless stems up to 40cm (16in) tall. A second flowering often occurs in late summer.

Propagation is usually by seed.

SALVIA JURISICII
Kosanin (1926), Feathered sage
In the wild, this species is found in the mountainous terrain of the south of former Yugoslavia, Albania and northern Greece. A low-growing, much-branched plant, it is quite resistant to cold, but may nevertheless die out over winter in wet soil.

When in flower, the plant can reach up to 60cm (24in) high, though it is usually dwarfer. Plant spread is up to 50cm (20in). The stems are white. The distinctive foliage, to which the plant owes its common name,

A sunny position in a rock garden is ideal for *S. taraxacifolia*.

PLATE V   *Salvia splendens* Sizzler Series

'Sizzler Red'

'Sizzler White'

'Sizzler Purple'

'Sizzler Burgundy'

'Sizzler Salmon Bicolour'

'Sizzler Dark Red'

'Sizzler Orchid'

All specimens are shown at approximately ⅕ life size

is as much an incentive to grow this very attractive plant as its long display of flowers. Olive-green in colour, the upper leaves are finely divided into narrow, almost ribbon-like parts, rather like those of some ferns. Each leaf consists of 4–6 pairs of widely spaced segments, less than a centimetre (½in) wide, with a single terminal segment. The lower leaves are up to 10cm (4in) long and undivided but deeply toothed.

The inflorescences are freely produced in early summer, and flowering continues until early autumn. The flowers are borne on branched racemes, in closely spaced whorls of up to 7. Individual flowers, usually pale violet, are small – only about 1cm (½in) long – very hairy, and have the unusual feature of being borne upside down. The lips of the flowers are spreading.

Cultivation

This species does best in full sun and on a free-draining soil which is not too rich. It makes an attractive and unusual container plant, and is one of the relatively small number of salvias which looks in place in a rock garden. Its obvious garden locations otherwise are at or near the edges of beds and borders.

Propagation may be by seed or cuttings. The flower colour on plants from seed may vary from that of the parent. If a greenhouse sowing is made early in the year, the plants will flower in the same season.

There is a white form, **'Alba'**. As with the type species, there may be some colour variation if propagation is by seed, and the variants may not be acceptable to the gardener, i.e. the flowers will not be white!

SALVIA ARGENTEA
Linnaeus (1762), Silver sage

'The amazing young leaves are so heavily shrouded in white wool, especially the backs, they could be used as powder puffs.' So wrote distinguished plantswoman Beth Chatto, in her gardening classic, *The Dry Garden*. The specific epithet *argentea* means 'silvery', and the silver-grey of the handsome foliage is the primary reason why this species is so widely known and liked.

A native of southern Europe and North Africa, it is hardy to temperatures down to at least –10°C (14°F). It may, nevertheless, die out in much less severe winter weather because of prolonged wet conditions. Unsurprisingly, it does best in areas with relatively dry winters, and on fast-draining soils.

The ovate or oblong, wavy-edged leaves are large, with the leaf-blade up to 20 by 15cm (8 by 6in), and the petioles sometimes equally long. The margins are lobed or toothed, and both surfaces are densely covered with long white hairs, giving young foliage its silver-grey appearance. From a sowing early in spring, a large rosette will develop by the autumn and persist through the winter. Late the following spring much-branched stems with small, sessile leaves grow rapidly to a height of 90cm (3ft).

The inflorescences are also branched and bear widely spaced whorls, each of 4–10 short-stalked flowers, which are white with a hooded upper lip flecked with mauve. A pair of large and conspicuous greyish-white bracts subtends each whorl, cradling the cluster of flowers. The flowers themselves are up to 3cm (1¼in) long.

The main flowering period is early to midsummer, but if the stems are promptly removed at their base as the last flowers fade, some later flowers are also often produced. This removal should, in any case, be carried out for a more important reason: allowing seed to set increases the chance of the plant dying after flowering. It commonly behaves as a biennial even when this is done, and in almost all circumstances is relatively short-lived.

Cultivation

This species needs a well-drained soil in full sun to give of its best. It is quite drought-tolerant and can do well in dry-stone walls or on sunny banks. It is sometimes grown as an annual pot plant, purely for its foliage, and as such will overwinter perfectly well in an unheated greenhouse, given enough ventilation to avoid long periods of high humidity. S. *argentea* is very susceptible to slug and snail damage.

Propagation is usually by seed, though it is possible to separate lateral rosettes from the parent plant in spring: these latter are best started in individual pots until well established.

SALVIA AETHIOPIS
Linnaeus (1753), African sage

This species is found in southern and central Europe and western Asia. It has become naturalized in parts of the USA. Surprisingly, in view of both its common and botanical name (*aethiopis* refers to Africa), it is not found wild in Africa. Authorities differ as to whether or not this species is hardier than the closely similar *S. argentea*. In British conditions, for both species, in most winters, wet is more dangerous than cold.

S. aethiopis, like *S. argentea*, is marked out from other species of similar growth habit and hardiness by its white flowers and their thick-felted leaves, which appear silver or grey because of the dense covering of white hairs. In *S. aethiopis*, leaf colour is whitish-grey rather than the silver of *S. argentea*, which has the more densely hairy leaves of the two species. The leaves of *S. aethiopis* are similar in length to those of *S. argentea*, but rather narrower with coarsely and irregularly toothed margins.

The plant inflorescences usually reach a height of around 60cm (24in), rather less than *S. argentea*. The flowers are white, with the lower lip sometimes pale yellow, and are produced from early to midsummer.

Propagation is as for *S. argentea*.

SALVIA CANDIDISSIMA (syn. *S. odorata*)
Vahl (1804)

This little-grown species also has a good deal of similarity to *S. argentea*. As a young plant it too forms a rosette of leaves, grey in colour due to their dense covering of hairs. It is native to the eastern Mediterranean, mainly Greece and Turkey. Established plants reach a spread of up to 60cm (24in). Again, like *S. argentea* and *S. aethiopis* it is hardy but may succumb to wet winter conditions.

The plant can be up to 90cm (3ft) in height. The long-stalked leaves are up to 15cm (6in) long, and are strongly aromatic. Produced from early summer, its flowers are about 2.5cm (1in) long, and borne in much-branched inflorescences. The ground colour is white with small yellow and purple markings.

Propagation is by seed or division.

SALVIA LYRATA
Linnaeus (1763), Cancer weed

Like a few other species, *S. lyrata* is cultivated primarily for its attractive foliage rather than for its flowers: reputed therapeutic properties give it its common name. Alone among the hardy herbaceous perennials considered in this book, it is a New World native, growing wild in woodland areas in the northern and central states of the USA. In most of its native home, it

normally experiences winter temperatures well below those of England, or even most parts of Scotland.

In flower, the plant reaches a height of up to 50–60cm (20–24in). The basal leaves cover an area of about 30cm (12in) in diameter. They are up to 20cm (8in) long and lyrate, that is having a broad, rounded terminal lobe and a pair of lateral lobes, also rounded. The plant's most attractive aspect is the coloration of the leaves: they are dark green, but with maroon markings along the veins and leaf edges. In dry conditions the entire leaf may be maroon.

The main flowering period is early to midsummer, but some flowering may persist into the early autumn. The erect flowering stems, deep maroon in colour, arise from a basal leaf rosette, and each usually bears only a single pair of leaves, which are smaller than those in the rosette. The flowers, in widely spaced whorls of up to 10, are violet to purple and up to 3cm (1¼in) long. In themselves they are not very significant and are only a minor part of the attraction of the plant. The corollas do not always even match the length of the pendent calyces, and are then hidden entirely from view. The calyces are bristly toothed and marked with red, and persist after the corollas have fallen.

Cultivation

This species is well placed at the edge of a bed or border, or in a rock garden. Propagation is by division or by seed.

OTHER HARDY
HERBACEOUS SPECIES

The features of the seven species in this group do not conform with the general characteristics of the species in either of the two major groups described above. Therefore they are placed here in a separate category.

SALVIA GLUTINOSA
Linnaeus (1753), Jupiter's distaff, sticky clary

This very hardy perennial is one of the few cultivated species which have yellow flowers. Among its other characteristics are handsome foliage and a stickiness to the touch. It is native to a large area of central and southern Europe and to part of south-western Asia, and has become naturalized in parts of England and Scotland. Typically it grows in the shade of deciduous forest trees in mountainous areas, often in quite wet soils.

S. nubicola is closely related to *S. glutinosa* and is one of the few yellow-flowered species commonly cultivated. It is quite tolerant of shade.

The stems can reach a height of over 1m (3ft), while an equally large spread of growth may also be achieved. The dark green leaves are long-stalked, and up to 15cm (6in) in length. They are usually close to an elongated triangle in shape, with the tip drawn out narrowly to a sharp point. The margins are serrate and the upper surfaces rugose. As with the stem, sticky hairs are present both above and below.

The whorls of the 2–6 flowers are quite closely spaced on a raceme up to 45cm (18in) long. The flowers have a somewhat drooping poise on the very sticky stem of the inflorescence. They are up to 4cm (1½in)

long, with the lower lip forming a straight extension of the corolla tube. The base of the large upper lip is nearly at a right angle with the lower, but its upper end forms a pronounced hood. The flowers have pale yellow as their ground colour, but fine brown stripes and flecks result in a first overall impression of dull orange. The amount of striping and flecking can vary considerably.

The main flowering period is mid- to late summer, though some flowers are usually present until mid-autumn.

Cultivation

This plant is best used in a shady position among shrubs or other herbaceous perennials, or near the foot of trees. It thrives in moisture-retentive soils. It is one of few salvia species that are suitable for naturalizing in wild garden conditions.

Propagation may be by seed, cuttings taken in spring, or division.

SALVIA NUBICOLA
Wallich ex Sweet (1825–27)

S. nubicola is similar to *S. glutinosa*, but has narrower leaves and is found in the wild on the southern slopes of the Himalayas and in Afghanistan. Specimens I have seen made a less impressive floral display than *S. glutinosa*. This experience is not universal: the owners of the largest of the National Collections in France rate it as much superior, with a longer flowering period.

Propagation is as for *S. glutinosa*.

SALVIA KOYAMAE
Makino (1922)

As yet very little known in the British Isles, this yellow-flowered Japanese native has attracted considerable enthusiasm in the United States. Fairly hardy, it is a woodland plant in the wild and spreads by underground rhizomes.

Its most noticeable characteristics are yellow-green heart-shaped leaves, up to 15cm (6in) long, and whorls of pale yellow flowers in summer. Usually reaching 60–70cm (24–28in) high, the plant often has prostrate stems and is entirely covered in soft hairs. The stems and leaves die back to ground level in autumn.

The plant prefers a shady position and moist soil. Propagation is by seed, division or cuttings.

SALVIA VERTICILLATA
(syn. *S. regeliana* Trautvetter)
Linnaeus (1753), Whorled clary

One of the better-known of the hardy herbaceous perennial species, *S. verticillata* and its cultivars are distinctive plants of quiet but very real charm. This species is quite widely sold under its synonym. Unfortunately not all plants and seed with that name are *S. verticillata*: see also *S. virgata*.

Native to a large area of central and southern Europe and of western Asia, *S. verticillata* is fully hardy in the British Isles. It is naturalized in some northern parts of the USA. In flower, plants may attain a height of over 1m (3ft), though 'Purple Rain', the most widely grown cultivar, is a good deal dwarfer than the species.

The mid-green basal leaves are stalked and up to 13cm (5in) long. They are covered with short, whitish hairs which make the leaves soft to the touch. The outermost in each cluster usually have one or two pairs of basal lobes, while the shape of the main leaf-blade may be lyrate, ovate, elliptic or oblong. The leaf edges are often wavy, and the margins either almost entire or notched.

The flowering stems are leafy; the leaves are smaller than the basal ones, and are sessile and triangular. The inflorescences, often branched, and usually slightly arching, are up to 30cm (12in) long. The widely spaced whorls of flowers each contain a large number, 20–40, of small, violet or lilac flowers. The calyces are also violet-tinged, and after flowering is over they remain attractive for a long period. However, prompt removal of spent flowering stems is needed to promote a summer-long succession of flowers. Flowering usually occurs from early summer to early autumn.

Cultivation

The species and its cultivars are of easy culture, doing best in full sun. They are somewhat susceptible to powdery mildew in later summer. Along with plants like *Alchemilla mollis*, *S. verticillata* provides a visually relaxing neighbour for more flamboyant summer-flowering plants. It is a charming plant for front edge positions in borders and beds mainly planted with shrubs or roses.

Propagation may be by seed, though some variation in flower colour must then be expected. In favourable conditions self-seeding occurs. Divide or take cuttings of the named cultivars 'Alba' and 'Purple Rain'.

Cultivars

'Alba' is white-flowered with calyces untinged by violet. 'Purple Rain', a Dutch introduction of the early 1990s, has both flowers and calyces of a deeper purple than the species. It is also considerably dwarfer – around 60cm (24in) tall. For smaller gardens, this would be the usual variety of choice, and is the most popular. **subsp. amasiaca** is dwarfer still (around 40–50cm/16–20in) and its inflorescences are usually unbranched.

SALVIA JUDAICA AND SALVIA NAPIFOLIA

S. judaica (Boissier, 1853; Judean sage) is native to Syria, Lebanon and Israel, and is rather less hardy than *S. verticillata* but is otherwise very similar. It bears fewer flowers per whorl, but these are larger.

Some botanists argue that this species should be a subspecies of the Turkish native *S. napifolia* (Jacquin, 1773; syn. *S. verticillata* var. *napifolia*), which is again similar to *S. verticillata*, but differs from it in the same respects as *S. judaica*. The foliage of *S. napifolia* is distinct from both, however, as the leaves are broadly ovate in outline and bear an obvious resemblance in shape to those of the turnip (*napifolia* means 'turnip-leaved').

SALVIA NILOTICA (syn. *S. abyssinica*)
Jussieu ex Jacquin (1776)

This species is native to much of Eastern Africa where it grows freely in a range of habitats at altitudes above 1000m (3000ft). In habit, it more closely resembles *S. verticillata* than any other species in this book, but the inflorescences are quite unalike. *S. nilotica* is fairly hardy in gardens in southern England. All growth above ground dies down in winter.

The many-branching leafy stems can reach about 75cm (30in) high, but as they are quite weak the growth tends to sprawl and the plant develops a very bushy appearance. The leaves are lyrate to ovate.

Produced from midsummer to early autumn, the inflorescences are very compressed, being only about 5cm (2in) long and usually comprising six whorls, each bearing many small mauve flowers. Almost the entire length of each corolla tube is enclosed by the calyx, which is green.

Propagation is by seed. In favourable conditions self-seeding will occur.

7

HALF HARDY
HERBACEOUS PERENNIALS

alf hardy plants are those that are able to withstand temperatures down to 0°C (32°F), but are liable to damage or death at lower temperatures. This chapter also deals with some 'tender' species: those that may be damaged by temperatures below 5°C (41°F). I have used either half hardy or tender, as seems most appropriate, in the descriptions of individual species.

In terms of cultivation and garden use it is impracticable to distinguish between half hardy and tender; the distinction between them is inevitably blurred in any event. A species generally agreed to be tender, such as *S. confertiflora*, can be cultivated in just the same way as a half hardy species like *S. guaranitica*, given an appropriate situation in a garden in a favoured part of the country. Quite how climatically favoured the location needs to be depends on how appropriate the situation is. For example a border backed by a sunny wall, and with good shelter from wind from all directions, may be a prescription for potential success with a tender species even in cooler areas.

Many of the species dealt with in this chapter are natives of Mexico, and none of them can with complete confidence be depended on to overwinter outdoors in the British Isles, except in the very mildest areas. This, along with the fact that some do not come into flower before late summer, and a few of the most interesting species seldom before early autumn, has so far greatly limited their popularity in British gardens, and has resulted in most of them being still quite unfamiliar even to gardening enthusiasts.

A fine species, easily raised from seed, *S. canariensis* (p.92) has inflorescences that remain attractive over a long period.

Those marked * are true perennials but are usually grown as annuals and are described in chapter 5, pp.47–57.

BLUE-FLOWERED

RED-FLOWERED

FLOWERS OF OTHER COLOURS

Late flowering is obviously likely to be a problem in areas where the first frosts of autumn come early. It is wrong, though, to look too negatively at this characteristic, which in any case applies only to a small minority of the species described in this chapter. After all, how very nice it is to have new attractions adding themselves to the flower display as the summer draws to its close.

The need to provide somewhere for the overwintering of plants in this group should not prove too great a deterrent for most gardening enthusiasts. A coldframe will be sufficient protection for some of the most attractive species. Where a greenhouse is available, all that is required is just enough heating to exclude frost to ensure that all the species can be brought safely through the coldest months.

IN THE GARDEN

In the garden, half hardy herbaceous salvias may be used in all manner of reasonably sheltered situations, but perhaps look at their best in beds and borders mainly devoted to shrubs. Apart from the possibilities of particularly attractive visual associations, the shelter from wind provided by established shrubs is obviously an asset. Many less thoughtfully conceived plantings of shrubs can look a little dull in the latter half of the summer, the glories of new foliage in the early spring and of flowers in the months immediately following being over, and autumn colours and berries yet to come. This period is a sort of off-season, relaxing to the eye, perhaps, but lacking in clear focuses for interest, and this is just the time when most of the half hardy salvias come into their own.

INFORMAL TROPICAL BEDDING

A number of the half hardy salvias also have a time-honoured place in tropical bedding. Summer visitors to many large gardens open to the public will have met memorable examples of informal borders and beds largely or entirely devoted to half hardy and tender perennials. These, the present-day successors to the tropical bedding of the great Victorian gardens, are often planned to give an effect of exoticism and flamboyance, incorporating plants like cannas, *Fuchsia fulgens*, melianthus, *Plectranthus argentatus* and castor oil plant (*Ricinus communis*). In such company, some salvias look entirely at home, among them *S. conferti-*

flora, with its almost voluptuous foliage and velvety flower spikes, *S. fulgens*, with its glowing deep red tubular flowers, and *S. involucrata*. At the back of a sufficiently wide border or in the centre of a large bed, *S. atrocyanea* can produce a spectacular effect with its great drooping wands of deep blue flowers at the end of the summer.

Fine examples of this type of planting can be seen at Powis Castle near Welshpool in Powys, Bourton House in Gloucestershire, and Coleton Fishacre in South Devon. They are based on annual replanting, using quite large salvia plants raised from cuttings taken the previous summer and grown slowly over the winter in a greenhouse, with little more heating than is needed to exclude frost. Although by late winter these plants are usually not much more than large rooted cuttings, their subsequent growth is very rapid. The plants that are set into their final positions, usually in groups of three or five, as soon as the risk of spring frost has passed are large enough to make a real visual impact within a very few weeks.

Not many garden owners can begin to match the scale of these displays but dramatic effects of the same kind can be achieved in quite small areas. Do bear in mind, though, that these plants are native to warmer countries and will only give of their best in relatively warm and sheltered positions.

There is an almost endless series of pleasing combinations of half hardy salvias with other frost-susceptible perennials. In addition to those already mentioned, other examples include argyranthemums, a variety of dahlias, gazanias, grevilleas, heliotropes, lantana (*Lantana camara* cultivars) and osteospermums, as well as *Eucalyptus globulus* and *Hibiscus acetosella* 'Coppertone'. With some of these, red-flowered salvia species that are smaller in both flower and leaf than those so far mentioned can also look superb: examples are *S. darcyi* and *S. elegans*. There is also a range of blue-flowered species, such as *S. cacaliifolia*, the taller *S. guaranitica*, *S.* 'Indigo Spires' and *S. uliginosa*, which never fail to attract admiration for their colour. These can also, of course, be enhanced by a thoughtful selection of neighbouring plants. The last three mentioned will particularly benefit from well-chosen associated plants being placed in front of them to disguise their natural, but not particularly attractive, legginess.

GENERAL CULTIVATION TECHNIQUES

In cool temperate climates, the almost universal starting point for this group of species is a pot-grown plant for setting out in its flowering position when all risk of damaging frost has passed. The actual technique of planting and aftercare to secure good establishment of plants is dealt with in Chapter 4. Both before planting out and for some while afterwards, it is well worth pinching out the growing points of the more strongly developing shoots of the taller species as this encourages a bushier shape.

Many of the species in this group respond well to liberality in watering throughout the summer months. On naturally hungry soils like sands, many also respond to supplementary feeding. Liquid fertilizer is most effective but, failing that, dry fertilizer can be spread around the plants and watered in well and this will also achieve good results.

SUPPORTING

Some of the best-known species in this group do need support. S. *uliginosa*, for example, is a favourite among salvia enthusiasts; the upper parts of its tall thin stems almost appear to flow as they flex with the wind. To make sure that the entire plant does not finish up almost horizontal, however, some form of secure stiffening for the lower half of the stems is needed.

With species that have somewhat thicker stems, such as S. *atrocyanea*, S. *guaranitica* and S. *elegans* 'Scarlet Pineapple', the object of any support is more to avoid breakage of stems at their bases and the keeling over of entire plants.

Support from convenient neighbouring plants often makes a valuable contribution. When staking is required, there is still nothing more effective and natural in appearance than brushwood. However, with care metal stakes, canes and string are all perfectly acceptable.

It is important to put support in place well before the plants need it. This simplifies and speeds the job itself, avoids the plants being caught out by unexpected high winds in early summer, and also gives developing stems and leaves the best opportunity to conceal the presence of the support. A last-minute supporting operation can leave a previously handsome group of plants looking quite ugly.

OVERWINTERING

When frost in autumn has brought the flower display of these species to its end, there remains the question of overwintering the plants. In climatically favoured gardens, many species may overwinter successfully *in situ*, especially if they are given some protection over the soil surface in the form of a deep mulch. The prospects of success in this obviously depend much on the species' inherent tolerance to cold, the location of the garden, the soil type and the severity and wetness of the winter.

The best advice must be: if in doubt try it and see whether your plants overwinter to your satisfaction. If they fail, you are no worse off than if you had dug them up and consigned them to the compost heap. Many gardeners in milder areas find species like S. *guaranitica*, S. *involucrata* and S. *uliginosa* come through one winter after another to their full satisfaction. One important point to realize is that plants may overwinter successfully, but not recommence growth until very late. Do not be over-hasty in deciding that they have succumbed to the rigours of winter.

It does sometimes happen that the flower display of plants that survived winter in the open is later and poorer than that of plants which were propagated from cuttings towards the end of the previous summer and taken through the winter in a cool greenhouse, as described on pages 131–35. By the time frost risk has passed the latter may be quite large plants already promising a fine show. This is why outdoor overwintering of plants is not even attempted in many gardens that are open to the public and well known for their salvias. Again, if in doubt, there is no substitute for experimenting with overwintering plants *in situ* to see how they fare in your particular conditions.

An overwintering technique that will appeal to some gardeners is to dig up entire plants and put them under cover until spring. They can be lifted once the first frost of autumn has damaged the top growth. Cut the stems back to 15cm (6in) or so, and transfer them to a frostproof greenhouse or frame, either just as they are or, more conveniently, planted into potting compost in a deep box or put individually into large pots. In spring the plants can be used either as a source of cuttings – just like chrysanthemum stools – or re-planted as they are, or divided beforehand to increase their number, or both.

Because entire plants are relatively large, they may be regarded as too space-consuming to be kept in a greenhouse all winter. A coldframe may serve just as satisfactorily for the purpose of overwintering the less tender half hardy species, but remember that slugs are more likely to cause trouble in coldframes, and take precautions accordingly.

BLUE-FLOWERED HALF HARDY SALVIAS

SALVIA ULIGINOSA AGM
Bentham (1833)

Among half hardy salvia species that have achieved a notable popularity among enthusiasts, *S. uliginosa* was one of the last to come into cultivation in Britain, early in the twentieth century. Its current widespread availability reflects both its qualities as a garden plant and the fact that it can overwinter successfully outdoors over much of southern England.

A native of Argentina, Brazil and Uruguay, it is found in the wild in wet soil conditions; *uliginosa* literally means 'inhabiting swampy places'. It does not, however, survive readily from one growing season to the next in Britain on soils that naturally lie wet in winter.

The plant is notable for its lovely pale blue flowers, which are borne freely on slender, much-branched stems. In even quite gentle winds, the upper flowering parts of the stems flow with all the grace of weeping willow. The height may, in very sheltered positions, reach 2.5m (8ft), but is more ordinarily about 1.5m (5ft). The narrow, dark green leaves vary from lanceolate to ovate and are up to 9cm (3½in) long. Their upper surfaces are smooth, and the margins are usually quite markedly saw-toothed. The leaves bear some resemblance to those of the ordinary garden spearmint, *Mentha spicata*, and, coincidentally, emit a minty odour when rubbed.

Short, dense inflorescences, up to 12cm (5in) long, bear the sky-blue flowers in whorls of up to 20. They are short-tubed, up to 1cm (½in) wide, and the horizontal lower lip of the corolla has prominent white

Among the most popular of the herbaceous species, valued for its graceful habit and pale blue flowers, *S. uliginosa* will overwinter outdoors in southern England on well-drained soil.

markings to guide pollinating insects (as is also found in *Nemophila* or *Myosotis*, for example). Flowering commences in mid- or late summer and continues until the first frosts.

Cultivation

In southern England on free-drained soils, *S. uliginosa* can be treated as hardy if given a protective dry mulch in autumn. Slug damage can be a serious problem once shoot growth recommences in early spring. The slender growth needs support, which is ideally provided in part by neighbouring plants.

The plant spreads freely by rhizomes just below the soil surface. Propagation is most easily done by division, or by potting up the tips of the rhizomes, just as can be done for *S. guaranitica* (see below). Cuttings taken in late summer root readily and provide the usual means of multiplication, and of overwintering plants where this cannot safely be relied upon outdoors. Plants can be successfully overwintered in a coldframe if greenhouse space is unavailable.

SALVIA GUARANITICA
(syn. *S. ambigens*, *S. coerulea*)

St. Hilaire ex Bentham (1833), Anise-scented sage Along with *S. uliginosa*, this species must now be the best known of the half hardy perennials. It was introduced to Britain in 1925, quite a long time after most of the other relatively popular half hardy and tender species, and, despite its garden value, remained little known until after the Second World War. Its qualities as a garden plant – intensely blue flowers, clearly displayed and freely produced over a long period – received overdue recognition in 1996: the cultivars 'Black and Blue' and 'Blue Enigma' both earned the AGM following the RHS trial at Wisley.

S. guaranitica is native in a large area of South America, including Argentina and Brazil. In favoured areas of the British Isles, it commonly overwinters outdoors, though all top-growth is destroyed by frost. Elsewhere in the country it is usual to take cuttings in late summer and overwinter the resulting young plants under cover to ensure the continuity of the plant from one year to the next.

The plants reach 1.25–2.50m (4–8ft) in height, according to cultivar and conditions. An individual plant set out in spring may achieve a spread of up to

50cm (20in). The growth habit is erect but freely branching. When successful overwintering occurs, the plants spread to form a clump, by means of rhizomes that develop just below the soil surface. A proportion of the roots will form elongated tuber-like swellings, but unlike the rhizomes these cannot be used as a means of propagation. They are just simple food storage organs.

The bright dark green leaves are slightly hairy and rather nettle-like in appearance. They may attain 13cm (6in), but are usually much shorter. Ovate to broadly lanceolate, they have pointed tips and crenate-serrate margins, and when crushed they exude an anise-like scent.

The bright deep blue flowers are borne in whorls of up to 8, spaced closely together on spike-like inflorescences up to 25cm (10in) long. The tip of the inflorescence is curved over before flowering commences but straightens as flowers begin to open. The narrow, tubular corollas are up to 5cm (2in) long with the upper lip longer than the lower. The calyx, tinged blue in the species, is much shorter than the corolla. Flowering of the cultivar 'Blue Enigma' can commence as early as midsummer and continues until the first frosts of autumn.

Cultivation

A cluster of three or more plants, or an established clump, forms a commanding feature towards the back of a border or in the centre of a bed. This species associates well with small-flowered dahlias with dark foliage, such as the red 'Bishop of Llandaff' and orange-bronze 'David Howard', and with some of the taller perennial asters with white, pale pink or pale blue flowers. They can also look well with Japanese anemones – 'Géant des Blanches' ('White Queen') for example.

S. guaranitica does well on clay soils, partly because the plants need a reasonably good supply of water to support their growth. Gardeners on naturally dry soils should improve moisture retention with compost, leafmould or peat and should attach priority to watering the plants generously during any prolonged rainless periods. This species is happy to have some shade, especially on sandy soil.

Although growth is naturally stiff it is also brittle so some support should be given up to about half of the mature height of the stems.

PLATE VI

BLUE-FLOWERED HALF HARDY SALVIAS

S. cacaliifolia

S. uliginosa

S. guaranitica
'Purple Majesty'

S. arizonica

All specimens are shown at approximately ⅗ life size

S. *urica*

S. 'Indigo Spires'

S. *guaranitica* 'Blue Enigma'

Propagation of the species itself may be achieved by seed, but cuttings, which root easily, are the preferred means of multiplication and overwintering for the species and the cultivars. An easy alternative is to use the rhizomes. These can be found by careful shallow forking of the soil round the plant base in late summer. Division in spring can be carried out in countries with warmer, drier winters than Britain.

Cultivars and hybrids

The most widely grown variety **'Blue Enigma'** AGM 1996 (syn. *S. ambigens*) is similar to the species, but has an entirely green calyx. Height 1.2–1.7m (4–5½ft). The flowers of **'Black & Blue'** AGM 1996 are larger and deeper coloured, and have almost black calyces. The plants are more vigorous but come into flower a good deal later than 'Blue Enigma'. Height 2–2.5m (6–8ft). It is sometimes wrongly known as *S. coerulea*. **'Argentine Skies'** has light blue flowers with a slight mauve tint. A similar height to 'Blue Enigma', it performs less satisfactorily in British conditions.

'Purple Majesty' is an American hybrid between *S. guaranitica* and *S. gesneriiflora*. It has large, very deep purple flowers with prominent exserted stamens. These are not produced until early autumn. Less hardy than *S. guaranitica*, it performs better in countries with summers that are warmer than those of Britain.

SALVIA CONCOLOR
Lamb ex Bentham (1833)

Two distinct salvias are sold under the name *S. concolor*. One is simply an incorrectly named, vigorous form of *S. guaranitica*, similar to the variety 'Black & Blue', but having green calyces. The true species is a native of Mexico, having calyces and corollas of a similar colour to each other (*concolor* means 'of the same colour').

S. concolor can reach a height of up to 2.5m (8ft), and makes a spectacular autumn-flowering display in favourable conditions. The large flowers are deep bright blue and are in whorls of 6–12 on inflorescences that can reach a length of 50cm (20in).

This species is a woodland native, and even in the comparatively less sunny conditions of Britain, does best in partial shade. It has flowered in almost breathtaking style in woodland conditions at Abbotsbury Gardens in Dorset.

Propagation is by cuttings.

SALVIA ATROCYANEA
Epling (1935)

This tall, blue-flowered salvia has a similar habit of growth to the very much better known *S. guaranitica*. A Bolivian native, it is probably a good deal less likely than that species to survive the winter in the open in Britain, although it does have some frost tolerance. It also tolerates fairly shady conditions.

Growing up to about 1.75m (nearly 6ft), its distinctive feature is its long, drooping inflorescences, which are densely packed with rich bright blue flowers. Both the large green calyces and the persistent blue-tinged bracts also contribute to the overall impact. Flowering begins late, in early autumn, but if the onset of frosts is sufficiently delayed the inflorescences can exceed 50cm (20in) long.

Cultivation

This species is probably seen at its best when planted among medium or tall shrubs. Because of its late flowering period in the British Isles, it is most worthwhile for gardeners along the south coast or in London. The best specimens I have seen were growing in the Chelsea Physic Garden.

Propagation is by cuttings.

SALVIA URICA
Epling (1939)

This is among the least seen of the species described in this book but seems worth its place if its performance in my own garden is in any way typical. A Mexican native, its habit is similar to that of *S. guaranitica* although it is probably less hardy.

Plants of this species reach a height of around 1m (3ft). The dark green leaves, up to 10cm (4in) long, are ovate to lanceolate, tapering to a pointed tip. Both they and the upright, branched stems are covered in sticky hairs.

The bright, deep blue flowers, up to 2.5cm (1in) long and with a flared lower lip, are in well-spaced whorls of about six. Although the number of flowers that open at the same time in any one raceme is never large, this species flowers consistently over a long period, from early summer to early autumn, a feature which, along with the number of racemes per plant and the flower colour, should justify it to a wider public.

Propagation is by cuttings.

SALVIA MEXICANA
Linnaeus (1753), Mexican sage

Over a quarter of all salvia species are native to Mexico, as are 24 of those described in this book. Unfortunately, the very species that bears the name of the country so important to salvia enthusiasts is disappointing for gardeners in cooler countries, simply because it flowers so late. In the wild it grows in forest environments up to 2500m (8000ft) above sea-level. It is, nevertheless, unlikely to overwinter outdoors in Britain.

A perennial of considerable vigour, plants can exceed a height of 3m (10ft) by the time they come into flower. It is very variable, however: a less vigorous variety, **S. mexicana var. minor**, is the one normally grown in Britain because it comes into flower earlier, but even this may reach around 2m (6ft) in height.

The leaves are usually grey-green and covered with very short hairs on both surfaces, but in some forms of the plant the upper surface is glabrous. Leaf shape varies also, but they are usually ovate with a long-pointed tip. The leaf stalks are often tinted mauve. The foliage has an agreeable slight aroma of – according to my younger daughter – juniper and ginseng. The larger leaves, near the base of the plant, can be up to 15cm (6in) in length.

The upright flowering racemes are long, usually 30–50cm (12–20in), bearing whorls quite close together, each of up to 12 flowers. These are dark blue to purple, and may exceed 4cm (1½in) in length. Calyces may be either green or dark reddish-purple. Flowering, even of var. *minor*, does not commence until early autumn.

Cultivation
The species will grow well in positions that are in shadow through a good deal of the day. Nevertheless, outdoor cultivation is only worthwhile in warm, sheltered gardens in locations where the first frosts are unlikely before mid-autumn. Otherwise, this fine species is suitable only for appropriately large greenhouses. Propagation is by cuttings, which root easily.

SALVIA 'INDIGO SPIRES' AGM 1996
This fine addition to garden salvias is a chance hybrid found growing in the 1970s at Huntington Botanical Gardens in California. It is presumed that its parents are *S. farinacea* and a species rarely cultivated in Britain, *S. longispicata*. Its distinctive appearance and long flowering period should in future earn it a place in far more gardens than it enjoys at present. It is unlikely to overwinter in the open in any but the most favoured situations.

Of lax habit, it reaches a height of 1.25–1.5m (4–5ft) and a spread of up to 1m (3ft). The branching stems are purple tinged, as are the petioles and the leaf veins. The mid- to dark green aromatic leaves are up to 8cm (3in) long and slightly hairy underneath. The margins are coarsely serrate.

A chance hybrid, S. 'Indigo Spires' produces deep violet-blue flowers with purple calyces over a long period.

Long, slender-stemmed inflorescences curve or bend over under their own weight, in an engagingly informal fashion, from midsummer until the first frosts. They are remarkable for their length, up to 50cm (20in), and are densely furnished with small flowers. These are in many-flowered whorls, and are deep violet-blue with purple calyces that persist after the corollas fall. Flowering starts earlier than that of many species native to Mexico, although both parents are Mexican. This is probably because of the genetic influence of S. farinacea, which itself may come into flower from early summer.

Cultivation

The lax stems need some support. During the spring, pinching out the growing points of the more vigorous shoots will encourage the plant to develop a bushier habit. It is among those salvias that are particularly susceptible to attack by capsid bugs. Propagation is by cuttings, which root easily. The hybrid is reportedly sterile, though I have known seeds offered for sale.

SALVIA AZUREA

Michaux ex Lamarck (1792), Prairie sage

This lovely plant, universally admired for the clarity of colour of its flowers, is native to a large area in the centre and south-east of the United States. It has been widely grown for many years in gardens over much of that country.

As with many species in the genus, authoritative estimates and opinions of quite how winter-hardy S. azurea is in British conditions vary quite widely. It is certainly not dependably capable of overwintering outdoors, even in areas with very mild winters. It may be winter wet rather than winter cold that determines survival or decease.

The plant attains a height of about 1.25–1.75m (4–6ft) and a spread of 60–80cm (24–32in). The stems, often quite numerous, are woody at their bases, slender, erect and usually more or less unbranched up to the height at which inflorescences develop. The long narrow leaves are up to 10cm (4in) long and linear or lanceolate. The upper surface is often slightly downy, giving a greyish effect.

Whorls contain 3–6 flowers each and are usually close together on slender, spike-like racemes. A number of these may be borne at the upper end of a stem.

The flowers are not large – about 1.5cm (½in) long – but the lower lip is of a width about equal to the overall length. The colour is clear blue with a white marking in the lower lip, in the throat of the flower. The flowers last quite well when cut. The flowering period is from late summer, at the earliest, to autumn.

S. azurea subsp. **pitcheri** (syn. var. *grandiflora*) is found in the wild to the south of the main area of distribution. Compared with the species, it has slightly larger and paler flowers in whorls closer together in the inflorescence. Hairy stems and calyces are other points of difference.

At the time of writing I have not yet seen a recent Californian selection that flowers much earlier on very upright stems, reaching a height of only 60cm (24in). It could be an outstanding addition to the garden.

Cultivation

S. azurea requires a sheltered, sunny spot in the garden. Despite the glorious colour of the flowers, their characteristically very late production tells heavily against this species in Britain. Even in the most sheltered position, the slender stems need some support. For the fortunate owners of a sufficiently large greenhouse, S. azurea can be grown in a large container to provide a fine autumn display.

Propagation is by division, basal cuttings in spring, or seed. Plants raised from a winter sowing in a heated greenhouse will flower in the same year.

SALVIA LEUCANTHA AGM

Cavanilles (1791), Mexican sage, velvet sage

The meaning of *leucantha* is white-flowered, but as the prominent calyces of this species are covered with a violet to pale purple woolly down, the botanical name does less than justice to the attractiveness of its bicoloured flowers.

The plant is a low-growing shrub found wild in Mexico and tropical Central America. It was introduced into cultivation in the mid-nineteenth century. Although tender, it can thrive outdoors in favoured situations, but flowers too late to be worth trying where the first frosts are comparatively early. It also makes a fine container plant for a greenhouse or conservatory in autumn and winter.

In very favourable conditions, S. leucantha can attain 1.2m (4ft) in height, though a half to a third of this is a more ordinary range. As flowering commences, the plants spread outwards, commonly achieving a spread of 1m (3ft).

The entire plant is hairy, with the inflorescences very noticeably so. The attractive mid-green leaves are narrow and pointed, measuring up to 10 by 2cm (4 by ¾in). They have short stalks, rugose upper surfaces and finely toothed margins. The foliage smells rather like blackcurrants.

The inflorescences can be up to 30cm (12in) long, the tips bending over gracefully, after the fashion of those of *Buddleja davidii*. The dense covering of long woolly hairs on the inflorescence stems changes in colour from white at the base to purple violet at the tip. The sessile flowers, up to 3cm (1¼in) long, are borne in widely spaced whorls of 6–8. The wide calyces are about half the length of the flowers and are also very densely covered with long woolly hairs, again purple-violet in colour. The white corollas, also densely hairy, are not in themselves very showy, but they contrast well with the more conspicuous calyces. In flower, the overall effect is soft in both appearance and texture: the common name velvet sage is apt. Flowering does not usually commence until late summer or early autumn but in greenhouse conditions will continue throughout autumn, winter and spring. Plants are usually out of flower in summer because this species is unable to initiate and develop flowers during the longest daylengths of the year.

There is a form in which the corolla is almost the same colour as the calyx. It is named **'Midnight'** in American catalogues, while the similar or identical **'Purple Velvet'** is obtainable in the British Isles.

Cultivation

To thrive planted out in the garden, this species needs a border position backed by a wall with a southerly aspect. It does well as a container plant outdoors on a sheltered sunny patio, and the flowering period can be extended for many months if there is conservatory or heated greenhouse space for them to be moved into in early autumn. It lasts quite well as a cut flower, and is grown commercially for the purpose in the USA.

Propagation is easily achieved by means of shoot-tip cuttings taken in late summer. Shoot tips of young plants should be pinched out to encourage the development of a bushy habit.

S. semiatrata is a Mexican species, popular in gardens along the north Mediterranean coast. It has potential as a pot plant.

SALVIA SEMIATRATA
Zuccarini (1832)

Widely grown as a shrub along the French and Italian Riviera, this blue-flowered Mexican species deserves wider attention in Britain. Naturally a shrubby species, it is treated as a herbaceous tender perennial in Britain.

The species is characterized by attractive foliage and small but striking blue flowers. Naturally up to 1.5m (5ft) tall, in Britain it is unlikely to exceed 1m (3ft). On the freely branching stems the leaves are only about 3cm (1¼in) long at most. Shaped like a triangle with gently rounded corners, they are dark green and the attractively textured leaf surface is rugose.

The flowers, up to 2cm (¾in) long, are borne in whorls of up to six on short – 10–15cm (4–6in) – inflorescences. The pinkish-red calyces nicely complement the colour of the corolla. The corolla tube is half white and half blue, which gives the plant its specific epithet *semiatrata*, meaning 'half-darkened'. The beauty of the flowers is additionally enhanced by the very deep violet-blue middle lobe of the lower lip.

Cultivation

A plant for a sunny, sheltered situation, this species may prove outstandingly successful as a container plant. As such, it has been recorded as flowering quite freely through the winter in Australia. More interestingly still, it has flowered in England from midsummer to early autumn outdoors, then continued until January following a move of the container to an unheated greenhouse. It is a brittle plant, and is vulnerable to slugs and snails.

Propagation is by cuttings. In my experience, the young plants hate 'wet feet' in winter: for preference overwinter them in clay pots, and water with caution.

SALVIA KEERLII
Bentham (1833)

Like the previous species, S. semiatrata, this is also a shrub native to Mexico that is insufficiently hardy to be treated other than as a herbaceous perennial, tender in most British gardens. However, in a favoured position in Chelsea Physic Garden it does survive most winters outdoors without serious damage.

An aromatic plant of branching habit, it does not usually exceed a height and spread of 1m (3ft). The greyish leaves are ovate-lanceolate and up to 4cm (1½in) long.

The small lilac flowers are borne in many-flowered whorls on short inflorescences. The flowering period extends from midsummer until early autumn.

Propagation is by cuttings.

SALVIA CANARIENSIS
Linnaeus (1753)

Like S. broussonettii, which is also a native of the Canary Islands, this species is a shrub in its natural habitat. In areas with mild winters, established plants can attain a height of 2m (over 6ft). Outdoor survival in climates such as that of the British Isles is only likely in particularly mild areas, and for that reason the plant is normally cultivated as a half hardy perennial or as an annual.

The young stems and leaf stalks are quite a feature as they are densely covered with long, soft white hairs. The handsome greyish-green arrowhead-shaped leaves, up to 12cm (5in) long, are covered in short white hairs.

Varying from violet to purple, the flowers are up to 2.5cm (1in) long, with a hooded upper lip. They are borne in whorls of 4–8 in densely branched racemes. Individual racemes are quite short, their visual effect enhanced by the calyces and large bracts. These persist after the flowers have fallen, darkening to purple as they age, and the entire inflorescence remains attractive for a long period.

S. canariensis var. candidissima has foliage with a denser, whiter covering of hairs, so that the plant appears silver-grey.

Cultivation

Propagation is easy by cuttings or seed. In their first year, plants raised from seed do not flower until late summer, but the young plants are very attractive for their particularly large leaves on which the hairy covering is very well developed.

Plants raised by cuttings taken the previous year and set out in late spring will grow to about 1m (3ft) and flower in summer.

SALVIA CACALIIFOLIA
Bentham (1848)

This blue-flowered species is one of the more widely available, tender salvias. It enjoys the affection of many enthusiasts for the attractiveness of its foliage as well as of its flowers, which open over a long period.

S. cacaliifolia AGM is a native of forested mountain land in Mexico, Guatemala and Honduras, and plants are unlikely to overwinter outdoors in British gardens except in the very mildest areas of the country. In the United States the species has survived temperatures down to –7°C (20°F) where the crowns were protected by a mulch.

Growth in very young plants is initially quite stiff and upright, but the freely branching stems are quite slender and the plant soon develops a loose, almost sprawling growth habit. Height can exceptionally exceed 1m (3ft), but is more usually 40–50cm (16–20in). Spread is 40–60cm (16–24in). The fleshy rootstock is the natural means of spread, and in climates allowing overwintering, many stems are produced to form a large clump. The entire plant is hairy, though hairs on the upper leaf surfaces are very short and inconspicuous.

The long-stalked, mid-green leaves are triangular, creating a pleasing impression of arrowheads or aces of spades. The leaf shape is similar to that found in some

Deep bright blue flowers and handsome foliage are the attractions of *S. cacaliifolia*.

species of the tassel flower, a tropical genus now called *Emilia* but formerly *Cacalia*. The leaf-blades are up to 10cm (4in) long, and have entire margins. Flowers are freely produced and a deep bright blue. They are tubular and up to 2cm (¾in) long. Each widely spaced whorl comprises only two flowers, but they are borne on a many-whorled, branched inflorescence. The flowering period usually commences in midsummer and is ended by the first frosts in autumn.

Cultivation

S. cacaliifolia does best in fertile, water-retentive soil and a sunny, sheltered position, although it will grow and flower quite happily in partial shade.

It makes a striking container plant, and I have seen it successfully grown in a large hanging basket. It profits

from watering in dry periods, and in containers regular feeding is also needed for it to do well.

Propagation is by cuttings, which root readily. For overwintering, they are usually taken in late summer.

SALVIA DISCOLOR **AGM**
Kunth (1817)

A Peruvian native, the unusual qualities of this species have resulted in its quite wide availability. 'If one could only grow one salvia, it would have to be this one,' wrote Beryl Davies, a noted enthusiast and authority on the genus. A 'flopping oddity' was the description accorded it by Christopher Lloyd, doyen of gardening writers and a member of the judging panel for the RHS salvia trial in 1995–96.

S. discolor is a tender plant, and very unlikely to survive a British winter in the open, even in exceptionally favoured locations. In a warm climate and a sheltered position it can attain a height and spread of around 1m (3ft). In Britain, grown outdoors even in the best circumstances it is unlikely to exceed 60cm (24in).

The thin, lax and branched stems are conspicuously white with a dense hairy covering. The leathery, slightly scented leaves are quite widely spaced and long-stalked, up to 6cm (2½in) long and oblong-ovate. Their undersides, like the petioles, stems and calyces, are densely covered in white hairs, contrasting strikingly with the green of the upper leaf surfaces. The meaning of *discolor* in plant names is 'of two different colours' and here applies primarily to the leaves.

The small flowers are deep indigo and appear almost black against the large pale green, white-hairy calyces. The flowers are in well-spaced whorls of up to 9, on long pale green stems which look, and are, very sticky. They are also slender and droop under their own weight and that of the flowers, which themselves have a drooping poise. It is accordingly difficult to get a good view of the flowers, without having the plant itself well above standing level. This is why its cultivation at the edge of a raised bed or in a large hanging basket has much to commend it.

Cultivation

S. discolor is a summer-flowering species but if grown in a container and moved to a slightly heated greenhouse or conservatory by early autumn it will also continue to flower well into the winter. Outdoors the plant needs a

Strikingly different from other species in both foliage and flowers, *S. discolor* is a distinctive plant for a hanging basket.

very sheltered and sunny position. Support – ideally with some bushy twigs – is needed to display the plant to best effect.

Propagation is by cuttings.

SALVIA ARIZONICA
Gray (1886)

This low-growing species is little known in the British Isles. A ground covering plant, spreading by rhizomes, it deserves a trial by anyone looking for a different, blue-flowered plant for the front of a sunny border, or a rock garden or raised bed where its trailing stems can spill over the edge. Cannington College's walled gar-

den in Somerset is one place where it thrives impressively. A native of Arizona and Mexico, it grows up to altitudes of almost 3000m (10,000ft), and is sufficiently frost-tolerant to have a fair chance of surviving winter outdoors in milder areas.

Producing numerous thin-branched, semi-prostrate stems, the plants are generally no more than 30cm (12in) high but, in favourable conditions, they can be widespreading. The small, lanceolate leaves completely hide the ground from view and act as an attractive foil for the small, indigo-blue flowers, which are borne from midsummer until the first frosts. When handled, the leaves have a minty aroma.

Propagation is by seed, division or cuttings. It is important not to take cuttings too late in the growing year: I have tried and failed in the early autumn, probably because they had become too woody.

SALVIA MISELLA (syn. *S. riparia*)
Künth (1818)

A native of South America, from the West Indies and Mexico in the north to Peru in the south, *S. misella* has also become naturalized in Australia, Indonesia and Zaire. Experience with it in Britain is very limited so far, but plants have overwintered outdoors in southern England. In the wild it favours dry river banks.

It deserves much wider trial in Britain as it is a pretty sight in flower – midsummer to early autumn – the numerous small flowers foiled by a dense mass of attractive foliage. Numerous thin stems grow up to 75cm (30in) and bear mid-green, narrowly ovate leaves to 3cm (1¼in) long, which taper elegantly to a sharp point. The whorls of flowers, up to eight in each, are quite close together on racemes up to 20cm (8in) long. They are mid-blue, the dark calyces and a white marking in the throat of the flared lower lip enlivening the effect.

Propagation may be by seed, division or cuttings. Established plants spread naturally by rhizomes.

SALVIA CHAMAEDRYOIDES
Cavanilles (1793)

Unusually among salvias, much of the growth of *S. chamaedryoides* is more or less prostrate, and plants can appear almost mat-like in the autumn (*chamae* means 'on the ground'). The plant spreads by means of subterranean rhizomes.

In cultivation by the middle of the nineteenth century, this species is found in dry, rocky habitats in its native Mexico, at altitudes of 2000–3000m (6500–10,000ft) above sea-level. It is capable of surviving quite low winter temperatures, authoritatively given as below –10°C (14°F), but this potential is likely to apply only in relatively dry soil conditions.

In the wild, it is a sprawling, evergreen shrub up to 60cm (24in) high. In British gardens, plants usually reach only half that height, and spread to 50–60cm (20–24in). Growth above ground dies back each winter. As the numerous thin, woody stems extend, their basal parts become prostrate or nearly so, with only the upper ends remaining upright. The short-stalked leaves are usually under 2cm (¾in) long, grey-green, and elliptic to triangular. The surface is rugose and the margins crenate.

The intensely coloured, deep violet-blue flowers are in whorls of 2–6 on slender unbranched racemes which are up to 20cm (8in) in length. Up to 2.5cm (1in) long, the flowers have small upper lips, but relatively larger, widespreading lower ones. Flowers are mostly produced from late summer until mid- or late autumn, though an early summer show may also occur.

S. chamaedryoides var. isochroma is more upright than the species, and has greyer leaves.

Cultivation

The edge of a sunny border, an informal paved area, a raised bed or a rock garden are the logical and most pleasing situations for this species. In all cases, good drainage and a sunny position are assets, though I have known it do well where it was in shade throughout the middle of the day.

Propagation is by seed, or by cuttings taken in the summer, but not so late that they have become woody. It is also possible to detach young shoots with roots at their bases from growing plants.

SALVIA REPTANS (syn. S. leptophylla)
Jacquin (1798)

Reptans means 'creeping' which, strictly speaking, this salvia does not do but, nevertheless, it gives a fair indication of its appearance. It came into cultivation early in the nineteenth century.

Although a native of Mexico and Texas, *S. reptans* is fairly hardy in Britain. Significantly, in the National

S. reptans makes a good groundcover plant, enlivened from midsummer by mid-blue flowers.

Collection at Kingston Maurward College it is grown with the hardy species, rather than with the other Mexican species, which constitute most of the half hardy part of the collection.

Growing from tuberous roots (like *S. patens*), its numerous lax stems form a dense sprawling groundcover about 60cm (24in) across. Its height is usually less than 50cm (20in). The dark green, very narrow, pointed leaves are without stalks and up to 8cm (3in) long and only 5mm (¼in) wide at most. The only other species mentioned in this book with a comparable leaf shape (linear) is *S. azurea* (p.90), to which *S. reptans* is quite closely related.

The flowers, which are borne from midsummer to early autumn, are in whorls of 3, quite widely spaced, on slender-stemmed inflorescences up to 30cm (12in) long. They are mid-blue, up to 1.5cm (½in) long and have a widely expanded lower lip, often with white marking in the throat where it joins the tube. The upper lip is small.

PLATE VII

RED-FLOWERED HALF HARDY SALVIAS

S. elegans

S. oppositiflora

S. blepharophylla

S. splendens 'Van Houttei'

S. fulgens

S. darcyi

S. confertiflora

All specimens are shown at approximately ⅔ life size

Cultivation

A sunny situation and well-drained soil should ensure success. If it is possible to place it at the edge of a raised bed or in a rock garden or large container, its naturally sprawling habit will be seen to best advantage. The front of a bed alongside a wide path on which there is space for it to encroach is also an attractive situation. *Nepeta* (catmint) species are often used in the same way: *S. reptans* is less floriferous, but less liable to be troubled by cats, and is pleasingly different from other plants that are suitable for the same situation.

Propagation is by seed or cuttings.

SALVIA SINALOENSIS
Fernald (1900)

This low-growing plant is another example of the diversity of growth habit and foliage in the genus, bearing very limited resemblance to any other species described in this book. A Mexican native, it grows in the province of Sinaloa, after which it is named. Like other Mexican salvias, it does have some tolerance to winter frosts, but outdoors is likely to succumb to the British winter combination of cold and prolonged wet.

S. sinaloensis spreads by means of underground rhizomes. The lower parts of the stems trail loosely on the ground, but in flower, the plant reaches a height of 15–30cm (6–12in). The leaves are notable for their colour – a beetroot-red – when young. As they mature, the upper surfaces usually lose most of this attractive coloration to become dark green, but in cool or very dry conditions the reddish-purple colour remains. Up to 6cm (2½in) long, they are elliptic in shape and – unusually for salvias – almost stalkless. The margins are finely serrate.

The upright inflorescences are displayed well clear of the foliage. The flowers, in well-spaced whorls of 3, are an intense, almost pure, deep blue. They are about 2cm (¾in) long, which is quite large in proportion to the size of the plant. In the throat, on the lower lip of the flower, is a pair of white markings. Flowering commences in mid- to late summer, and continues until mid-autumn.

Cultivation

This is an attractive plant on account of its foliage alone, but is really outstanding when flowers are present, as the intensity of their colour is accentuated by the contrasting hues of the leaves. It does best in a sheltered sunny spot: if you can provide this in conjunction with an edge position in a raised bed, your appreciation of its qualities will be enhanced. It also makes a good pot plant, and overwintering is then simply a matter of transfer to a cool greenhouse. *S. sinaloensis* is reputed to thrive better in an acidic peaty soil.

Propagation is by cuttings or division.

RED-FLOWERED
HALF HARDY SALVIAS

SALVIA ELEGANS
Vahl (1805), Tangerine sage

This is a species of great charm with quill-shaped, scarlet flowers produced quite freely over a long period in the summer and into autumn. Though never a mass of colour, it is a distinctive border plant with attractive foliage which foils the flowers very effectively. The cultivar known as 'Honey Melon' in the USA is a selection of the species as it is described below.

S. elegans is a native of Mexico and Guatemala and has been in cultivation since early in the nineteenth century. It is a bushy plant, with branched stems, which does not usually exceed 60cm (24in) in height in British conditions. The branches are quite slender and are brittle, so the plant really needs some support up to about half its height.

Sometimes surviving through winter outdoors in the British Isles, tangerine sage is capable of living through temperatures of –5°C (23°F) and probably lower. Even so, in the RHS salvia trial at Wisley, plants failed to survive the 1995–96 winter, which was one of average character for south-eastern England.

The leaves are broadly ovate, with pointed tips, and up to 4cm (1½in) long and almost as wide. They are mid-green, sometimes tinged with dark purple, and are usually hairy. The margins are finely toothed. When crushed, they emit an agreeable smell, fairly close to that of oranges. In British garden conditions this aroma is not very strong but James Compton tells me that it is very noticeable in the wild.

The bright scarlet flowers are borne in 2–6-flowered whorls on quite long inflorescences (up to 20cm/8in). They are characteristically slender, creating the impression at a casual glance of short scarlet quills. They are up to 3.5cm (1½in) long, with relatively short lips. The calyx is very short, about a fifth of the length of the corolla tube. Flowering can begin in early summer in favoured localities, and continues until terminated by autumn frosts.

Cultivation

Outdoors, S. *elegans* does best in full sunshine, and a sheltered position is desirable in view of the plants' natural brittleness. As a container plant in a slightly heated greenhouse, it will flower in autumn and winter from cuttings rooted in summer. Propagation is usually by cuttings, though division is also practicable.

'Scarlet Pineapple' (syn. *S. rutilans* Carr)
Pineapple sage

A good deal of confusion has existed for many years about the differences between the species S. *elegans*

and its later-flowering and taller variety 'Scarlet Pineapple', still very widely known as S. *rutilans*. Both can be found growing wild in Mexico.

The first record of this plant in cultivation is in 1873, but there is no note of its initial introduction. It is reputed to be more tender than the species, with little frost tolerance, although this reputation may not be entirely justified as plants quite often survive the winter outdoors in the National Collection at Kingston Maurward College in Dorset. The flowers are slightly larger than, but otherwise identical to, those of the species. Vegetatively, the plant looks considerably different. It is more robust in growth, more erect in habit, and taller, reaching a height of up to 1.5m (5ft).

The hairier leaves are ovate-lanceolate, i.e. much narrower in relation to their length than those described for the species itself. Their actual length may be up to 10cm (4in), with a width only about half as great. The foliage differs also in its marked – and very pleasing – pineapple scent, which is both different from and stronger than that of the form of the species known simply as S. *elegans*. 'Scarlet Pineapple' is among the select few members of the genus that could well be grown for the pleasure of its scent alone.

One of this plant's most important horticultural characteristics is the lateness of its flowering, which rarely commences before the autumn. In the 1995–96 RHS trial at Wisley the first flowers opened on 18th October. For this reason it is best grown in a container in most British gardens, using plants from cuttings taken in late spring or early summer, and moved into a greenhouse or conservatory in early autumn: flowering will then continue into the winter. In exceptionally favoured garden conditions this does occur in the open, as at Abbotsbury on the Dorset coast, where most winters are almost frost-free.

'Frieda Dixon'

The S. *elegans* hybrid 'Frieda Dixon', with pearly-red flowers, is popular in California, but is currently unobtainable through commercial channels in the British Isles. It is in origin a chance seedling, and the pollen parent is unknown.

S. *elegans* is one of the most attractive of the half hardy herbaceous perennials. It has agreeably aromatic foliage and produces its quill-like, red flowers over a long period.

SALVIA FULGENS (syn. *S. cardinalis*) **AGM**
Cavanilles (1791), Cardinal sage

This is in many respects a larger version of *S. elegans* (p.98) and is also a Mexican native. The greater size of the flowers results in a more striking visual impact than *S. elegans* can provide.

The plant is of a similar hardiness to *S. elegans* and, like it, sometimes overwinters successfully in favoured situations outdoors. It nevertheless failed to overwinter in the open in the RHS salvia trial in 1995–96. Such cold tolerance as it has it owes to its native habitat, at altitudes sometimes exceeding 3000m (10,000ft).

The much-branched stems can reach a height of up to 1.5m (5ft). The leaves are dark green, ovate-lanceolate and up to 12cm (5in) long. They are white-hairy beneath and have crenate margins. When crushed, their slight scent is reminiscent of apples.

Vivid scarlet flowers are borne in 2–6 flowered whorls in loose inflorescences, which are usually quite short – often only 10cm (4in) long. The individual flowers are up to 5cm (2in) in length, with a long, broad upper lip, and are hairy. The reddish calyces are around half the length of the corolla tube. Flowering usually commences in late summer and continues until the first frost.

Cultivation

A sunny, sheltered spot is needed for this plant to show itself to best advantage. In dry weather, it responds well to liberal watering. It is very susceptible to attacks by capsid bugs.

Propagation is by cuttings. Growth in suitable conditions is rapid: it will make a good-size specimen and flower in the same year from cuttings taken in early spring.

SALVIA GESNERIIFLORA
Lindley & Paxton (1851)

This species, which has been in cultivation for many years, does not differ greatly in appearance from *S. fulgens* (above). It is a larger plant with slightly bigger leaves and longer petioles. Leaf shape is slightly different, with the tips narrowly pointed, a feature seldom found in *S. fulgens*, in which they are normally rounded. The flowers are also larger and can reach 6cm (2½in) in length. However, these physical differences are not very obvious to a casual observer.

There is a substantial difference in flowering time between the two species, though. While *S. fulgens* usually commences flowering quite late in the summer, *S. gesneriiflora* is truly autumn-flowering: one Midlands enthusiast wryly remarked to me that he took its commencement of flowering in his garden as a sign that the first serious frost would soon be wreaking its customary havoc. For this reason, the species can only be recommended unreservedly as an outdoor plant in Britain for sunny, sheltered positions in areas where the first autumn frosts do not normally occur before, say, the start of Advent, four weeks before Christmas.

Both purple- and green-calyxed forms of *S. gesneriiflora* are quite widely available. The purple-calyxed form is known as **'Tequila'** in the USA.

S. fulgens is among the larger-flowered salvias and has an upright habit. In dry weather it appreciates liberal watering.

Cultivation

In the wild, *S. gesneriiflora* flowers in autumn and spring. This characteristic shows when the species is grown in a greenhouse, and it can make a striking display there in early and mid-spring.

I have had small plants in flower in spring from cuttings taken as late as the beginning of autumn, but propagation in early summer is the usual practice for container-grown plants for spring display. Cuttings are best taken in late summer to produce plants for outdoor cultivation the following year.

SALVIA SPLENDENS 'VAN HOUTTEI'
(syn. *S. vanhouttei*) AGM 1996

This is a nineteenth-century selection of *S. splendens* (p.48), now the only form of this very popular species that is treated as a tender perennial. It is not at all hardy, and overwinters outdoors only in frost-free cli-

mates. Van Houtte was a distinguished Belgian nurseryman and botanist of the nineteenth century.

S. splendens 'Van Houttei' is grown for its deep red inflorescences, foiled by luxuriant foliage. Flowering commences very late in the summer, so the flowering period is accordingly short. At the RHS trial at Wisley in 1995–96, it began on 25th August.

The inflorescences are up to 25cm (10in) long, with 3–6 wine-red flowers at each whorl, their colour complemented by the deep purple-red of the calyces. The whorls are well-spaced on a dark red inflorescence axis which droops elegantly at its tip.

The plant reaches the full height natural to the species, about 1m (3ft) or rather more. It grows vigorously, a single specimen achieving a spread almost equal to its height.

Cultivation

In flower this plant produces a dramatic effect in late summer, ideally towards the back of a herbaceous border or in a central position in an island bed. Grown in a large container and moved to a greenhouse or conservatory in early autumn, it will continue flowering at least into the early part of the winter.

It does best in a moisture-retentive soil, and will appreciate watering in prolonged dry conditions. It tolerates some shade quite happily.

Propagation is by cuttings, which are easily rooted in late summer.

SALVIA DARCYI
Compton (1994)

This species, one of nearly 300 that are native to Mexico, was not collected until 1991. British botanist James Compton, an authority on the genus, found *S. darcyi* growing among some limestone rocks in a mountainous area in the north-east of Mexico. He named it after his colleague on the expedition, John d'Arcy. At the time of writing, it is not certain how *S. darcyi* will overwinter outdoors in Britain. There are indications that it may prove rather hardier than most other red-flowered Mexican species: however, it may not prove more resistant to soil that is wet as well as cold.

The plant, which has a pleasing aroma, reaches a height of up to 1.5m (5ft) in the wild, but about half to two-thirds of this in Britain. It spreads by stolons –

stems that creep on or just below the soil surface, just as are found in *Vinca* and *Monarda*. The stems are sticky-hairy and branch in their upper parts. The dark green leaves, also sticky-hairy, are triangular or heart shaped, and about as wide as they are long (4–8cm/1½–3in). The margins are crenate to crenate-serrate.

The upright, unbranched inflorescences may be up to 25cm (10in) in length and occasionally more, with widely spaced whorls of 4 or 6 flowers. The corolla is bright scarlet and 3.5–4.5cm (1¼–1¾in) long. Flowering usually commences in midsummer.

Cultivation

Although found naturally in alkaline soil on limestone, the species does not seem to be sensitive to soil acidity. A sheltered situation is desirable, because it is among the many salvia species with brittle stems.

Propagation is by cuttings or seed. Cuttings taken and rooted in a heated greenhouse in early spring usually commence flowering within five months.

SALVIA REGLA
Cavanilles (1799), Mountain sage

A native of Mexico and a small part of Texas, this species is of fairly compact but upright habit. Although known to horticulture since the first half of the nineteenth century, and hardier than *S. fulgens* and *S. gesneriiflora*, it is much less seen in British gardens than they are. Several cultivars are available in the USA, where they are proving very successful as deciduous shrubs. British experience of the ability of *S. regla* to overwinter outdoors has so far been very limited. On the other side of the world, in New Zealand, it has proved capable of surviving considerable frosts.

The plant reaches a height of up to 1.2m (4ft) in a favoured spot in the open in a single growing season, but in warmer countries it will grow half as high again. Before flowering commences, it looks distinct from the other red-flowered species described above in having more or less hairless leaves and stems. The much-branched stems are dark red, and the rather small, dark green leaves are as wide, or nearly so, as they are long. They are mainly 2–5cm (¾–2in) in length and are mostly rather triangular in outline, though some are more nearly kidney shaped.

The flowers are borne in loose, few-flowered clusters at the ends of the stems. They are scarlet, with a touch of orange, and up to 4cm (1½in) long. The upper lip is the longer of the two, and the well-exserted stamens and stigma are a noticeable feature. Much more conspicuous are the attractively coloured calyces. These are orange, and particularly striking because they are inflated, considerably larger in diameter than the base of the corolla tubes which they surround. The calyces persist for some time after the corollas have withered and fallen. Flowering does not usually begin until the late summer and continues until the first frosts.

Plants have only become available in recent years: in *The RHS Plant Finder* (1998–99) only one nursery lists it. It is very unfortunate that the species was not included in the RHS trial at Wisley in 1995–96.

S. regla is closely related to **S. sessei**; this is rarely seen in Britain, but is popular as a shrub along the French and Italian Riviera and in Madeira.

Cultivation

In particularly favoured situations, it may prove suitable for growing as a shrub in just the same way as *S. microphylla* or *S.×jamensis*. It is, in other circumstances, an outstanding candidate for those minded to experiment with it as a half hardy perennial and as a container plant. The Americans appear to be very favourably impressed by it and have several cultivars, even though it was scarcely seen in US gardens before the 1980s.

Propagation is usually by cuttings. These should be taken when flowers begin to develop in midsummer; if taken any later rooting is likely to be difficult. Propagation is also possible by seed, which are unusually large.

SALVIA CONFERTIFLORA
Pohl (1831)

Even in a genus well-endowed with species of striking character, this native of Brazil stands out prominently. Its first mention in British horticultural literature came late in the nineteenth century as a shrubby species for greenhouse culture; it is more often now seen grown outdoors in summer in warm, sheltered positions in gardens in the southern half of England and Wales. Effectively a tender herbaceous perennial in cultivation, the plant's base does become woody by autumn. It is usually overwintered as young plants from cuttings taken in late summer. If you have space, entire specimens can be lifted and accommodated in a slightly heated greenhouse.

The Peruvian species *S. oppositiflora* is found in arid, sunny places in the wild. Its large orange-red flowers are a delight.

Plants reach a height of 80–120cm (32–48in) with a spread that is usually not much less. The dark green leaves are ovate with pointed tips. They are large – up to 20cm (8in) in length, and half that width. When crushed, they emit an unpleasant odour. The leaf surface is rugose, and thinly covered with short, tawny hairs. The hairiness is more marked on the undersides of the leaves. The petioles of the youngest leaves, and the uppermost part of the stem, are also covered with reddish hairs.

Flowering starts quite late – towards the end of the summer. The same reddish, hairy covering of the stems and leaves is also a feature of the inflorescence stem and the calyces, which appear deep red. The unbranched inflorescences are commonly up to 30cm (12in) long and sometimes longer, each with many whorls of between 6 and 15 flowers (*confertiflora* means 'with crowded flowers'). Blunt, short-lipped and densely hairy, the orange-red flowers are complemented by the darker calyces. The overall effect is a rusty-orange, almost glowing in sunshine. The upper and lower lips of the corolla are about the same length.

Cultivation

This is a species for the larger garden, and needs both a sunny, warm position close to a wall, and shelter from wind. To achieve its full potential, plenty of soil moisture is necessary. In flower, a well-grown plant presents a dramatic appearance.

Propagation is by cuttings taken in late summer.

SALVIA OPPOSITIFLORA AGM
Ruiz & Pavon (1798)

To see this low-growing Peruvian species flowering happily is to experience yet another of the multifarious delights offered by the genus. A shrub in its natural environment, it must be treated as a tender herbaceous perennial in Britain. The outstanding feature of the plant is its large orange-red flowers, which can be produced over a long period from midsummer onwards.

The plant may reach a height of up to 60cm (24in), but more typically is dwarfer. It is spreading, with lax stems tumbling over any edges they encounter. The flowers, borne in short inflorescences, are in whorls of two only. They are on opposite sides of the inflorescence axis, giving the plant its specific epithet. Their colour glows against the background provided by the small, pale green leaves.

Cultivation

In the wild, this is a plant of arid, sunny places and flowers in winter. As Peru is at tropical latitudes, somewhere dry, warm and sunny is clearly called for if it is to do well. I have no experience of it as a container plant, but suspect it would repay investigation.

Propagation is by cuttings.

SALVIA BLEPHAROPHYLLA
Brandegee ex Epling (1938–39)

Vividly coloured flowers are commonplace among salvias, but S. blepharophylla additionally provides a foil of dark green, glossy foliage to heighten the intensity of its orange-red floral display, which can last throughout the summer in favourable conditions. A half hardy native of Mexico, it can sometimes survive winter outdoors in the warmest areas of England.

The name blepharophylla means 'eyelash-leaved'; each leaf carries on its margin a projecting fringe of long, fine hairs. In other respects – habit, stems and leaves – the species differs little from S. buchananii (p.106) when not in flower.

The plant, which is herbaceous in cool climates, reaches a height of up to 50cm (20in). The lower part of many of the stems lies flat on the ground, or at a low angle to it, so the growth habit appears somewhat spreading. In favourable circumstances the spread may exceed 75cm (30in) across. In the wild, and in mild climates, S. blepharophylla spreads widely by rhizomes, in much the same fashion as Monarda (bergamot) or Physalis (Chinese lantern).

The stems are thin and purplish and are covered in fine hairs. The dark green glabrous leaves are up to 5cm (2in) long, and are usually narrowly ovate. Their margins are serrate, as well as having the distinctive fringe of fine hairs already mentioned.

Where the growing conditions are ideal for it, the flowering period of S. blepharophylla can extend from early summer to the first frosts of autumn.

Each whorl produces 2 to 6 flowers up to 4cm (1½in) long, which is large in relation to the size of the plant. They are borne on short racemes up to 12cm (5in) long. The upper lip of the flower is a straight extension of the corolla tube and is covered in fine scarlet hairs, while the lower lip is quite broad. The impact of the flower colour is further heightened by the purple-tinged calyces.

Sometimes shy-flowering in Britain, S. blepharophylla is an unforgettable groundcover plant at La Mortola in Italy.

Cultivation

In a sunny position this can be an outstanding plant for the front of a border. In climates that are warmer than the British Isles it does best in partial shade. S. blepharophylla is very well worth a try if you have a good spot for it, but does not always flower freely. It can do well as a container plant. Although the naturally lax growth habit is less than ideal, the plants respond to the pinching of the longer stems to encourage more compact development. Providing support with short twiggy prunings enhances the plant's appearance, too.

Propagation is by cuttings, though, during the summer, it is usually possible to remove young stems with roots attached, which arise from the rhizomes.

HALF HARDY SALVIAS WITH FLOWERS OF OTHER COLOURS

SALVIA INVOLUCRATA AGM
Cavanilles (1793)

Among the best known of the half hardy species, this plant is notable for the speed and vigour of its growth and its long succession of tubular flowers of vivid pink colours which might well belong in an ambitious range of lipsticks. The name *involucrata* marks the conspicuous nature of the involucres – pairs of bracts that enclose the flower buds.

The flowers of this species in their colour and shape come near to a charge of nature outdoing art. Yet, foiled by abundant large leaves, they retain a certain refinement. The flowering period is normally from midsummer until the first frosts.

A native of Mexico, where it usually grows in positions shaded by trees, this salvia is herbaceous in the British climate; in warmer countries it behaves more nearly as an evergreen shrub. It will overwinter successfully where frosts are relatively slight, for example in many parts of southern England, particularly in positions backed by a wall of southerly aspect. Long-established specimens can be found at Hadspen Garden and at Cannington College, both in Somerset.

Plants in favourable conditions reach a height of up to 1.5m (5ft), though two-thirds of this is a more ordinary attainment. The slightly hairy stems are initially little branched and erect in habit, though the plants in later summer tend to spread sideways in pleasing fashion, resulting in plants quite as wide as they are tall. The ovate leaves are relatively large for the genus, with the leaf-blades up to 15 by 7cm (6 by 3in). Their midribs and undersides are purplish. Leaf tips are sharply pointed, and margins minutely serrated.

The inflorescences are unbranched, spike-like racemes up to 30cm (12in) long, with closely spaced whorls of 3–6 flowers. A characteristic feature is the prominent coloured bracts, a pair enclosing the flower buds of each whorl. In a young inflorescence, only the bracts are visible, ensheathing all the buds; they fall as the flowers open. The flowers are up to 3cm (1¼in) long, and have noticeably inflated corolla tubes which are pink or purple. The form of S. *involucrata* that was awarded the AGM has magenta-red flowers and calyces.

S. involucrata var. puberula (syn. S. *puberula*) is bushier in habit, later-flowering and may prove rather hardier than the type species. It has bright pink flowers.

Cultivation

S. *involucrata* is a good feature plant for a warm spot, and will tolerate some shade. It can also look impressive on a sheltered patio in a large container. From cuttings taken for the purpose in spring, the flower display can extend into the winter if there is space in a slightly heated conservatory or greenhouse.

S. *involucrata* 'Hadspen', with its deep pinkish-red flowers, makes a large feature plant for a warm, sheltered position.

The plant is otherwise propagated by means of cuttings taken in late summer; the young plants need cool greenhouse conditions for survival. Division of the rootstock is also possible as a means of propagation, and in warmer countries is a convenient method of increasing plants in spring.

Cultivars

'**Bethellii**' is the most widely grown cultivar. It is notable for the large, almost spherical cluster of deep pink bracts at the tip of each inflorescence. The flowers are bright purplish-pink. '**Boutin**' AGM 1996 has strong purplish-red flowers and purplish-pink calyces. It is not as tall as the other cultivars. '**Hadspen**' has deep pinkish-red flowers, which are rather larger than those of 'Bethellii' and are in less congested whorls. '**Mrs Pope**' is identical to 'Hadspen'.

SALVIA SPATHACEA AGM 1996
Greene (1892), Pitcher sage

Extensive cultivation of this Californian species only started in the 1970s so experience of overwintering it outdoors in Britain is limited. From available evidence it seems likely that in gardens where *S. guaranitica* 'Blue Enigma', *S. involucrata* and *S. patens* survive satisfactorily, so will this species. It did so successfully during the trials at Wisley, in a winter in which –6°C (21°F) was the lowest recorded temperature.

Considerably vigorous in favourable circumstances, *S. spathacea* spreads by underground rhizomes. In flower, plants are 1–1.2m (3–4ft) tall, and achieve little less in spread. The large and long-stalked leaves, up to 25cm (10in) in length, are rather pale green when young, and are mostly basal. Lanceolate, with sagittate bases, they have a rugose upper surface, white-hairy undersides and are soft to the touch.

In late summer and autumn, on the uppermost 30–40cm (12–16in) of their length, the bold, erect flowering stems carry many-flowered, widely spread whorls. Each whorl is subtended by large bracts, and both these and the large calyces are tinged maroon. Even before the showy flowers begin to emerge, the conspicuous whorls of buds give the inflorescence a characteristic profile. The flowers are up to 4.5cm (1¾in) long, but the lower half of the large corolla tube is concealed by the wide-mouthed calyces. The purplish-red flowers have an erect poise; the stamens

and stigmas are exserted. Bracts and calyces persist after the corollas have fallen and continue to contribute to the handsomeness of the inflorescence. In each whorl only a few flowers open at any one time, but the inflorescence remains a strikingly attractive feature for many weeks. Stems, leaves and calyces all have sticky hairs, which release a marked aroma.

Cultivation

An imposing and distinctive plant, *S. spathacea* looks well in mixed plantings in which shrubs predominate and serve as a late summer foil to its floral display. It will tolerate some shade.

Propagation is by seed, by division, or by cuttings taken early in autumn.

SALVIA BUCHANANII (syn. *S. bacheriana*) AGM
Hedge (1963)

Among the smaller and less vigorous species, this is notable for the size of its flowers and the vividness of their colour: glowing magenta. Like so many other salvias, it originated from Mexico, but unusually has never been found in the wild. Seed obtained in the 1950s from a garden plant in Mexico City was sent to Sir Charles Buchanan in Leicestershire, who – so far as is known – became its first cultivator outside Mexico.

In habit and foliage *S. buchananii* is closely similar to *S. blepharophylla* (p.104). It is unlikely to overwinter outdoors in Britain. It attains a height of 30–50cm (12–20in) and a spread of 25–30cm (10–12in). The dark stems are woody at their bases, much branched and quite slender. They are fairly numerous and tend to sprawl outwards from the base. The glossy dark green leaves are rather leathery, up to 6cm (2½in) long, and ovate to ovate-lanceolate with serrate margins.

The flowers, borne well above the foliage – usually from midsummer to early autumn on outdoor plants – are in widely spaced whorls on spikes up to 20cm (8in) long. There are 3–6 flowers in each whorl, but only one or two of these open at any one time. Densely covered with short velvety hairs, they are about 5cm (2in) long and droop gracefully. The upper lip is slightly hooded, the lower quite widely spreading. The colour has been variously described as magenta, rose-purple and cerise, but beyond dispute is memorably intense: the intensity is reinforced by the dark green of the foliage.

Cultivation

This species makes an attractive container plant, best given support by twiggy prunings. If it is grown with other plants, they might well provide it with sufficient support. As with S. blepharophylla, judicious pinching out of the tips of the longer shoots will result in an an improved growth habit for containers. Planted out, a sunny, sheltered spot is needed at the front of a border, though it will tolerate some shade. S.buchananii can easily become almost lost in the unintended overspill of vigorous neighbours, so these should be chosen for appropriate height and lack of aggression.

Propagation is by cuttings. When grown in more or less frost-free environments, the plant spreads by fleshy rhizomes.

SALVIA DIVINORUM
Epling & Jativa (1962)

This is a book for gardeners rather than seekers of alternative states of being. Nevertheless, a book on salvias might perhaps scarcely be complete without a mention of this tender Mexican native. Suggestively, divinorum means 'of the seers', and refers to the plant's hallucinogenic properties. It is used for these effects in those parts of Mexico where it grows in the wild.

The large leaves have no special attractiveness, and the flowers, which are an intense deep blue, are only likely to be seen if the plant is given heated greenhouse space in winter. Though it is a fine plant in flower, better use of the space might be made with S. dorisiana (see below).

SALVIA BROUSSONETTII
Bentham (1833)

This Canary Islands native is a salvia to grow for its lovely foliage rather than its white flowers, pleasing though these are. A shrub in its natural environment, it has little tolerance to frost and must be treated as a tender herbaceous perennial in British gardens.

Plants reach a height of 1m (3ft) and a spread of up to 60cm (24in). The thick, hairy leaves, to 15cm (6in) long, are shaped like an elongated heart. Pale grey-green in colour, their particular interest lies in the deep indentation of the main veins below the upper surface, which provides a very attractive, minutely reticulate patterning effect. The leaf margins are slightly irregularly notched.

Flowering may occur throughout the summer and early autumn. The upper lips of the flowers are hooded. Although white in cultivation, pink-flowered forms are found in the wild.

Cultivation

The plants will tolerate some shade, though almost certainly at the expense of flower production. S. broussonettii would be a delightful inclusion for anyone seeking to emulate the effect of the famous white garden at Sissinghurst.

Propagation is by seed or cuttings.

SALVIA DORISIANA
Standley (1950)

This is among the most tender species described in this book, and one which does not ordinarily flower at all as an outdoor plant in Britain. The foliage is, however, very attractive, both for its appearance and its very pleasing fruity scent, which is released on contact with the leaves. The plant also makes a fine large winter-flowering specimen for a heated greenhouse or conservatory.

A native of Honduras, in Central America, the species is of recent introduction. The Doris after whom the species is named features in Greek mythology as the mother of 50 nereids, or sea nymphs.

Reaching a height of up to 1m (3ft), S. dorisiana is freely branched and has an upright habit, generally similar to species such as S. guaranitica and S. mexicana. The ovate leaves are an attractive lime-green and notably large – up to 18cm (7in) in length – with serrate margins. The stems and both leaf surfaces are densely hairy.

The large, magenta flowers, to 6cm (2½in) long, are in whorls of up to ten on spike-like inflorescences as much as 15cm (6in) long.

Cultivation

S. dorisiana can be grown outdoors in a sheltered spot. As a container-grown plant for winter flowering, it is usually sited outdoors for the summer months and brought under cover before any risk of frost arises. The stem tips of the young plants are best pinched out at intervals, to promote increased branching.

Propagation is by cuttings. For winter flowering, early summer is the most suitable time for taking them.

8

SHRUBS

In their native climates many salvia species are shrubby because their stems survive from year to year and become woody. In cooler climates all growth may be cut back to ground level annually by frosts. Hence *S. elegans*, *S. involucrata* and *S. leucantha*, which are effectively herbaceous perennials in Britain (see pp.98, 105 and 90), are all described as shrubs in the catalogue of the French salvia specialists, Pépinière de la Foux, whose nursery is located a few kilometres from the Mediterranean coast.

Nearly all of the small number of salvia species that are cultivated as shrubs in Britain fall quite tidily into two groups. One comprises Old World species, which are mainly native to countries surrounding the Mediterranean, and the other consists of a small number of Mexican species. The kinship of species within each group is quite obvious from their appearance, and the differences between the two groups are very striking. A small third group consists of two South African species, which are also very distinct from the other two groups.

EUROPEAN AND ASIAN NATIVES

This familiar group is characterized by one of the two best known members of the genus, common sage (*S. officinalis*). Of all the shrubby salvias, this is one of the hardiest and certainly the most accommodating. The ideal situation to grow it in is full sunshine on free-draining soil, but it is tolerant of a wide range of sites and soils. The variegated cultivars and – even more so

S. officinalis Purpurascens Group, perhaps the most popular cultivar of common sage, is eye-catching in foliage and flower.

– the golden-leaved sage *S. officinalis* 'Aurea' are less vigorous and rather more demanding than those that have the normal leaf pigmentation of the species. For these, where the natural soil of the garden is slow draining, a much better prospect of survival is achieved by planting into raised beds. In Scotland and comparably cool parts of England and Wales it may be best to grow them as container plants, providing greenhouse conditions over winter, or to propagate annually.

S. blancoana, *S. fruticosa* and *S. lavandulifolia* are almost as hardy as *S. officinalis*, and can well be treated in just the same way. *S. candelabrum* has very similar general characteristics to *S. officinalis* but is somewhat less cold resistant. In southern England, though, it will commonly do well in a sunny, sheltered spot backed by a wall. At the end of each winter, pruning may be needed to cut back frost-damaged shoots to healthy older wood. S. *ringens* and S. *multicaulis*, a smaller shrub, are similar in hardiness to S. *candelabrum*, though if anything they are less cold resistant. They need the same kind of favoured siting to give them a good chance of success. This is also true of S. *interrupta*, a Moroccan native which is probably the least hardy of the group.

All the species mentioned usually become less attractive after a few years. Unlike most shrubs, therefore, they are all best regarded as relatively temporary and can be very effective in beds or borders otherwise devoted to herbaceous perennials, where they will have a similar lifespan to most of their neighbours, which is particularly convenient when it comes to replanting with new specimens.

These shrubby species are available in garden centres and nurseries in spring, and this is generally the most favourable period for planting. Plants of S. *officinalis* can be bought at most other times of the year as well, and for this species early autumn planting may be quite as good as spring, so long as the soil is fast-draining.

The habit of the popular, fast-growing S. *officinalis* cultivar 'Berggarten' is quite spreading, and that *of S. blancoana* and S. *lavandulifolia* is even more so. Accordingly, spacing these around one and a half to two times their expected eventual height is appropriate.

Once established, the plants in this group are drought-tolerant, but if planting is undertaken in late spring or in summer, frequent watering may be needed at first.

In the first spring after planting all are best cut back hard once new shoots are seen around the base of the plant: the previous year's shoots should be reduced to about 5cm (2in) in length. It is possible to repeat this drastic treatment each spring, but ordinarily pruning is a matter of cutting out between a third and a half of the branch system. Start by removing any growth that is broken, straggling, frost-damaged or relatively bare of leaves and which detracts from the overall appearance of the plant. Then cut others back hard enough to encourage the vigorous production of new shoots.

On poor soils, an application of general fertilizer late in winter each year is worthwhile. In autumn, a dry mulch around the base of each plant provides useful protection against the freezing of roots and basal shoot buds. This is particularly recommended for the less hardy cultivars of S. *officinalis* and for S. *interrupta*.

Any specific requirements are given under the individual species descriptions below.

SALVIA OFFICINALIS
Linnaeus (1753)

Long before S. *splendens* became established as *the* salvia in the mind of the general public, S. *officinalis* was well known as a medicinal and culinary herb. Its medicinal uses date back at least to the days of the ancient Greeks and Romans. Claims made then and over the following centuries cite its value in the treatment of wounds, spots, colds, fevers, constipation, infant diarrhoea and snake bites. It was also supposed to help in the promotion of conception, the relief of asthma and the whitening of teeth.

In cooking, its best-known uses today are in sage and onion stuffing, in traditional mixed dried herbs, and as a flavouring in cheese. Sage bread and sage tea are less familiar. The choice of *officinalis* as the specific epithet is unsurprising in view of its various uses over so many centuries: the meaning of the word is simply 'sold in shops'.

A native of Spain, the Balkans and North Africa, and widely naturalized in southern Europe, the first reference to its cultivation in Britain was in AD955 in Aelfric's *Colloquy* (*Nominum herbarum*). In all probability it would have been present long before that, perhaps introduced by the Romans. More of the history of this species can be found in chapter two. Strangely, although Shakespeare mentions many herbs in his plays and poems, sage is not among them.

The plant is well known as an evergreen, aromatic shrub. It is generally quite hardy in most areas of the British Isles, although some cultivars need a favoured position to thrive. At maturity, the height of the rounded bushes is 60–80cm (24–32in) and the spread is around 1m (3ft). The white-hairy stems are much-branched and well furnished with leaves. These are oblong to elliptic and up to 6cm (2½in) long. The grey-green upper surfaces are rugose, the lower ones are white, and hairs are present on both, but especially on the lower surface.

The short-stalked flowers are borne in whorls of 4–20, fairly close together on the flowering stems. Individual blooms are up to 2.5cm (1in) long. Violet or purple are the colours commonly found in the wild, but white and pink occur also. The flowering period extends from early to late summer, but the primary garden interest in this species is in the foliage.

Not many salvia species have more than a very few cultivars: S. officinalis is among the small number of exceptions. Cultivars differ in leaf colour and shape, in vigour and in flower colour. Some flower seldom, or not at all. All are suitable for use as a herb.

Propagation

Propagation is easily achieved by cuttings. These may be taken at any time between late spring and late summer. Success can readily be achieved both with basal cuttings, pulled away from their point of origin on older wood, and with shoot-tip cuttings. It is also possible to earth up the lower parts of the plant in spring, when the shoots subsequently pushing through the surface will be found to have formed roots from their bases. These can be detached and replanted immediately into their permanent positions.

Grey-green leaved cultivars

The species itself is widely listed by nurserymen. The selections offered as 'broad-leaved' (syn. S. officinalis latifolia) are the ones generally chosen for cultivation as a herb. They have leaves which are up to half as wide as they are long, compared with the quarter to one-third that is typical of the species. They do not normally flower.

'Berggarten' is low-growing and spreading in habit, seldom exceeding 40cm (16in) high. Its leaves are broad and have characteristically rounded tips. The flowers are blue, though not very freely produced. It has been reported as particularly long-lived. 'Herrenhausen' is probably identical. 'Albiflora' (syn. 'Alba') and 'Rosea' are respectively white- and pink-flowered forms of the species. 'Grete Stolze' has pointed, pale grey leaves and mauve-blue flowers.

Variegated cultivars

'Icterina' AGM seldom flowers, but is valued for its green and gold foliage. Basically, the central area of the leaf is green, and a broad margin pale golden-yellow, but the proportions and patterns of the two colours vary widely from leaf to leaf. The plant is lower-growing and less robust than the grey-green leaved cultivars.

'Tricolor' AGM 1996 has mid-blue flowers but is primarily grown for its foliage, which is very aromatic.

The leaves are grey-green with broad cream margins. When young they are hairy and have a marked and attractive pink to purple flush which fades as they age. A vigorous plant, it typically reaches a height and spread of 30 by 100cm (1 by 3ft). In particularly cold or exposed conditions, where it may fail to overwinter, it is easily good enough to justify the effort of annual propagation and replanting.

'Purpurascens Variegata' is a sport of 'Purpurascens' (see below) and has cream markings on some of its leaves, contrasting strikingly with the purple ground colour.

Coloured-leaved cultivars

'Purpurascens' Group AGM, commonly known as purple sage, and sometimes red sage, is possibly more widely grown than any other S. officinalis cultivar and has been well known for centuries: it was remarked on by Philip Miller, in the eighteenth century, as being 'the most common in English gardens'. It has reddish-purple foliage and violet-purple flowers. 'Robin Hill' is a selection of it.

'Kew Gold' AGM 1996, a sport of 'Icterina', to which it sometimes reverts, has leaves which are, at a casual glance, pale gold. A closer inspection reveals an underlying green, particularly in the younger leaves. It makes a considerably smaller plant than the species, not normally exceeding 30cm (12in) in height and 60cm (24in) in spread.

'Aurea' is a much older cultivar than 'Kew Gold', which has superseded it. It is very similar but inferior in vigour.

SALVIA FRUTICOSA (syn. S. triloba)
Miller (1768), Greek sage

This species is very similar in broad terms to S. officinalis. It is native to much of the Eastern Mediterranean, including Israel, and is also found wild in Algeria and the Canary Islands. Although first described in 1768, it was certainly known to the Greeks well over three thousand years ago and has been identified in a fresco on Crete, painted in the second millenium before Christ. Despite its southerly distribution in the wild, it appears to be comparable in hardiness to S. officinalis.

An evergreen shrub, S. fruticosa usually grows slightly taller and tends to spread more slowly than

S. officinalis. In leaf shape there is a good deal of naturally occurring variation, but a notable point of difference from *S. officinalis* is that on many plants some of the leaves are pinnatifid. These have a relatively large, elliptic or oblong terminal lobe, while at the basal end of the leaf-blade there are one or two pairs of smaller lateral lobes. The former name of the species, *S. triloba*, was given because of the prevalence of the 3-lobed form of the leaf. The overall size and other characteristics of the leaves are similar to those of *S. officinalis*. On some plants the leaves are simple (with no lateral lobes), reducing the obvious differences in leaf appearance between the two species. The leaves, both dry and fresh, are used to make herbal tea.

S. fruticosa flowers rather earlier and more freely than *S. officinalis* but the flowers themselves are similar. They vary from pink to mauve. Calyx colour also varies, both green- and – more attractively – red-calyxed forms being found.

Propagation

Propagation from cuttings is the only reliable way to ensure that you secure the flower and calyx colours and the leaf form that you prefer. It can also be easily raised from seed, though it may need a period of exposure to low temperatures before germinating freely.

Salvia lavandulifolia
Vahl (1804), Spanish sage

In the wild, this species has a similar distribution to *S. officinalis*, but is less widespread: it is native to Spain, south-east France and possibly also north-west Africa. It is so closely related to *S. officinalis* that it has in the past been regarded by some botanists as a subspecies of it, and, like *S. officinalis*, has been very long in cultivation. The most obvious point of difference is that in Spanish sage almost all the leaves are clustered together at the base of the plant, with the flowering stems virtually leafless. The leaves are also narrower (hence lavender-leaved) than those of *S. officinalis*.

An evergreen shrub, *S. lavandulifolia* is equal in hardiness to *S. officinalis*, but is lower growing. A mature plant reaches a height of 30–40cm (12–16in) when in flower, and may achieve a spread of 75–100cm (30–40in). The narrow, oblong leaves are whitish-grey above, and white and densely hairy below. Their length may be up to 5cm (2in) and their petioles are often longer than the leaf-blades. They smell rather like rosemary when crushed.

In early summer the plant produces flowering stems which bear pale blue-violet flowers with the split lower lip marked white where it joins the corolla tube. The whorls of between 6 and 9 flowers are widely spread on short racemes. The flowers are rather smaller than those of *S. officinalis*, but in common with that species, *S. lavandulifolia* is grown more for the value of its foliage effect than for its flowers.

Cultivation

The propagation, cultivation and garden uses of this species are just as for *S. officinalis*. It is particularly effective where a low-growing foliage plant is wanted to provide a contrast with the deep green leaves of others of similar or slightly greater height. It seems quite susceptible to infection by powdery mildew.

Salvia blancoana
Webb & Heldreich (1850)

This species, which is very variable in the wild, is similar enough to *S. lavandulifolia* to be regarded by some authorities as a subspecies of it. While prevailing expert opinion gives it the status of a distinct species, yet other botanists have argued that it is a subspecies of *S. candelabrum*. All three are found in the wild in Spain, and in the case of *S. blancoana*, and probably *S. lavandulifolia* also, in north-west Africa.

One of the principal differences between the two latter species is in habit. *S. blancoana* is almost prostrate, as distinct from simply being low-growing. This means that *S. blancoana* is among the few salvias that look entirely at home in a small to medium-sized rock garden. Another difference is that the flowers of *S. blancoana* are in whorls of 2–6: in *S. lavandulifolia* the count is 6–9, and the whorls are noticeably bolder. The flowers are otherwise very closely similar indeed. *S. blancoana* is a very close equivalent to *S. lavandulifolia* in the garden.

Salvia candelabrum AGM
Boissier (1838)

When not in flower, this fine species shares its general habit and appearance with the common sage, *S. officinalis* (p.110). Both are native to Spain and are evergreen shrubs with strongly aromatic foliage. They

S. candelabrum is worth a place for its foliage alone, the early summer flower display further enhances its value.

are fairly similar in hardiness; although *S. candelabrum* is the less cold-resistant of the two, it did overwinter in the open without serious damage in the RHS trial at Wisley in 1995–96, on the fairly open site on which it was held. The species has been in cultivation at least since the middle of the nineteenth century.

Mature plants are up to 90 by 90 cm (3 by 3ft). The bases of the erect stems are woody, and most stems either branch just once or twice, or not at all. The greyish-green leaves are up to 9cm (3½in) long and lanceolate or elliptic to oblong. Occasionally there is a pair of small lobes on the petiole just below the leaf-blade. The leaf margins are notched; the upper surface is rugose, and the lower hairy.

A distinctive feature of *S. candelabrum* is its fine display of flowers in early summer. These are borne in tall, candelabra-shaped inflorescences of large flowers, bringing the plant temporarily to a height of up to 1.2m (4ft). As the inflorescence develops, widely spaced pairs of short lateral stems arise from its main axis, each up to 10cm (4in) long. At the end of each of these a loose cluster of up to seven flowers is borne, the terminal one opening first. The flower colour is dominated by the dark purple of the lower lip, while the upper is paler. Individual flowers are large for the genus, at up to 4cm (1½in) long, and much longer than those of *S. officinalis*. The main flowering period is early to midsummer, but some further flowering may occur until early autumn.

Cultivation

Its soil and site preferences and its garden uses are just as for *S. officinalis*. The species has a dual role aesthetically: during the flowering period, established plants are a focal point of interest in their own right, at other times their foliage provides a valuable foil and accompaniment to neighbouring plants, and with its muted grey-green tones, contributes to the overall effect created by a planting.

Propagation may be either by seed or by cuttings.

SALVIA INTERRUPTA
Schousboe (1800)

Introduced to the botanic gardens of Cambridge University in 1798, *S. interrupta* is quite closely similar to *S. candelabrum* and the two species have often been confused. They are easy enough to tell apart, though: *S. interrupta* has few or short branches while *S. candelabrum* has long, lateral ones, and the fine foliage of *S. interrupta* is pinnate – each large leaf consists of a single terminal leaflet with usually two pairs of lateral lobes arising from the leaf-stalk close to the stem.

Native to the Atlas Mountains of Morocco, *S. interrupta* is less hardy than *S. candelabrum*. It can survive winters in a sheltered position in southern England, but even there its hardiness is not dependable.

The plant at maturity is 60–90cm (2–3ft) tall and has a spread of around 60cm (24in), but the inflorescences may reach a height of up to 1.2m (4ft) or occasionally more. The stems are woody based and much branched. The terminal segment of each grey-green leaf is much the largest, and may be up to 11cm (4½in) in length. There are usually two pairs of stalk-less lateral segments, but sometimes three or only one. The leaf segments are ovate to oblong, with the upper surface rugose and the lower white-hairy. The margins are crenate. A markedly disagreeable odour arises from the foliage on contact.

PLATE VIII

SHRUBBY SALVIAS

S. microphylla 'La Foux'

S. × *microphylla*
unnamed seedling

S. × *jamensis*
'Devantville'

All specimens are shown at approximately life size

S. microphylla 'Oxford'

S. × *jamensis* 'Pat Vlasto'

S. × *jamensis* 'La Luna'

Produced in late spring and summer, the fine, airy inflorescences have the same structure as those of S. candelabrum. The flowers are violet with a white throat, and in size approach those of S. candelabrum – the corolla is up to 3.5cm (1½in) long and the 3-lobed lower lip can be as much as 2.5cm (1in) wide. The slightly hooded upper lip is relatively small.

Cultivation

This species is best overwintered by taking cuttings in late summer and growing them through the winter in a frost-free greenhouse. In cool areas of the country, it is quite handsome enough to treat as a container plant for a large greenhouse.

Propagation is by seed or cuttings.

SALVIA RINGENS
Smith (1806)

This native of south-east Europe differs little in habit and stature from S. candelabrum and S. interrupta. Much less commonly grown in Britain than either of these species, it is probably of similar hardiness to S. candelabrum. It stands the best chance of overwintering safely if growing on fast-draining soil.

The leaves are pinnate, as in S. interrupta, with 2–3 pairs of lateral segments. There are differences in detail, however, with S. ringens having longer petioles and lateral segments more nearly matching the terminal segments in size; the tip of each segment is pointed.

The inflorescences also show minor differences in structure from those of the other two species. The flowers are purple in some plants, but there is considerable variation in colour within the species and it is necessary to take cuttings to be certain of having a specific shade. Otherwise the plants can be propagated by seed.

SALVIA HELDREICHIANA (syn. S. benthamiana)
Boissier (1852)

A Turkish native, little seen in cultivation, S. heldreichiana is also similar to S. interrupta. As in this species, the leaves are pinnate but normally comprise three leaflets only: a large terminal segment and a single pair of lateral lobes.

It is hardy enough to withstand mild winters outdoors in the south Midlands without damage.

Propagation is by cuttings.

SALVIA MULTICAULIS
(syn. S. acetabulosa) AGM 1996
Vahl (1804)

This low-growing shrubby species has been undeservedly neglected in the past, though it is known to have been in cultivation before 1930. The attainment of an AGM as a plant generally hardy in the British Isles should help it to achieve a much wider popularity. A native of Turkey and adjacent countries, it can succumb to wet winter conditions: exposure to the winter temperatures encountered in most parts of Britain is not of itself likely to be a problem.

Mature plants form mats, up to 90cm (3ft) across, of erect unbranched woody-based stems. Plant height is only about 15cm (6in) when out of flower, but the flowering stems attain 30–45cm (12–18in). Once seen, the leaves are unlikely to be confused with those of any other species in this group. They are oval, usually about 3cm (1¼in) long and 2cm (¾in) wide, on petioles about 3cm (1¼in) in length. In other respects they are similar in appearance to those of S. officinalis: grey-green, the upper surface rugose and the lower white and densely hairy.

The small, violet flowers are borne on unbranched, usually leafless stems. They are in whorls of 4–10, usually well spaced from one another. The bracts, up to 1.5cm (½in) long, are fairly conspicuous and reddish-brown; the persistent calyces are similarly coloured. The flowering period is generally early to midsummer, but more flowering stems may develop in late summer.

Cultivation

Distinguished by its unusual foliage, this plant will appeal where space is at some premium. It would, for example, look well on a sunny patio, particularly in a raised bed, or as one of the occupants of a large tub.

Propagation may be by seed or cuttings. Once plants are established, layering as described for S. officinalis may be the most convenient means of multiplication.

SALVIA CAESPITOSA
Montb. & Aucher ex Bentham (1836)

This very low-growing Turkish species is a natural rock-garden plant, found on the limestone and volcanic slopes of Anatolian mountains around 2000m (6500ft) above sea-level. If there were a term 'microshrub' it would serve well to describe this plant which forms woody-based mats of growth only 10–15cm (4–6in) high. In favourable conditions in the wild these may be up to 60cm (24in) across: in cultivation a 25cm (10in) spread would be a typical expectation. *Caespitosa* means 'growing in tufts'.

The hairy grey-green leaves are pinnatisect – the single leaf-blade deeply cleft into a lanceolate terminal segment about 2cm (¾in) long, and 2–4 pairs of smaller lateral segments. The lilac-pink flowers are borne in 3–6-flowered whorls in very short terminal racemes. For the size of the plant, the flowers are surprisingly large – up to 3cm (1¼in) long – and are held in an upright poise. The flowering period is early to mid-summer.

Cultivation

Although hardy, plants of this species may fail to overwinter because of wet conditions, and are commonly short-lived. They are best grown either in pots in an unheated greenhouse – ideally an alpine house – or in a drystone wall.

Propagation is by seed or cuttings.

MEXICAN NATIVES

This section consists of S. *greggii*, S. *microphylla* and their hybrids S. × *jamensis* and S. *greggii* × *lycioides*, which are deciduous, small-leaved, bushy plants with thin stems, looking so different from the evergreen S. *officinalis* and its Mediterranean neighbours that one can be forgiven for surprise that they belong to the same genus. They are all in the same broad category of inability to overwinter without risk of serious frost damage as S. *candelabrum*. If you cannot plant them at the base of a sunny wall, these shrubs may well be excellent candidates for containers, but they are not suitable for the long-term rigours of the open in most British gardens. Outdoors in a suitable situation, or container-grown and moved into a greenhouse at the end of the summer, they are notable for the length of their flowering period in summer and autumn.

These species can retain an attractive appearance over many years. They are best planted out in late spring, and generally demand no more attention than mulching for frost protection in autumn and pruning each year in early spring to remove frost-damaged shoots if grown permanently outside. Regrowth takes place quite readily from the base of the plant, in much the same way as occurs with outdoor fuchsias that have suffered from frost killing some shoots. When S. *microphylla* suffers little or no frost damage over a period of years, it can become quite large: there are some fine specimens, up to 3m (10ft) tall, growing close to the foot of high walls at Cannington College in Somerset.

Salvia greggii, Salvia microphylla
(syn. S. *grahamii*) and related species

Joint treatment seems very appropriate for these species: S. *greggii* (Gray, 1872), and S. *microphylla* (Kunth, 1817) are both shrubby natives of Mexico and the southernmost states of the USA, and are probably closely related. They are almost identical in their cultivation requirements and their garden value.

S. *microphylla* var. *microphylla* is notably long flowering.

Natural hybrids between the two species were recently discovered in the wild. These have been named S. × jamensis, and are valuable in the garden in the same way as their parents (see below).

Both the species and their hybrids are wiry-stemmed, small-leaved shrubs, which are usually deciduous in the British climate. None is fully hardy, but in sheltered positions in gardens in the southern half of England and Wales, they can generally be counted on to over-winter with little harm. Frost-damaged stems can be cut back in spring. Authorities differ as to whether one species is more cold-tolerant than the other, though some of the best informed opinion is that S. microphylla is hardier than S. greggii. The winter of the RHS trial was of average severity for the area, with the lowest air temperature recorded being –6°C (21°F): all the trial entries for S. greggii, S. microphylla and S. × jamensis survived successfully.

One of the outstanding garden attributes of the group is the long flowering season – from midsummer until the first hard frosts. Another is the commencement of flowering – and that freely – in the first season after propagation. A third is the rapid growth of young plants so that by the middle of their second full year – usually the season after planting – they are well on their way towards achieving their final size.

Of the two species, S. greggii is generally of smaller stature, achieving a plant height and spread up to about 75cm (30in). S. microphylla commonly attains 1.2m (4ft) in height, with the cultivars 'Kew Red' and 'Newby Hall' being taller.

Leaf shape and hairiness vary within both species. Those of S. greggii seldom exceed 3cm (1¼in) in length, and have entire margins. They are usually glabrous, and are narrow in relation to their length. Those of S. microphylla are larger, up to 5cm (2in) long, and have finely toothed margins. They are usually slightly hairy, and are between ovate and almost triangular in shape.

Flowers are usually borne in whorls of two (occasionally four in S. microphylla), on racemes 10–20cm (4–8in) long. Flowers of the two species are generally up to 2.5cm (1in) long. The upper lip is hooded, while the much larger lower lip is widely spreading. Colour range in S. greggii is red to purple, pink, yellow and violet; there is also a white variety. In S. microphylla, deep crimson, pink, purple and magenta are found, with cherry-red in 'Kew Red', bright red in 'Newby Hall' and

S. microphylla 'Kew Red' (p.119) is among the most outstanding of all shrubs, though not fully hardy in Britain.

vermilion or magenta in var. wislizeni (syn. S. lemmonii). All the colours mentioned are found in S. × jamensis, the hybrids between the two species.

There is one detail of the flower structure that reliably serves as diagnostic for S. microphylla as opposed to S. greggii: this is the presence of two small protuberances (papillae) within and near the base of the corolla tube of each flower of the former species. These do not occur in the flowers of S. greggii.

Salvia microphylla and its varieties and cultivars

S. microphylla var. microphylla (syn. S. grahamii) makes a slightly shorter and more spreading plant than the cultivars described below, and also has smaller leaves. Flower colour is a purplish-red and the mid-green leaves are around 2.5cm (1in) long and half that width. It was praised by William Robinson in his classic book *The English Flower Garden*.

In North America this, representing the named type, is widely known as Graham's sage, and is identical to the species described and named *S. grahamii* by the great nineteenth-century botanist George Bentham. However, unknown to him, the first scientific description of the species, which had been named *S. microphylla*, had already been published. Thus, according to the rules of nomenclature, the name *S. microphylla* is accepted as correct. Unfortunately, in Britain, the illegitimate name *S. grahamii* passed into currency and became specifically applied to the vigorous cultivar now known as 'Kew Red', which was formerly called *S. microphylla* var. *neurepia*. The name Graham's sage, therefore, means something different, according to which side of the Atlantic you are on.

'**Alba**' is white-flowered. '**Cerro Potosi**' was found growing in the wild and has magenta flowers.

'**Kew Red**' AGM 1996 remains widely known both by the salvia enthusiast and much of the nursery trade as *S. grahamii* (see above). It is characterized by its vigour, its large, hairless, mid-green leaves, and its large flowers of a vivid red. It has long been recognized as a slightly tender shrub of outstanding worth. Height and spread attained at the Wisley trial was 90 by 140cm (3 by 5ft).

'**La Foux**' is similar, but has a different, more intense flower colour enhanced by blackish calyces. It bears the name of a French nursery near Toulon, which holds one of its country's National Collections. Under British conditions, if not more widely, it is less free-flowering than 'Kew Red' or the following cultivars.

'**Newby Hall**' AGM 1996 is again of similar vigour to 'Kew Red', with slightly hairy leaves and still larger flowers of a bright red colour. '**Oxford**' has deep crimson flowers. '**Ruth Stungo**' is a variegated-leaf sport of 'Oxford' and shows the reduced vigour typical of variegation.

'**Pink Blush**' AGM 1996 and '**Pleasant View**' AGM 1996 are both pink-flowered cultivars. They showed high qualities of freedom of flowering, good growth habit and attractive flower colour at the Wisley trial.

Five new varieties are being introduced in 1999 to commemorate the total eclipse of the sun in Cornwall.

All of upright habit, they are: '**Trebah**' lilac-white, '**Trelawny**' rose-pink, the particularly vigorous '**Trelissick**' creamy-yellow, '**Trenance**' lilac-pink, and '**Trewithin**' cerise.

S. microphylla var. *wislizenii* (syn. *S. lemmonii*) is a smaller-leaved variety of the species. It may be a little hardier than other varieties and cultivars of *S. microphylla* and has triangular, narrow-tipped, glabrous deep green leaves not normally exceeding 1.5cm (¾in) in length. The small flowers, on a relatively short inflorescence, are vermilion or magenta.

Salvia greggii cultivars

'**Alba**' is white-flowered. '**Peach**' AGM 1996 produces vivid-red flowers very freely, although the plant tends to make rather sparse growth. The height and spread are around 60cm (24in). The flowers of '**Strawberries and Cream**' have yellow outer areas on the lower lip; the corolla tube and the upper lip are pink.

S. × *jamensis* 'Raspberry Royal' is an American introduction that is among the best cultivars of this interspecific hybrid.

Salvia × jamensis cultivars

Large numbers of plants that had arisen in the wild as hybrids between S. greggii and S. microphylla were found in Mexico late in 1991 by an English plant-hunting expedition including John d'Arcy, James Compton and Martyn Rix. The name jamensis (pronounced hamensis) is after Jame, the nearest village to the mountain pass area, 2400m (8000ft) above sea-level, in which both the parent species and their hybrid off-spring were growing. It was already known that it was possible for the two species to hybridize, because James Compton had obtained interspecific hybrid cultivars during the 1980s by deliberate cross-fertilization.

At the site of the expedition's find in a natural habitat, the form of S. greggii present had red flowers; those of the S. microphylla plants were bright magenta-pink: their hybrids bore flowers in a very wide range of colours. The expedition members collected seed from plants of almost 30 different colour forms, ranging through crimson, reds, orange, pinks, and two shades of yellow. One of the yellows has been chosen as the type of the interspecific hybrid, and has been given the cultivar name 'La Luna'. Less than seven years after this discovery, eleven cultivars were listed in the RHS Plant Finder. Those more widely available are: 'Devantville' orange-red, 'El Duranzo' orange-red, 'James Compton' deep crimson, 'La Luna' pale yellow, 'La Siesta' pink, 'La Tarde' also pink, 'Los Lirios' AGM 1996 purplish-red, 'Pat Vlasto' peach-red, and the American introduction 'Raspberry Royale' which freely bears flowers with purplish-red upper lips and dark red lower ones. Plant habit, height and leaf characteristics vary to some extent between cultivars, however, in stature these hybrids closely resemble S. greggii, and do not exceed 1m (3ft) in height.

Three years before James Compton and his colleagues made their discovery, John Fairey and Carl Schoenfeld, of the Texan Nursery Yucca Do, also found plants of S. × jamensis in the wild, and in 1991 introduced three selections in their catalogue. It was only subsequent to the discoveries of the English party later that year that it was realized that these, too, were of the previously unknown natural hybrid S. × jamensis.

SALVIA GREGGII × LYCIOIDES

S. lycioides is a rarity as a garden plant in both Britain and the USA. Though plants are sometimes offered under that name, these are in fact usually of the interspecific hybrid S. greggii × lycioides.

Like both parents, it is a small-leaved dwarf shrub, differing from S. greggii in making a smaller plant, not more than 50cm (20in) tall, and having thinner stems and a lax, spreading habit. It is also rather more cold-tolerant. The plant tolerates some shade.

Both leaves and flowers are smaller than in S. greggii. The narrow, dark green leaves are hairless and have a leathery appearance. The flowers are reddish-purple and the calyx is purple. Plants flower over a similarly lengthy period to S. greggii, from midsummer until the frosts.

This is one of the few salvias that looks very much at home in a rockery because of its growth habit. Its flowering period provides bright colour in a period of the year when the majority of rock-garden plants are out of bloom. Otherwise, it is a plant for positions at or near the edges of beds or borders. The darkness of foliage and flower colour is most appreciated next to appropriately chosen neighbours such as silver-foliaged gazanias, Anthemis punctata subsp. cupiana or white-flowered Cuphea hyssopifolia.

Propagation is best by cuttings since not all seed-raised plants will come true.

SOUTH AFRICAN NATIVES

The two other noteworthy species that behave as shrubs in the open in British conditions are S. africana-lutea and S. aurita.

In terms of cultural needs they fit quite well with their distant Mexican relatives, from 8,000 miles away on the opposite side both of the Atlantic Ocean and the Equator. Where a suitably sheltered, sunny spot can be found for it, the flowers of S. africana-lutea are often a talking point because of their colour – yellow when young, ageing to brick red.

The principal object of pruning is to maintain good shape and encourage new growth. S. africana-lutea and S. aurita begin to become unsightly after a few years and are best then replaced.

SALVIA AFRICANA-LUTEA (syn. S. aurea)
Linnaeus (1753)

Native to South Africa, this shrub was among the earliest of the non-European species to come to the notice of botanists. It is included in the classic forerunner of horticultural encyclopaedias, Philip Miller's eighteenth-century *Gardeners' and Florists' Dictionary*. Known in South Africa as the beach salvia, it is found growing wild in a coastal area of the Cape of Good Hope. The latitude concerned corresponds to that of Lebanon and Los Angeles in the northern hemisphere, so it is not surprising that in British gardens it is a plant only for the foot of a sunny wall in the south. It will survive a few (Celsius) degrees of frost unharmed, although not so many as *S. microphylla*.

A much-branched evergreen shrub, it is unlikely to attain a height and spread of more than 1m (3ft) in cultivation in Britain: in its native area it approaches twice this size at maturity.

The stems are stiff, short-jointed and numerous, and in their younger state quite hairy. The rounded, aromatic leaves are grey-green, up to 3.5cm (1¼in) long and covered in fine hairs, which are easily visible on the petioles. At their basal end many of the leaves have an almost torn appearance, owing to the presence of a pair of irregularly shaped, backward-pointing lobes. The leaf margins are both toothed and markedly undulate (wavy).

The flowers are borne on whorls of 2, closely packed on racemes that are only 5–10cm (2–4in) long. The flowers are yellow as they emerge, but soon turn to a golden- or rusty-brown. They are large – up to 5cm (2in) in length – with a falcate upper lip. The calyces persist, enlarging considerably after the corollas have fallen, and change from green to brown, developing an interestingly paper-like appearance.

There is a cultivar **'Kirstenbosch'**, which is dwarfer than the species.

Cultivation

Flowering may occur throughout the summer, but unfortunately the plant does not flower freely in Britain. Planted out in a warm, sheltered spot as a permanent occupant of bed or border, this shrub does best in light soil and full sun. Any pruning should be simply to maintain an attractive appearance, and will obviously include removal of frost-damaged shoots in spring.

The Surrey nurserywoman Margaret Hiley suggests that *S. africana-lutea* is well worth trying as an annual container plant, propagated afresh each year. She believes that the plant's flowering may well respond to all the light it can be given, and suggests standing the container on a piece of expanded polystyrene, for the value of the reflection from the white surface. It is obviously true that a South African coastal native must find the British summer a rather dark experience!

Propagation is by cuttings.

SALVIA AURITA
Linnaeus (1781)

This South African shrub has the distinction of being the only species described in this book of which neither plants nor seeds are available commercially in the British Isles at the time of writing. (A similar species, *S. scabra*, also from South Africa, was catalogued by three British nurseries in 1998.) The species is, however, no stranger to botany or to horticulture. It was described over 200 years ago and was listed in Loudon's *Encyclopaedia of Plants* in 1855.

In the wild, *S. aurita* is found on streambanks, flowering from spring to late autumn. It makes a height of 1.2m (4ft). The pretty flowers are borne on numerous short racemes, in widely spaced, few-flowered whorls. Blue-, lilac- and white-flowered forms occur naturally.

Cultivation

Like many other visitors to the Chelsea Physic Garden in recent years I have been much impressed by the long-sustained and abundant display of pale blue flowers on the compact, bushy plants grown there. The Head Gardener, Fiona Crumley, is an enthusiast, and it is easy to see why. At Chelsea, flowering commences in midsummer and continues until the first frosts. By autumn, plants are about 75cm (30in) tall. It must be said that the plants enjoy a well-favoured position, in a sheltered border backed by the south wall of the main Physic Garden building. Chelsea, of course, has the benefit of the artificial warmth of its central position in London.

With all this taken into account, *S. aurita* must be a species that deserves trial by gardeners in southern England who are able to offer it anything like the environment the Physic Garden provides. It may well give a more rewarding response than its shy-flowering compatriot, *S. africana-lutea* (above).

Propagation is by cuttings or seed.

I hope at least one or two English nurserymen will add this species to their catalogues.

9

PROPAGATION

Salvias are not only among the easiest groups of plants to propagate but for most of the species described in detail in this book there are at least two methods of propagation and for some, three. The salvia enthusiast does not suffer the problems of complexity and skill that confront the rose-lover who has an urge to multiply his plants, nor the sheer timespan it takes to multiply irises or lilies. There are few salvia species that could not be propagated in one way or another with facilities as unsophisticated as a sunny kitchen windowsill and a coldframe.

The main methods of propagation are by seed, by division and by cuttings. This chapter provides the basic practical information on each technique that the would-be salvia propagator needs to ensure a successful outcome. More specific details for each species are given under the individual plant description.

SEED

Many cultivars of salvia species will not come dependably true from seed, but apart from this, propagation by seed can be used successfully for almost all species. In many cases, the only practical restriction on multiplying plants in this way will be one of availability. In Britain the best seed companies offer a very small range of species: around thirty in 1998. (See the specialist suppliers listed in the appendices.) Although you can use seed from your own plants or those of fellow enthusiasts, in the British Isles and countries with similar climates, many of the tender species never, or very rarely, succeed in ripening seeds.

S. nemorosa subsp. *tesquicola* (p.61) is a tall plant that comes true from seed, unlike the cultivars of *S. nemorosa*.

Presuming you actually have seed of what you want, getting it to germinate and growing on the seedlings and young plants is not generally a difficult matter. Both at and beyond the seedling stage, salvias seem generally quite tolerant of root disturbance, given suitable care after transplanting.

LIGHT AND COLD REQUIREMENTS
Before looking at the raising from seed of specific groups of species, two general requirements need consideration – light and exposure to cold.

First, salvia seeds – or those of many species at least – respond to exposure to light during germination. This is simply provided by not covering the seeds after sowing.

Many sources say that light is a necessity for salvia germination, but to the best of my knowledge and experience, this is not so. However, for many species the most rapid germination, and perhaps the highest percentage of seeds germinating, will be secured by leaving them uncovered after sowing. You do need to take particularly great care of seeds left to germinate on the surface, because of the risk of their drying out at a critical stage. My own opinion, backed by experience with many species, is that it is better to cover the seeds with a shallow depth of compost, say 3 to 6 mm (⅛ to ¼in) according to size. This gives seedlings in the very early stages of their development some protection against drying out. A suggestion that I have not tried, but which seems a sound one, is to use vermiculite as the covering layer. This allows some light penetration to the seed, while retaining moisture effectively.

The second requirement is for the seeds of many species to undergo a period of exposure to cold before germination is able to occur. This is precisely what happens in natural conditions in cool temperate climates and at high altitudes in warm climates, when seed ripens and is shed towards the end of the summer. It provides a means of ensuring that the next generation of plants passes through the winter in relative safety, in the form of dormant seeds, rather than in the exposed form of seedlings. There is no definitive guide as to which species require this period of exposure to cold and which do not. Confronted by seed for which you have no definite information, I recommend that you make a trial sowing in a small pot at a suitable germination temperature as soon as you obtain your seeds. Ten seeds is a sample of perfectly adequate size for the purpose. If there is no germination after three weeks, or if only one or two seedlings have emerged, there is probably a dormancy problem.

Sowing in late summer or early autumn and leaving the container out of doors over winter mimics the natural way of breaking dormancy, but if you have obtained seed in late winter or early spring, and do not want to wait another year for plants, it is often possible to overcome dormancy artificially. First allow the seeds to absorb moisture in warm conditions and then place them in a refrigerator for a period before transfer to normal conditions for germination. In practice you can sow the seed in small pots in the normal way, watering well, allowing the compost to drain thoroughly, and leaving in ordinary room temperatures for three days. At the end of this time, place the pots in an unsealed polythene bag, with the open end loosely folded over, in an ordinary domestic refrigerator (not freezer). Remember to check every ten to fourteen days. If the compost begins to dry out, re-moisten it. If you observe seedling emergence, despite the cool conditions, move the pot in to suitable temperature and light conditions.

Seed of many species may not germinate in refrigerator conditions because of the low temperature, even when their dormancy has been broken. They will need to be removed and placed in temperatures ordinarily favourable for germination at some stage. Without experience or definite information, it is a matter of guesswork when you should remove them. I suggest that you divide the seed into, say, three equal lots, and sow each at the same time in a separate pot. Treat them identically as described above. If no seedling emergence is observed meantime, transfer one pot to warm conditions after two months, the next, if necessary, after three, and the last, if you have still had no success, after four.

Germination of some salvia species can be improved and hastened by a short period of treatment with gibberellic acid. In a few cases, germination may be very difficult to achieve without its aid. Gibberellins, which are produced naturally by certain fungi, stimulate germination in many species and have wider growth-promoting properties. Soak the seed in a very dilute solution – 0.02–0.10 per cent – of gibberellic acid 3 for up to two hours. An alternative has been suggested by American professor of chemistry and leading researcher on seed germination, Norman Deno: apply a very small quantity of the crystals to seeds 'sown' on a pad of folded, wetted paper towelling, then enfold the whole thing in more moistened paper and place it in an unsealed plastic bag. As seeds begin to germinate they are removed and grown on in pots. (Gibberellic acid has a very low toxicity to humans, but is only available in Britain from specialist chemical suppliers, see p.155. It is easier to obtain in some other countries.)

PERENNIAL SPECIES
FLOWERING IN THEIR FIRST YEAR

Five salvia species in this group – S coccinea, S. farinacea, S. patens, S. roemeriana and S. splendens – are almost invariably propagated from seed exactly like the wide range of frost-susceptible, annual bedding plants, such as French marigold and zinnia. Although these five species are, in fact, all true perennials, only S. patens is ordinarily retained for a second year, as greenhouse protection is needed to ensure their survival over winter. There seems little point in going to this effort as they all come true from seed and swiftly reach flowering from a late winter greenhouse sowing.

There is also a number of hardy perennial species that can be grown to flower successfully for the first time in the year of sowing, provided that this is carried out early enough. These species include S. forsskaolii, S. jurisicii, S. × superba, S. × sylvestris and S. verbenaca. They need the same initial treatment as S. splendens and the other species grown for bedding but, unlike them, they normally remain in the garden as long-term occupants. Because of their hardiness, it is possible to plant them out before the risk of the last spring frost has passed.

S. coccinea 'Coral Nymph' (p.53) is a pretty plant that is easily raised from seed in a warm greenhouse.

If the plants of any of these species are to start flowering much before late summer, a heated greenhouse is needed so that sowing can be carried out by early/mid-spring at the latest. The critical requirement for them all is a sufficient temperature in the seed compost for germination – at the very least 15°C (59°F) and preferably 20–23°C (68–74°F) – and a minimum air temperature of 13°C (55°F) for the development of seedlings and young plants. These factors, coupled with sufficient light, dictate the earliness of sowing.

There is seldom a problem about the germination temperature, which can be provided in an airing cupboard or warm kitchen if you like. However, sowing in late winter will produce seedlings just two weeks or so later, and these will need light conditions that can only be found on a greenhouse bench. So an early start will be unprofitable unless you have heating equipment and are willing to pay for its use to maintain 13°C (55°F) in at least part of the greenhouse.

Failing this, you will do far better to sow later, say in early spring or even later. The same heating equipment in the same greenhouse will then maintain a considerably higher temperature than it would have done a month earlier. Not only are nights shorter and on average warmer, but in Britain solar radiation in mid-March is on average about twice as great as it is in mid-February, and in mid-April about three times as great. Because of this, later-sown plants usually go a long way towards catching up those sown earlier. So long as plants are in sufficient warmth, they will grow at a speed roughly in step with the amount of daylight.

Sowing techniques Use a proper seed compost for sowing these salvias. The popular universal composts contain more fertilizers than seed composts, and the germination of some species is delayed and impaired by the resulting higher concentration of dissolved nutrients. Most composts are based on peat; for gardeners who prefer not to use them, there are alternatives in which the bulky component is coir, the husk material of coconuts.

Seed should be sown thinly, to lie about 1.5cm (½in) apart in pots or seed trays. After sowing, the best watering is achieved by standing the pots or trays in a shallow container of water for the first night. As already noted, a sufficient temperature for rapid germination may be provided in the home. Alternatively, proprietary electric propagators or an electric soil-warming cable installed in a sand bed, or electric foil are all ways of providing bottom heat. This will ensure warm enough compost without the need for raising the greenhouse air temperature to a costly level.

Once the seedlings are large enough to handle easily – from 2–3 weeks after sowing – they should be pricked out, 5cm (2in) apart, into seed trays. An alternative, often regarded as better because there is so little root disturbance at the time of planting out, is to prick out each seedling into its own cell in a cell tray or into a small pot. This is potentially the best practice, but it will only be better than putting, say, 24 or 30 seedlings in a shared standard tray, if you are confident that you will never let the plants suffer from water shortage. Every gardener who has tried it, will tell you that it is easier to look after the watering of a group of plants in a seed tray, sharing their root run through the compost, than it is to ensure that seedlings in individual pots or

PLATE IX

SHRUBBY SALVIAS

S. officinalis
Purpurascens Group

S. officinalis

S. officinalis 'Tricolor'

All specimens are shown at approximately life size

S. blancoana

S. interrupta

S. multicaulis

S. officinalis 'Icterina'

S. lavandulifolia

cells are properly watered. Underwatering at one end of a tray may be tolerated for the following day with little harm to the plants affected. No water at all arriving for 5 of 25 plants in cells or pots will do no good at all to those unlucky specimens. If you do opt to prick out your seedlings into a tray rather than cells or individual pots, and this is deeper than the standard seed tray, so much the better (growers' tomato boxes are quite good). More compost means a proportionally larger reserve of water.

The plants will benefit from liquid feeding as they grow: S. *splendens* is notoriously hungry for nitrogen. And on this species particularly, watch for aphids, which cause severe puckering and distortion of young leaves, from which the plants can take quite a long time to recover.

As usual with plants raised in spring in a greenhouse, do your best to harden them off and acclimatize them to outdoor conditions as planting-out time approaches. Ideally, a move from greenhouse to coldframe should take place during frost-free weather about a fortnight before planting out. Increasingly free ventilation should then be allowed, until the complete removal of the frame lights a few days before planting.

In practice, this is something of a counsel of perfection, and because most established gardens are fairly sheltered it is not usually necessary to go to great lengths to harden plants off. Once they have been taken out of the greenhouse, a sunny corner out of the wind may do well enough for this phase of their lives. If frost threatens, covering overnight with a synthetic fleece will protect sufficiently against slight frosts. Nevertheless, a single hard frost can kill tender species, so their planting should not anticipate too confidently the beginning of the frost-free period of the year.

Tender perennials flowering the year after sowing

For most of the frost-susceptible perennial species that are actually grown as perennials, flowering does not take place in the year of sowing, or if it does, satisfactory plant size is not achieved. These are among the reasons why such species are unsatisfactory for use as bedding plants raised from seed annually.

In raising the plants it is quite possible to treat them exactly as has already been described for the perennial species that are normally treated as half hardy annuals.

This has the advantage of giving the plants the longest possible first growing season and thus achieving the greatest possible plant size by its end.

Unfortunately, sowing in late winter or early to mid-spring does mean that plants will be occupying heated greenhouse space at precisely the time of year when it is at the greatest premium. Accordingly, preference might be more sensibly given to a rather later sowing, say in late spring. By this time little or no artificial heat will be required and, indeed, successful raising, just like successful overwintering of the resulting plants, will demand no more than a greenhouse from which frost

The very compact S. × *sylvestris* 'Blauhügel' (p.62) can be propagated by division or cuttings.

can be reliably excluded. That said, there is everything in favour of dependably warm compost for actual germination, and the use of an electric propagator, or an equivalent, is still well worthwhile.

Plants can be grown on over the summer in pots between 9 and 13cm (3½ and 5in) in diameter, according to speed of growth, and they can remain in these until planting out the following spring. There is no need for these plants to remain in the greenhouse throughout the summer. A coldframe or a sheltered sunny spot outdoors will serve at least equally well for the 2–3 months of high summer. The quality of plant growth is likely to be better out of the greenhouse than in it during this time and pest problems are usually much less.

HARDY PERENNIALS

Among the hardy perennial species are the clump formers such as S. × superba and S. × sylvestris, and the rosette-formers such as S. argentea and S. sclarea.

For this group of salvias, no greenhouse or coldframe is necessary. The seed can be sown outdoors in a well-prepared seedbed in late spring or early summer. Make sure the soil is moist enough, as well as fine and firm. If necessary, a V-shaped drill, 5cm (2in) deep, can be opened out with the corner of a draw hoe, and filled with water trickled into it through the spout of a watering can. By allowing the water to soak in, and then repeating the watering, the soil onto which the seed is subsequently sown is thoroughly moistened, even though the surface of the seedbed is left dry. Drills can be 15cm (6ins) apart.

In practice, however, most gardeners prefer to sow seed of these species very thinly in pots or seed trays, and keep them where they can be conveniently and frequently observed. The chosen location can have the advantages an outdoor seedbed usually cannot, such as being away from slugs, cats and the competition of weed seedlings. A coldframe – not necessarily with a covering light – does very well.

Once the seedlings are well established, transferring to a nursery bed at a spacing of, say, 10–15cm (4–6in) square is the most convenient way to care for them. Planting out in final positions can then be done in early spring the following year.

This is, of course, the standard treatment for a very wide range of herbaceous perennials and biennials, and is a very inexpensive way of acquiring large numbers of plants. A reminder, though, is not inappropriate, that the fine cultivars of S. nemorosa and S. × sylvestris such as 'Ostfriesland', 'Blauhügel' and 'Mainacht' do not come dependably true from seed. For these there is no alternative to an initial plant purchase – or a gift! – and multiplication by division or cuttings.

SOWING IN SITU

In the British Isles only one salvia species, S. viridis, is ordinarily raised by sowing the seed where the plants are to remain; readers in warmer countries may enjoy wider possibilities for sowing in situ, perhaps with one or more of the species that in cooler climates are treated as half hardy annuals raised in glasshouses.

S. viridis (syn. S. horminum), sometimes known as clary (although this name should properly be reserved for S. sclarea), is a true annual and is hardy enough to be sown outdoors in mid-spring while some risk of frost still remains. The most practical method of sowing where the plants are to remain begins with marking out the outline of the intended drift of plants on the surface of the prepared soil. This is conveniently done with a trickle of sand or lime. Then the corner of a hoe is used to draw out V-shaped drills running diagonally to the most usual line of sight. These should be 20cm (8in) apart and 1.5–2cm (½–¾in) deep. The seed is sown thinly in them and the displaced soil pushed back, using the back of a rake. If the soil is too dry for germination to start, water the drill beforehand as described for hardy perennials.

The virtue of sowing in drills is that the salvia seedlings can be easily identified from their inevitable close neighbours, the weed seedlings. The reason for the diagonal siting of rows is that, after thinning, the effect will be of informality. Thinning itself should be carried out in two stages, to allow for any accidental loss of plants, finally leaving young plants 20cm (8in) apart.

All this said, there are many soils – the stiff clay loam of my own garden included – on which it is not easy to make a good seedbed. In that case, you will probably do better to treat S. viridis in the same way as a half hardy species, sowing the seeds and growing on the seedlings in pots and planting out in late spring. Sowing seed in a coldframe in early spring will be quite satisfactory if you do not own a greenhouse.

DIVISION

Division is the method of propagation almost invariably chosen for the cultivars of the well-known hardy perennials S. nemorosa and S. × sylvestris, which will not come true from seed. Examples include 'Blauhügel' 'Lubecca', 'Mainacht' and 'Ostfriesland'. However, there is also a number of other hardy perennial species that do come true from seed but are, in practice, more often multiplied by division.

Compared with growing plants from seed, division brings about gratifyingly rapid results, with flowering achieved just as quickly as would have been the case had the original plant been left undivided. If you already possess plants and you want more, the multiplication possibilities are usually entirely sufficient for ordinary needs.

Multiplication is one reason for dividing plants: rejuvenation is another. As clumps of perennials enlarge, the central area of the clump tends to lose vigour. Left long enough, you will have an outer circle of strong young shoots and an increasingly extensive central zone of inferior ones. Lifting the clump, breaking it up and discarding the central area gives each relatively small replanted piece its own growing space, and the natural vigour of each new young cluster of shoots will rapidly exploit this to the best possible effect. If perennial weeds have become established within the clump, the process of division gives an ideal opportunity to extract wanted plants from the competition of very unwanted ones.

The two periods of the year in which division can be done are autumn and early spring. On free-draining soils in warmer and drier areas, the advantage of autumn division is a well-established plant by the time favourable conditions for growth commence in early spring. On other soils, and where winters are usually cold and wet, the usually preferred choice of time for division is early spring, just as active growth is commencing.

Division in autumn inevitably leaves young plants with minimal supporting roots. These must then spend a period of 3–4 months in cold, and usually wet, soil before conditions become favourable for the active extension of whatever root system originally survived the division process. The risk of losses from slug attack is particularly high: an established clump might not be impaired too much if some of its shoots are eaten, but a small division may become a total casualty. If, for any reason, you do opt for autumn division and your soil is naturally wet and slow draining in winter, your safest procedure would be to pot the divisions in, say, 10cm (4in) pots and put them in an unheated greenhouse or a coldframe or under cloches, for planting out in early or mid-spring.

The same deluxe treatment of new plant divisions – potting and re-establishment under protection – can, of course, also be applied for spring division. It may particularly be worthwhile if you have divided your plants down to very small pieces in order to multiply their number as much as possible. More commonly, in early spring, the divisions can be perfectly well planted out where they are to remain.

DIVIDING TECHNIQUES

Division itself is not a very difficult matter. Lift the plant to be divided retaining as much root as possible. For species with a more or less fibrous root system, the initial division, into two pieces, is best achieved by inserting the tines of two forks, back to back, into the centre of the clump. Pulling the two handles together will lever the two halves of the clump apart with the least possible destruction of roots. The process can then be repeated on the two half clumps, to produce four quarters, and, if appropriate, so on.

For species that form a relatively woody rootstock, division is best achieved by the use of a small spade or a stout long-bladed knife. The aim is to have as much root as possible attached to the shoot or shoots. In all circumstances, the older parts of the clump are best discarded. The end result may vary from a single shoot to a piece with 4–6 young stems.

Ideally, replant the divisions immediately. If this is impracticable for any reason, a temporary home in a plastic bag is the best place for them, as their worst enemy is dehydration. Once they are planted into their permanent positions, do not neglect to water them in thoroughly. Even if the soil is moist, there is no substitute for an initial post-planting soak to settle the soil particles into intimate contact with the roots. Do not rely on rainfall to provide this service – if there is anything less than a positive downpour just after planting, there will not be nearly enough to do what water from a can or hosepipe will achieve at once. Precautions against slugs may be wise at this stage.

CUTTINGS

For the cultivars of shrubby salvia species, which will not dependably come true from seed, cuttings are the only practicable means of propagation. For the tender herbaceous perennials and the shrubby species, as distinct from their cultivars, cuttings are by far the most commonly used method. Cuttings are also occasionally used for the propagation of many hardy herbaceous species and their cultivars. Propagation in this way is not only used for increasing plant numbers: for the many species that may fail (or definitely will fail) to survive the winter, cuttings are the commonest means of overwintering stock.

Happily, salvia cuttings in general root easily and quickly.

SUCCESSFUL ROOTING

Before going into detail on how to take cuttings, and on the special needs of particular groups of species, now seems an appropriate juncture to summarize what is needed to ensure successful rooting of cuttings, whether of salvias or of any other plant.

Material First must come suitable material – shoots that have the potential to root quickly. Fortunately, the genus presents no special problems here, with perhaps the worst mistake being to leave seeking cuttings material too late in the season. I remember a completely vain search in late autumn for any even remotely promising shoots on a large clump of S. *guaranitica*: six weeks earlier it would have been easy.

Equipment Assuming that good cuttings have been taken and prepared, the next priority must be keeping the atmosphere around the tops of the leafy cuttings (and all salvia cuttings fall in the leafy category) sufficiently humid to prevent dehydration winning the race against new root formation. In this respect, polythene film is a great friend of cuttings and their human propagators. This is true to such an extent that we may well wonder how people managed in the past without it! What they did, of course, was to enclose the atmosphere around their cuttings in other ways, such as with propagating frames, which are still seen on the greenhouse benches of amateur enthusiasts and professional gardeners, and which give very good results. At their simplest, propagating frames need be no more than a

25cm (10in) deep, topless box with a sheet of glass or rigid plastic serving as a lid. The lid is kept closed during the vulnerable phase between inserting cuttings and the formation of enough roots to maintain the turgidity of the foliage. The modern proprietary propagator is no more than a ready-made and more portable version of the traditional propagating frame.

An effective alternative to the propagating frame is simply a pot with 3–4 labels inserted round the rim and a polythene bag inverted over the assembly. It is even quite possible to dispense with the labels and leave the cuttings to support the polythene themselves. A tidier option is a suitable large, clear plastic container – such as a large water or fizzy drink bottle with its top cut off – inverted over the pot.

Professional nurserymen and gardeners use automatic mist propagation in preference to either polythene covers or propagating frames. Amateur-scale mist propagation kits are available, and may be well worthwhile for compulsive propagators. For salvia propagation alone, though, it is hard to imagine that their expense would ever be justified by their use, even for a very large private garden.

One word of caution. High humidity is the friend both of unrooted cuttings and of botrytis, the ubiquitous fungus responsible for grey mould disease. Whichever way you contrive to provide high atmospheric humidity, it is extremely important to maintain a hawk-like vigil for the disease, and to remove at once any leaves that show the symptoms.

Conditions Next come the right conditions around the base of the cutting, to encourage roots to initiate and grow. To begin with, this means moisture and oxygen; that in turn means a coarse, freely draining rooting medium which is, nevertheless, moisture retentive.

You can, of course, buy proprietary ready-mixed composts for rooting cuttings. My own favourite homemade mix is a 50:50 blend by volume of perlite and peat. Equally satisfactory as an alternative to peat in this mixture is a peat-based seed and potting compost. The presence of fertilizers in the compost does have some retarding effect on root formation, but if other conditions are as they should be, this has no practical consequence, and, of course, once the cuttings are rooted, is actually beneficial. If you are a traditionalist, you may prefer a 50:50 mixture of peat and very coarse sand, and why not? Cuttings in their untold millions worldwide have been rooted in such a preparation, and doubtless still are in places where perlite is as yet unheard of.

Timing Cuttings taken in or near high summer are the easiest and quickest to root. As summer draws towards its end, two factors may make success rather more difficult to achieve. One is too low a temperature in the rooting medium around the base of the cutting. Warm bottoms and cooler tops has rightly been an axiom among professional plant propagators for many years. Ideally the temperature of the rooting medium should be in the range between 20°C and 25°C (68–77°F), and without any special provision this will probably be the case on a greenhouse bench in mid- to late summer.

Outside this period, the artificial aid of electric bottom heat can make a world of difference. The available alternatives have already been mentioned in the section on propagation by seed. Electric propagators are the most popular for small-scale use. Electric soil-warming cable buried at mid-depth in a 10cm (4in) deep layer of sand is a well-tried and durable method of maintaining a temperature in the desired range on a larger scale. Thermostatic control is available, but if keeping expenditure to a minimum is an important factor, try just using a thermometer as a regular check, and see how you get on: you may find that the additional expense of a thermostat proves unnecessary.

The other factor that may militate against success in late summer and early autumn has been mentioned already. This is an adverse change in the nature of the shoots available for use as cuttings. This may apply quite obviously – because the shoots look tough and are all bearing flowers – or it may not be at all obvious – the shoots, promising though they may look, simply fail to produce roots.

The only advice, in the absence of experience or positive information, is to spread your risks by taking cuttings at various times and see how they get on. You will learn rapidly what you can get away with in timing, and what you cannot.

Light Finally, a word about light. Shortage of light, like the lack of artificial bottom heat, is unlikely to be a problem in high summer. In late summer and autumn,

a poorly illuminated environment can seriously affect the cuttings as they begin to root. Most likely to offend in this respect is the windowsill: light is the basic energy source of the growing plant and making sure plants get enough is a major objective of the people who design greenhouses. Windowsills, even sunny ones, compare very poorly for light with greenhouses.

Artificial lighting is not necessary for salvias in greenhouses, but like most other plants in autumn and winter their growth will certainly benefit from it, provided that they are warm enough. Sodium vapour lamps are the most satisfactory choice, although they are far from cheap. Tubular fluorescent (strip) lights are an alternative. The ordinary household electric light bulb does not give good results.

CUTTING TECHNIQUES

The ideal salvia cutting is usually the tip of a vigorously growing shoot that has developed in a favourable

S. *blancoana* (p.112) has a near-prostrate habit which makes it valuable as a groundcover plant and in larger rock gardens.

joints) of the stems. Although rooting in most salvia species occurs so easily that the precise position of the base of the cutting is immaterial, it makes sense as a precaution to treat them as if this might matter: make a cut with a sharp knife just below a leaf joint, and then remove the pair of leaves arising from it.

All other leaves are best left on, and usually best left entire. The practice of removing leaves other than the basal pair, and of shortening leaves, does have a justification as a means of reducing water loss from the cutting before roots develop. However, as leaves are the food factories of green plants, a better idea is to provide conditions in which little or no water loss occurs from the, as yet, unrooted cuttings. An atmosphere at, or very close to, 100 per cent relative humidity is needed. This can be achieved under a polythene cover or in a closed propagator or propagating frame as discussed above (p.131). (At 100 per cent, air is holding the maximum possible quantity of water vapour; above this, water will condense on relatively cool surfaces, or form a mist.)

Although, in good conditions, salvia cuttings will often root easily without the use of a rooting hormone, it seems silly to me not to make use of this inexpensive adjunct to successful practice. The formulations that are available all contain an added benefit, a fungicide that is often well worth using in its own right to protect against stem-rotting fungi, which are common in greenhouse conditions.

WEANING ROOTED CUTTINGS

Once the cuttings begin to show that characteristic perking-up that tells you there are effective young roots growing from the base, there remain two stages to complete their transition to independent young plants, capable of thriving under normal conditions. The first is to wean them away from a very humid atmosphere, the second to pot them up.

Taking off the polythene cover or removing newly rooted cuttings from their propagating frame or electric propagator will result in an abrupt fall in the humidity of the air around the leaves. Such abruptness is not desirable; the acclimatization process should be carried out in stages. If it is happening in bright sunny weather, first give your plants two nights without benefit of humid atmosphere, re-covering them with polythene or replacing them in a frame or propagator by day. After

position on the plant, not overshadowed by larger, stronger neighbours. Typically, it will have 4–5 pairs of expanded leaves, though the optimum number varies with species. If you are in doubt, take cuttings with a variety of numbers of leaf pairs: if your rooting conditions are good, you may well find that it makes little or no difference. Ideally, a shoot chosen as a cutting will have no flowers or flower buds, but if you have no choice in this respect, do not despair: simply remove them before inserting the cutting. As I write, I have S. *leucantha* and S. *uliginosa* cuttings that have rooted freely, with flower spikes coming into prominence which must have been there, tucked into the growing point, when I originally took the cuttings.

Root formation from cuttings in most genera is well known to take place most readily from the nodes (leaf

a couple of days of this treatment, it is usually safe enough to remove the polythene cover completely or to take the plants out of the frame or propagator for good. In the most dangerous weather conditions – bright and sunny – a sheet of newspaper or a piece of thin synthetic fleece laid loosely over them for another couple of days is a wise precaution. Likewise, occasional damping-down with a fine mist is a real kindness to soft foliage that is only supported by a small root system.

This weaning process complete, plants can be potted up. A 9cm (3½in) pot for each is usually an appropriate size, but for plants that are initially very small, such as S. arizonica, S. chamaedryoides, S. greggii, S. microphylla

S. greggi × lycioides is an interspecific hybrid, readily propagated by cuttings. Here it is seen to full advantage, tumbling over the edge of a raised bed.

or S. reptans, two or three to a pot might be a better bet initially. Further separation and individual potting-on will be needed once the plants begin to compete with one another.

SHRUBS

S. officinalis, S. lavandulifolia, their less hardy counter-parts S. candelabrum and S. interrupta, and the small-leaved species S. greggii and S. microphylla, and their hybrid, S. × jamensis, are all readily propagated by cuttings taken in early summer. These are taken by pulling away young shoots from the growth of the previous year from which they have arisen, so that a small heel of older tissue is at the base of the cutting.

Cuttings of S. officinalis and S. candelabrum should be about 10cm (4in) long; those of the small-leaved species, 5–7cm (2–3in). Under good growing-on conditions, the resulting young plants of the larger species can reach a height of 25cm (10in) or more before the end of the summer.

Ordinary stem cuttings, without a 'heel' at the base, can be successfully rooted at any time in the growing season. I have had excellent rooting of S. officinalis 'Berggarten' from cuttings taken in mid-autumn.

HALF HARDY PERENNIALS
FOR OUTDOOR CULTIVATION

Cuttings of S. guaranitica, S. uliginosa, and the many other species that cannot be depended upon to over-winter satisfactorily outdoors, are best taken in late summer or early autumn. The objective is to have securely established young plants by late autumn, when growing conditions, even in greenhouses, become unfavourable until late in the winter.

Propagation earlier in the year, from cuttings taken in early or midsummer, works equally well. Its unfortunate aspect is that you will then have quite large plants, already necessarily in quite large pots, to take through the winter. If you have abundant greenhouse space, all well and good. My observation of the greenhouses of keen plantsmen and plantswomen leaves me, though, with an indelible impression of demands on space forever outrunning supply. In this case, 30 young salvias each in a 9cm (3½in) pot, form a much more acceptable proposition than half the number of older, larger plants, each in a 13cm (5in) pot, which will require the same space in total.

Because early autumn is the usual potting time for newly rooted cuttings of this group of species, care is needed in two respects. First, watering: during the autumn and winter months, the best maxim is when in doubt don't. Secondly, avoid over-potting (the use of a pot that is large in relation to the size of the plant being put into it). This can be a menace in winter, when plants are growing very slowly or not at all. The menace lies in much of the compost lying very wet for long periods of time because roots have not yet spread far

enough to extract water from it. It is far better to leave the young plant in a relatively small pot until early spring brings about a rapid acceleration in water uptake and root growth: then is the time for moving on into a larger pot. (If you need a large number of cuttings of any individual species, you may find it worthwhile to grow one or more stock plants, specifically for their production; Nigel Hewish explains his method of producing stock plants on p.140.)

HALF HARDY PERENNIALS
FOR CONTAINERS

Half hardy perennials specifically destined to become container plants warrant particular mention only in terms of time of propagation. Suitable species for this purpose include S. elegans and its variety 'Scarlet Pineapple' (syn. S. rutilans), S. leucantha, S. discolor and S. involucrata. If they are grown as plants for bed or border, the cuttings are typically taken in late summer. Although there is nothing to stop the resulting plants being used in containers to flower in the following year – outdoors in the summer and under cover in the autumn and winter – the disadvantage of doing so is that they will, by then, be very big: large plants need correspondingly large containers if they are to be kept in good condition.

By taking cuttings in early or mid-spring instead, there is still plenty of growing time for impressive plants in full flower to be produced within four or five months. These will be a much more readily manageable and appropriate size for the greenhouses and conservatories – and even patios – of most modern households.

HARDY HERBACEOUS SPECIES

Propagation of hardy salvia species by cuttings is unusual in private gardens, as division and seed meet all normal requirements. But if there is a need, there is no reason why cuttings of species such as S. nemorosa, S. × superba, S. × sylvestris and S. verticillata should not be taken from the spring flush of growth, as soon as the shoots have reached a length of about 10cm (4in).

This enables sizeable plants to be grown in the same year, which will perform well in their permanent positions the following year. Division achieves the same result, of course, but more plants can be obtained from the original stock by taking cuttings.

10

NATIONAL COLLECTIONS

In the British Isles, National Collections are registered and co-ordinated by the National Council for the Conservation of Plants and Gardens (NCCPG). Founded in 1978, one of its objectives – and arguably its most important – is to foster the establishment of comprehensive collections of individual genera, including as many as possible of those species and cultivars that are in cultivation. The primary aim is to prevent the less widely grown of these being lost. Once this has occurred, future gardeners are not able to enjoy them, and they are no longer available for use in future breeding, or simply for multiplication if for any reason the demand for them revives.

The Dorset County Group of the NCCPG, the first of all such groups to be formed, came into being in the year following the establishment of the Council. At the time, there was much enthusiasm but considerable uncertainty about quite what such groups should be aiming to do. After consultation with the first general secretary of the NCCPG, Duncan Donalds, it was decided that the Dorset group should concentrate its efforts on three genera: *Penstemon*, *Primula* and *Salvia*. The energetic and resourceful founder member, Pat Vlasto, co-ordinated the group's activities over a period of years; ultimately around a hundred species of *Salvia* were brought together in her garden.

Ian Hedge of the Royal Botanic Gardens Edinburgh, an enthusiast for the horticultural potential of the genus and a world authority on its classification, was among Pat Vlasto's earliest contacts. He proved directly helpful by supplying plants of species then unobtainable except by the co-operation of botanic gardens. She and other group members also obtained plants and seeds from botanic gardens and other sources, particularly in Australia and North America.

Despite these successful efforts to establish the first British collection of salvias, Mrs Vlasto has always had strong reservations about the appropriateness of the private garden as a home for a National Collection: in the long term, its future is inevitably insecure due to the possibility of change of circumstances, or through accident or illness. Accordingly, in the early 1980s she arranged for the transfer of the collection to the nearby Abbotsbury Gardens. Here its care would be in the hands of the gardens' manager and his staff, and it would be protected from the vicissitudes inevitable when collections are in private hands. In 1982, the first year of its scheme for the recognition of collections, the NCCPG recognized as having national status both the part of the collection that was still in her own possession and the newly established collection at Abbotsbury.

Although it remains an outstandingly interesting garden for salvia enthusiasts to visit, Abbotsbury had difficulties in maintaining a satisfactorily wide range of species. These arose largely because it is very much a woodland garden, short of the relatively sunny sites needed for many of the Mexican and Mediterranean species to prosper. So, by mutual agreement, the collection was moved to the more satisfactory facilities available at Kingston Maurward College, just outside Dorchester. In its new home, the collection was recognized by the NCCPG in 1988. More details about the collection have been supplied by Head Gardener of the college, Nigel Hewish, see p.138.

S. coccinea (p.51) has been in cultivation for over two hundred years but is still little seen in gardens.

S. fruticosa, here at Kingston Maurward in Dorset, is represented on a Cretan fresco that dates from about 1400BC.

The collection at Kingston Maurward College was the first of the salvia collections currently in existence to be recognized by the NCCPG, but it is not alone. Nor is it, currently, the largest, since in 1992 the collection gathered by Christine Yeo at her Pleasant View Nursery in Devon was also recognized (see p.140).

In the same year as the Kingston Maurward collection was recognized by the NCCPG, so was a collection, originally restricted to hardy species, at Dyffryn Gardens at St Nicholas, six miles west of Cardiff. Owing to funding and staffing problems, it was decided by the current owners, the Vale of Glamorgan District Council Leisure Department, not to seek a continuation of NCCPG recognition after 1997. Fortunately, however, the Council has already begun to restore the fine historic gardens of the Dyffryn Estate, and has been successful in obtaining Heritage Lottery funding for the purpose. Some of this funding has been allocated towards enhancing the salvia collection, so Dyffryn Gardens should remain interesting for enthusiasts of the genus to visit.

With such a large number of species, and such diversity of hardiness and habit, there is abundant scope for three national *Salvia* collections in the British Isles. The original objective of the former Dyffryn collection, to concentrate on hardy species, could, for example, embrace the quite numerous cultivars of *S. officinalis*, *S. nemorosa*, *S. × superba* and *S. × sylvestris*. At present there is no single location in which such a collection exists.

A collection of salvias is also being assembled at the National Botanic Garden of Eire, at Glasnevin, Dublin. Although recognition by the NCCPG is not contemplated for the present, enlargement of the collection is being planned, and it is hoped to make it one of the more notable features of the botanic garden.

COLLECTIONS IN FRANCE

The French organizations most closely corresponding to the NCCPG are l'Association des Pépinièristes Collectionneurs (the Nurserymen–Collectors Association) and Le Conservatoire des Collections Végétales Specialisées (CCVS). There are three national collections in France, two under the aegis of the first organization and one of the second. See Where to See Salvias p.156 for addresses.

It is now legal within the countries of the European Union to take cultivated plants of most genera, including *Salvia*, across national boundaries for planting in the purchaser's garden. In the past, plant health legislation requirements made any such purchases a matter for planning well in advance and necessitated coping with a very unwelcome amount of bureaucracy. The latter days of a holiday can now be agreeably spent plant hunting in nurseries where species and cultivars as yet unknown at home may be acquired as living souvenirs. It is as well to bear in mind, however, the good old rule-of-thumb that woody plants purchased from a nursery north of one's own garden always have a better chance of survival.

KINGSTON MAURWARD COLLEGE
BY NIGEL HEWISH

There has been a collection of salvias at Kingston Maurward College for many years: the further gift of many plants by Mrs Pat Vlasto in 1988 gained it the status of a National Collection.

The species and cultivars grown here have been roughly divided into two groups: hardy and half hardy. I say roughly because we find that there are some in the half hardy group which will survive some winters outdoors with us, just as there are species in the hardy group that do not overwinter successfully every year.

Kingston Maurward gardens consist of three main garden areas. The open landscape that spreads out from the Georgian house built in 1720 by George Pitt consists of a lawn running down to a large lake surrounded by native trees. To the west of the house are the formal gardens, including the 'Balustrade Garden', built by the Hanbury family between 1914 and 1920. The other garden on the estate is the 'Demonstration Garden', which is set in the area enclosed by high walls behind the original Elizabethan manor.

Half hardy salvia species fit in well with the period of the Balustrade Garden. A series of gardens are divided by yew hedges and stone balustrading and it is in this sheltered area that the species in this group have been grown for the past few years. The protection from the prevailing south-westerly wind and from frosts has allowed several of the later-flowering varieties – such as

S. confertiflora and *S. dorisiana* – to make a show before being cut down by severe weather at the end of autumn.

The Demonstration Garden has a wide range of plants for all situations and is divided up by a variety of hedges. Here, the hardy salvia group is grown in a large rectangular bed devoted exclusively to the genus, so that the species can be compared with each other. They are left *in situ* permanently (meaning for as long as they live, which may be only a couple of seasons – as in the case of *S. sclarea* and *S. argentea* for example), or for as long as they stay within bounds. Some can be very invasive, either spreading or seeding among other plants. One such is *S. forsskaolii*: growing up to 1m (3ft) tall and almost the same across, and with large leaves that can easily smother weaker plants, this needs plenty of space.

For the many salvia species that come from rocky hillside habitats the soil at Kingston Maurward is ideally suited. It is very gravelly soil over chalk and is very free draining. The annual rainfall is an average of 990mm (nearly 40in), so we do not usually water the hardy salvias. Most of the species in the half hardy group, on the other hand, require regular watering during dry periods throughout the summer. We do not feed any of the hardy salvias other than by applying a mulch of well-rotted manure to the permanent beds; this is quickly lost into the open soil. The beds that are planted with half hardy species are dug during the winter months and well-rotted manure incorporated.

The half hardy group of salvias is planted out into the Balustrade Garden at the end of May when the risk of damaging frosts has disappeared. Most have already been growing well in a frost-free greenhouse and are by then potted into 2- or 3-litre pots. Some of the larger species like *S. mexicana* and *S. polystachys* will be in 5-litre containers and are nearly 1m (3ft) tall, having been pinched several times. Upon being planted out, they grow away very quickly because they have not been checked while in their pots.

Many of the half hardy species are late flowering, some – like *S. iodantha* and *S. longispicata* – growing up to 2m (6ft) before flowering in October. This means that they are just coming into flower as the frosts start. With the shelter of the wall around the garden, they are protected from these frosts and, given a favourable autumn, can flower into November and December. We allow all the salvias in the Balustrade Garden to remain

S. transylvanica (p.72) is an easily grown and very garden-worthy species. Seed is widely available.

in situ until they have been completely killed off by the winter weather. In severe conditions we will lose most of them, but during milder winters several will survive. Among those that most often do so are *S. gesneriiflora* and *S. elegans* 'Scarlet Pineapple'.

As we leave these half hardy plants out over winter it does mean that we have to make sure we have either young plants or stock plants in the greenhouse ready for the next season. We try to keep at least one stock plant from each species or cultivar, from which we can take our cuttings, in the nursery area. This is particularly desirable because so often when we come to take cuttings from the plants in the garden, they are in full flower and it is difficult to find material without flower buds. By keeping the stock plants cut back and fed they can be encouraged to grow good shoot material for propagation. Most of the cuttings are taken from July to September to give us well-rooted plants by early autumn for overwintering in a frost-free greenhouse. The plants are potted up as they require it and hardened off in spring prior to planting out.

Nigel Hewish has been Head Gardener at Kingston Maurward College since 1991. He was previously Head Gardener at Berkeley Castle, Gloucestershire. His formal training was at Cannington College, Somerset, itself notable for its fine salvias.

PLEASANT VIEW NURSERY
BY CHRISTINE YEO

My interest in salvias stems from 1978 when we moved house and found ourselves with a ¾-acre garden full of mature shrubs about which we knew virtually nothing. One plant in particular caught our attention as it flowered for such a long time, from July to December, or even longer if it didn't catch the frost. Unfortunately, it was unlabelled, but after much searching we found that it was a salvia. This was nothing like the annual salvia that we knew and had used as summer bedding; it was a shrub, known then as *S.grahamii* and now correctly called *S. microphylla*. It is now among the best-known members of the genus, but at that time knowledge of salvias beyond a handful of common species was very limited. The small number of people acquainted with a wider range were either professional horticulturists or botanists, or were well-to-do amateur enthusiasts with large private gardens.

My husband Bryan and I, inspired by *S. grahamii*, decided that it would be a good idea to collect more of these long-flowering plants. By the time we moved house again we had built up substantial collections of both salvias and abelias, another of our special interests. Once we were settled into our new garden, in 1992, we successfully applied to the NCCPG for recognition for collections of national status.

We grow all the salvia species that we come across, not just those that are of ornamental value as is usual in many genera collections. In the case of our genus, many of the less attractive species are among the most important medicinal herbs. Again, unlike many of the National Collections, ours is mainly of species rather than cultivars: with a genus of 900 species these must take priority. Recent years have seen the introduction of many cultivars of the *S. microphylla* and *S. greggii* alliance known as *S. × jamensis*, of *S. officinalis* and of *S. nemorosa* and its close relatives. As many cultivars are very similar, differing perhaps only in flower colour, and even then just slightly, we only collect those cultivars that are sufficiently special or distinctive. Currently our collection comprises about 200 species, and around 30 cultivars.

In the last few years we have travelled all over Britain in our search for plants and information. After corresponding for several years with the two collection holders in Australia, we decided to visit them to learn more about how growing conditions in different climates affect salvias. We have also visited one of the French collections – in Nice – and the Hanbury Gardens, La Mortola on the Italian Riviera. At La Mortola we were pleased to have been able to help restore the salvia collection. While staying in the garden for a few days we were able to check the names of the plants that they had grown from seed received from other sources.

We correspond with collectors all over the world and exchange seed and information. This liaison is important for plant collections, especially of a large and widely dispersed genus such as *Salvia*. Because of this we now regularly get visitors to the garden and nursery from all over the world.

Unfortunately, with a large proportion of the members of the genus coming from Central and Southern America, many of them are not hardy in the British Isles. Even in south Devon, which is usually thought of as being very mild, we are not close enough to the sea

to be frost-free, and in an average winter we experience temperatures of –6 to –10°C (14–21°F). As our nursery is at a height of 80m (260ft) above sea-level, and exposed to easterly and westerly winds, our salvias need to be planted with as much shelter as we can give them. Fortunately, we are on a well-drained, south-facing slope over limestone, which is ideal for a very large number of the species we grow.

As many are not hardy with us, we have to take cuttings every autumn so that we can overwinter small plants in the greenhouse. We also save seed of the rather hardier species, just in case we have an exceptionally bad winter. Any surplus seed we make available for purchase, and this is catalogued in our annual seed list. With many of the more difficult species we need to have several plants in different stages of growth to ensure that we do not lose any that we cannot replace.

In 1992 we created a special salvia garden in a sheltered position next to our plant nursery. We replant annually with different species, and aim to create a show garden changing in interest from year to year. This enables customers to see the plants in flower before they choose what to buy from the nursery. Many salvias are also dispersed throughout the surrounding larger garden. We have been responsible for introducing many new species into the British Isles and have bred many new varieties ourselves.

In 1995 and the two following years, we exhibited at Hampton Court Flower Show in the NCCPG Plant Heritage marquee, with a selection of other National Collections. During 1995–96 we assisted with the salvia trials at the RHS Gardens, Wisley. We sent many plants to the trials and one of these was given the accolade of the AGM. This was our own introduction, a *S. microphylla* variety named after our nursery 'Pleasant View'. The recognition of its excellence was a source of special gratification, since it means that this exciting genus now has such a close identification with the nursery.

Christine Yeo is author of the handbook *Salvias*, which was the first publication devoted exclusively to the *Salvia* genus. This described almost a hundred species, and was published in March 1995; *Salvias II*, which described over 80 more species, followed in March 1997.

11

SALVIAS IN NORTH AMERICA, AUSTRALIA AND NEW ZEALAND

I s there any other field of human activity in which amateurs and professionals come together so amicably and to such good effect as in horticulture? Whether in organizations like the Royal Horticultural Society or the Hardy Plant Society, or at shows or meetings, or writing books and articles – there they are, amateurs and professionals working side by side and to the observer often indistinguishable. It is not in the least uncommon to find that the professionals were themselves amateur enthusiasts before choosing to make their livelihoods from horticulture. Many a successful nursery is, in origin, the founder's overgrown hobby. It is very fitting, then, that of our three contributors to this chapter, two are nursery owners and one is a dedicated amateur of long standing and much esteem.

Sue Templeton owns a nursery with the inspired name 'Unlimited Perennials', in New South Wales, Australia. She also has the larger of the two National Collections of salvias in her country. Geoff Genge, in New Zealand, is her close counterpart, again being a nurseryman and also the holder of one of New Zealand's two National Collections, started by his wife Adair. Betsy Clebsch is a noted name, not only in American gardening circles in her home state of California, but also as a writer and lecturer throughout the USA. Her *Book of Salvias* is without competition for gardeners in climates similar to her own. It is also a mine of information for salvia enthusiasts elsewhere.

The inflated calyces of *S. africana-lutea* (p.121) make it a highlight in the collection at Nice Botanic Garden, France.

To give European readers a sense of climatic perspective: Old World cities at similar latitudes to Betsy Clebsch's home are Athens and Lisbon, while Sue Templeton's nursery is at a latitude corresponding to the Mediterranean coast of Morocco; and the French city of Lyon is about the same distance north of the equator as Geoff Genge's nursery is south – on the southernmost tip of New Zealand's South Island. He also mentions Auckland in North Island, which is on about the same latitude as San Francisco, 30 miles from Betsy Clebsch's garden. **NOTE:** Both Sue Templeton and Geoff Genge mention north and south: don't forget that they are in the southern hemisphere, where north means warmer and sunnier!

SALVIAS IN NORTH AMERICA
BY BETSY CLEBSCH

Since the 1970s, gardening has steadily been gaining the attention and the participation of the people who live in this vast and geographically divergent country. There are now dozens of monthly magazines that focus on gardening or include some aspect of it on a regular basis, as well as features in newspapers and journals.

A general awareness of the genus *Salvia* has come about as recently as the 1990s, mainly as a result of these publications: glowing with colour, their pictures and illustrations have allowed gardeners to visualize a variety of salvias in a garden setting. Once they have seen these images and learned of the unique qualities of the plants, including the ease of growing them, the quest for their own specimens follows quite naturally.

Unfortunately, there is no society in the USA devoted to the study of salvias nor is there a National Collection of plants to be seen. The formal approach of teaching the public about salvias has fallen into the hands of arboreta and botanical gardens. Their function is one of education, maintaining gardens for observation, and the dissemination of plants. On the other hand, and quite informally and spontaneously, a soaring number of enthusiastic gardeners with an inquisitive and lively interest in growing salvias has led to the sharing of cultural information about the genus as well as the exchange of cuttings, seeds and plants. These gardeners, with their passionate interest, are found from coast to coast.

The West Coast of the USA has a Mediterranean climate that is rather mild in winter and dry throughout summer and is especially amenable to growing a large number of salvias. In particular, the long-blooming species from Mexico and Central and South America do well in this area. It is not surprising that both public and private botanical gardens in California have established salvias in appropriate settings: from San Francisco to San Diego there is a rich source of arboreta and botanical gardens that contain and maintain collections of species from habitats as close as Baja California (the part of Mexico that is adjacent to California) and as distant as China and Africa.

STRYBING ARBORETUM

Strybing Arboretum in San Francisco is one such source, and has an interest in salvias that dates from the early 1970s. At that time it was relatively easy to get permits from officials in both Mexico and the USA to transport seed and plants, and throughout these early years, salvias from Mexico and Central America were obtained for Strybing. Don Mahoney, who is in charge of the gardens, particularly enjoys salvias and has encouraged growing them for the plant sales that are held at the Arboretum. At present, it is particularly the Mexican species, which have a long period of bloom, that are being propagated from the collections and offered to the public. Having a diversity of salvia species available, including S. *cacaliifolia*, S. *blepharophylla* and S. *purpurea*, has stimulated widespread interest in the genus among gardeners in the western USA.

Of especial interest to Don Mahoney is the encouragement of urban wildlife such as birds and butterflies.

In North America, the colourful tubular flowers of salvias are a major source of nectar for hummingbirds. There are many winter-blooming species so hummingbirds can rely on a year-round food supply from members of the genus. Yet another source of food for a wider range of birds is the nutritious seed. The nectar and pollen of salvias also furnish food for butterflies and moths. So planting salvias in city gardens, as well as larger gardens, helps to produce favourable conditions for the development of a healthy, balanced habitat with plants, insects and vertebrates all able to thrive.

RANCHO SANTA ANA BOTANIC GARDENS

Rancho Santa Ana Botanic Gardens in Claremont, California, is closely associated with the Claremont Colleges, and botanical studies and projects have long been joint endeavours of the two institutions. Salvias that are native to California and what is known as the California Floristic Province (plants that range beyond the borders of the state), are being grown in the botanic gardens. These plants are of vital interest to Californian gardeners because they grow actively in winter and remain dormant in summer, a pattern of growth that exactly coincides with California's periods of rain and drought.

Bart O'Brien, director of horticulture at Rancho Santa Ana, calls Californian native salvias outstanding garden plants and has made sure that both the species and the numerous cultivars are labelled and well positioned for viewing in the botanic gardens. 'The list of compatible plants that would harmonize well with California's salvias is endless,' says O'Brien, and adds, 'They offer their spectacular flowers, leaves, colours, fragrances, and growth forms to dry sunny gardens around the world.' He quickly makes a verbal list of companion Californian natives and then rapidly goes on to prove his point by adding a number of exotics. Shrubby Mediterranean plants not only complement the California native salvias, but also require the same cultural conditions.

Gardeners in the Los Angeles area flock to Rancho Santa Ana's yearly plant sale for they can be sure that many of the 19 native Californian salvias will be available. There are over 30 cultivars of these natives and some of these plants are available at this sale, as well as at nurseries.

DENVER BOTANIC GARDEN

North American gardeners, from the Atlantic to the Pacific Ocean, all share one thing in common: outrageous weather patterns from time to time. Mild maritime regions experience periods of frost, wind and drought. Immense interior regions are plagued with excessive temperatures, both hot and cold, as well as strong winds wind and severe drought. Across this continent, gardeners need both physical as well as emotional stamina in order to deal with nature's forces. Conversations typically begin with a litany of past and present weather!

The Denver Botanic Garden, in Colorado in the Rocky Mountains, is situated in an area that is noted for its fickle weather patterns. The thermometer can soar or plummet in a matter of hours. Panayoti Kelaidis is curator of the rock and alpine section of the garden. As early as the 1980s, he was growing and experimenting with salvias in order to widen the palette of plants that can be grown throughout the area. The seed lists of plants from Turkey, offered by Jim and Jenny Archibald of Wales, caught his attention because the native habitats of the salvias that were included had much in common with the Denver area. There were a number of species with captivating descriptions simply begging to be tried: S. cyanescens, S. hypargeia, S. macrochlamys and S. multicaulis, to name a few. Kelaidis's investigation continues not only with western Asian and eastern European salvias, but also hardy species from Mexico, such as S. microphylla var. wislizenii, that have proven adaptable to the area. Also, two species from the western USA, S. dorrii and S. pachyphylla, are being evaluated for cultivation at high elevation and in dry gardens.

SALVIAS AS ANNUALS

Throughout the USA, a large number of perennial salvias, the majority from Mexico, are being treated and planted as annuals. This is particularly the case in the cold climates of the northern and eastern states. From actively growing rooted cuttings, plants have been found to develop swiftly and to blossom for a two- to three-month period. This practice includes large salvias such as S. mexicana and S. microphylla and many of their named selections. S. cacaliifolia and S. involucrata are also in the same category. Medium to small salvias that are also suitable include S. chamaedryoides,

S. greggii and S. muelleri, to name but a few. Tucked into gardens at the time when annuals would normally be sown or planted, these rapidly maturing salvias flower from summer until frost.

Thus gardeners in our colder areas are making use of an old idea that speciality nurseries and dedicated horticulturists who live abroad put into practice many years ago. By this means it is now possible for them, as well as for gardeners and collectors elsewhere in this vast country, to grow a wide range of species, selections and hybrids in this impressive and fascinating genus.

SALVIAS IN AUSTRALIA
BY SUE TEMPLETON

For a young country with only one native species, the cultivation of salvias in Australia has a history of respectable length. Some species were certainly in gardens in the nineteenth century, among them S. patens and S. viridis (syn. S. horminum). Others introduced many decades ago are S. leucantha, S. microphylla (though under its pseudonym S. grahamii), S. rutilans (correctly S. elegans) and strangely, S. polystachya. Many older people have childhood memories of picking the flowers of S. rutilans to suck the nectar. As in other countries, extensive plantings of masses of red S. splendens have made the genus synonymous with the colour red in the mind of the public. Fortunately, in more recent times councils have made as much use of S. farinacea in such plantings, so this species is also getting well known. Sage is grown for kitchens but not many people make the association between the herb and the flowering salvias, or realise that sage is the English word for the Latin Salvia.

The Ornamental Plant Collections Association Inc. in Australia corresponds to the National Council for the Conservation of Plants & Gardens (NCCPG) in Britain. It was founded in 1988, following an initiative taken by some of the staff at the Melbourne Botanic Gardens. It is fortunate that the collections scheme was in place before botanic gardens began losing both government funding and the key people who cared for their collections. By 1991, the salvia group of the Herb Society of Victoria had collected roughly 50 species. Their collection is dispersed among several gardens.

Victoria calls itself 'The Garden State', and a large part of it has a better climate – more regular rain and cooler temperatures – than most of Australia. My home

PLATE X

HALF HARDY SALVIAS – OTHER COLOURS

S. atrocyanea

S. discolor

S. leucantha

S. involucrata 'Bethellii'

S. semiatrata

S. involucrata 'Boutin'

S.buchananii

All specimens are shown at approximately life size

and nursery is in a suburb of Albury on the border of New South Wales and Victoria, but inland of the mountains that extend from north to south parallel to the east coast. This means that my local climate is somewhat hotter and drier than that of the coast.

I have concentrated on collecting salvias since 1991 and now have more than 160 species. I believe that selling promotes the urgency to have correctly named plants, and that it also gives incentive and finances to seek more plants: I offer over 100 species for sale. One area of achievement is my introduction of many of the Mexican and American species that were previously unavailable in Australia, and which are usually the most showy; among them are S. blepharophylla, S. cacaliifolia, S. chamaedryoides, S. chiapensis, S. coahuilensis, S. confertiflora, S. fallax, S. gesneriiflora, S. iodantha, S. melissodora, S. mexicana, S. semiatrata and S. sprucei, as well as cultivars of S. microphylla and S. greggii. These have all been grown from seed, as I don't have quarantine facilities. Betsy Clebsch and associates in California have been particularly helpful with seed and shared information.

Other enthusiasts have also introduced individual, excellent salvias: in the late 1980s Marilyn O'Dowd brought in S. 'Indigo Spires' (unfortunately as S. regia so both names are used in Australia), Ken Gillanders brought S. corrugata from Ecuador, Natalie Peate introduced the South African species S. lanceolata and S. chamelaeagnea, Adelaide Botanic Gardens introduced S. wagneriana, and a couple of nurseries released S. buchananii. Other species have been made available through seed firms, such as Jelitto, Chiltern Seeds and Thompson & Morgan, and through rock garden societies. These have been grown in various parts of the country, though often incorrectly named.

NOMENCLATURE

It distresses me that the naming of some Salvia species is so confused, making it hard to get the correct plant. In my experience S. hians is the most often mistakenly identified. Australian nurseries are now taking more care to have informative labels (often the information is still incorrect, but at least the thought is there). With an accreditation scheme for plant producers spreading, and encouraging more accuracy, things can only improve. The easy exchange of information via the Internet should also help solve identification problems.

WINTER DISPLAYS

The majority of people live on the coast in Australia and so do most garden writers and all the influential nurseries. Here the climate is moderated by the sea, and the rainfall is usually fairly reliable. Accordingly there is not a lot of precise knowledge about what level of frost plants can tolerate, and in the past coastal nurseries have seemed not to care anyway, with perhaps enough sales in the larger cities. It is only by getting feedback about frost from clients all over Australia that I have begun to build a salvia frost-tolerance picture.

Usually sunny, dry summers occur in areas with cold winters so that plants get toughened up and maybe woody, and this helps them resist frost. I have temperatures to −5°C (23°F) at times and am still able to grow almost all species without covering. Admittedly some are sited at the foot of the north wall of the house for the better microclimate. If we have frost we generally have a clear sunny day, while rainy winters mean less frost. Because I live within 50 miles (80km) of permanent mountain snowfields, air temperatures are kept lower than they would be otherwise.

Many of the winter-flowering salvias are frost tender to an extent; they are also bulky plants. This means that it is not easy to poke them into a restricted area and some care is required to place them well and thus enjoy the flowers. Some, such as S. madrensis and S. iodantha, begin flowering in late autumn. S. madrensis continues throughout the winter, but S. iodantha only lasts a couple of months. Both are beautiful and I regard them as necessary for an Australian salvia lover. S. dorisiana begins flowering in late winter and needs frost protection if one is to see the deep pink flowers.

My winter favourite is a hybrid of S. karwinskii and S. involucrata as it begins flowering in late autumn and goes through to late spring. It originated from the University of California at Berkeley and has large spikes of cyclamen-pink blooms. Flowers that are already open when a frost occurs tend to fall, but the plant produces more so it has lovely displays when you need them most. S. gesneriiflora with its huge scarlet flowers and black calyces is another winter-flowering favourite.

There is a need to find out more about the frost tolerance of many species, and another area that needs study is flowering in shade. A number of species do flower well with little direct sunlight, but no doubt the summer temperature needs to be reasonably high.

Some species such as *S. fruticosa*, *S. interrupta* and *S. recognita* are difficult to keep going in our garden. We have very abrupt changes from cold to hot, and when the heat comes in November a few salvias give up on life. I think if I had an area I could leave permanently drier it would help. It frustrates me that some of the hilly areas near Melbourne suit some salvias better, although they are frequently moist and cooler. However, we do have some benefits. In our conditions there are species that flower year round such as *S. chiapensis*. This is a smaller plant, usually less than 1m (3ft) in height, with attractive olive-green shiny foliage and cerise tubular flowers. It is somewhat frost tender but is fine under an evergreen tree.

THE FUTURE

The release of Betsy Clebsch's *Book of Salvias* stimulated a lot of publicity about the genus. The gardening public is beginning to be aware that there are more salvias than 'the Bonfires', as *S. splendens* is widely known, after the variety that was so popular for so many years. I believe salvias are a very important group of plants for Australia, mainly because of their ability to be incredibly long-flowering, as well as for their winter colour. I hope to see them in most gardens, correctly named of course.

SALVIAS IN NEW ZEALAND
BY GEOFF GENGE

There are two National Salvia Collections in New Zealand, one at the Regional Botanic Gardens, Auckland (37°S), the other at my own nursery, Marshwood Gardens, Invercargill (46.5°S). The difference in latitudes within New Zealand allows a wide variety of salvia species to be grown, depending, of course, on location. Longer summers at 37°S make the cultivation of the more tender species successful, for example *S. concolor*, *S. madrensis* and *S. puberula*, whereas *S. argentea* and *S. patens* are among species that prefer the cooler climate at 46.5°S.

Many of the more tender species are also grown in the south, though usually as foliage plants, as they often do not commence flowering until the first frosts arrive. However, it is possible to grow some half hardy species successfully as flowering plants in the south. These include *S. azurea*, *S. guaranitica*, *S. involucrata*, *S. puberula*, and *S. microphylla* and *S. greggii* cultivars.

In my area of the country in 1996 temperatures as low as –14°C (6.5°F) over nine days killed many native plants to ground level and likewise the salvias. Most regenerated in the spring, the only casualties being *S. buchananii* and *S.* 'Black Knight'. *S. regla* and *S. microphylla* var. *wislizenii* proved to be hardier than previously thought, not being cut to ground level.

Salvias are suitable for a variety of sites and purposes in New Zealand. However, many gardeners have yet to 'discover' them as garden plants, their knowledge of the genus not yet having passed that of *S. splendens* 'Bonfire'. Fortunately, public parks are now planting, to great effect, the varieties of *S. coccinea* and *S. farinacea*, as well as this ubiquitous red-flowered annual.

Landscapers are using *S. aethiopis*, *S. argentea* and *S. officinalis* cultivars. The *S. officinalis* group and *S. nemorosa* group make excellent companion plants to old roses. This is also true of *S. bulleyana*, *S. castanea* and *S. przewalskii*, and these have magnificent foliage, in my opinion as good as any hosta. In shaded areas *S. forsskaolii* with its bold foliage is successful as are *S. glutinosa*, *S. nubicola*, *S. patens* and its cultivars, and *S. uliginosa*. In my exposed garden and nursery, *S. recognita*, grown from seed collected in Turkey, has proved a great success. Its 2m (6ft) stems of soft pink flowers take the gale-force winds that we often suffer in their stride.

NOMENCLATURE

Correct nomenclature is a problem. Both New Zealand collections obtain new species from overseas sources only to find, on flowering, that the seed has not been true to name: *Agastache*, *Stachys* and *Nepeta* have all arrived here as *Salvia*! Some mail-order nurseries are importing plant material, which is easier to identify, but quarantine regulations make this costly.

Identification remains a problem for New Zealand salvia enthusiasts, especially for those with no botanical training. Apart from floras, the publications of Christine Yeo and Betsy Clebsch have proved very helpful. Networking with other salvia growers has provided additional information.

THE FUTURE

For a country with no native salvia, the number of species available in New Zealand is ever increasing and the future potential of the genus here is encouraging.

APPENDIX 1
GLOSSARY

Ascending Stems growing in an upward direction only in their upper parts, the lower parts being almost prostrate or at an oblique angle to the ground.

Author The person who first described a species according to standard scientific practice. (See also **described/description**.) A full botanical name includes the author's name, usually abbreviated, after those of the genus and species.

Bract A leaf-like structure which has a protective function. In *Salvia*, bracts are found on the **inflorescences** of many **species**, e.g. *S. sclarea*, the flower buds in the developing inflorescence being sheathed by them.

Calyx (calyces) In *Salvia* the calyx is the outermost part of a flower, immediately within which is the **corolla**. The calyx consists of fused (joined) sepals and as the flower opens it usually expands into the shape of a tube, funnel or bell.

Corolla This consists of petals which in *Salvia* are joined to form a tube as the basal part. The tube has two **lips**, upper and lower. In *Salvia*, as in all members of the Labiatae, the ovary is enclosed by the corolla.

Crenate Leaf margins that are continuously round-toothed or scallop-edged. The teeth, small or very small in relation to the leaf-blade, are nearly semi-circular.

Cultivar A **variety** which has arisen in cultivation, either by deliberate selection or breeding, or by chance. An example of a cultivar in the last category is S. 'Indigo Spires'.

Cyme A form of **inflorescence** characterized by the terminal flower opening first. In *Salvia* a pair of cymes commonly form a **verticillaster**. In *Salvia* and in other members of the Labiatae, the **pedicels** or lateral stems

arise in pairs on opposite sides of the main stem of the cyme. See p.14.

Decumbent A stem that is prostrate on the soil surface, with the apex growing upright.

Deltoid A leaf-blade or bract, triangular in outline, with the three sides approximately equal in length.

Dentate Continuously toothed leaf margins. The teeth, small or very small in relation to the leaf-blade, are pointed (see also **crenate**, **serrate**).

Described/description In botany, a description (or diagnosis) is the first scientifically acceptable account of a species published (in Latin) in a recognized scientific journal. This is normally accompanied by the deposition of a preserved (usually dried) specimen in a declared place of collection and preservation, usually a herbarium. The years given in this book in relation to the description of species, are those for the first acceptable description according to this definition.

Elliptic Elongated leaf-blades with the margins of the two halves of the leaf, one on each side of the midrib, symmetrically curved in outline (see also **lanceolate**, **oblong** and **ovate**).

Exserted With the style and stigma and/or stamens protruding beyond the outermost part of the **corolla**. A feature of many *Salvia* species, e.g. *S. elegans*, *S. forsskaolii* and *S. semiatrata*.

Falcate The upper lip of a flower, curved in the shape of a sickle. This is common in *Salvia*, the lower portion of the upper lip then being usually at (or close to) a right-angle to the **tube**.

Family A group of **genera** that share certain key characteristics.

Form (forma, abbrev. **f.)** A naturally occuring population which differs from the **type** species only in one or two minor characters, e.g. flower colour.

Short-lived but deservedly popular, *S. sclarea* var. *turkestanica* is here shown in its glory at Bourton House, Gloucestershire.

Genus (genera) A group of **species** that share important common characteristics, sufficient to distinguish them from other plants in the same **family**.

Glabrous Smooth and hairless. Glabrous leaves are usually shiny in appearance, e.g. in S. *blepharophylla* and S. *buchananii*.

Glandular-pubescent With hairs which have a swollen cell or cells (glands) secreting oils. Glandular-pubescent **species** are commonly sticky to the touch.

Group A group is intermediate between a **species** and a **cultivar**. Individual plants within a group are closely similar, and distinct from other individual plants within the species, but nevertheless show too much variation from one another to be regarded as members of the same cultivar. Examples are S. *officinalis* Purpurascens Group and S. *pratensis* Bertolinii Group.

Half hardy Damaged by exposure to temperatures below 0°C (32°F). See also **tender**.

Inflorescence The flowering stem and the flowers (and **bracts**, if present) that are borne on it.

Lanceolate Spearhead-shaped leaves, with a length 3–6 times as great as the width, tapering to a pointed tip.

Lax Plants of lax habit have stems insufficiently stiff to be self-supporting in an erect position. Growth tends to be sprawling.

Linear A leaf shape characterized by its slenderness, and by parallel or almost parallel leaf edges.

Lips The outermost parts of the **corolla** (the fused petals).

Notched Leaf margins with large pointed teeth (see also **dentate**).

Oblong Oblong leaf-blades are 2–3 times greater in length than in width, the central portion of the leaf having edges parallel to one another. The end of the leaf is blunt.

Ovary The basal part of the **pistil**, containing the ovules which develop into seeds after pollination.

Ovate Egg-shaped leaves, widest below the middle and rounded at both ends.

Panicle In *Salvia*, a branched inflorescence that comprises short **racemes**, all of which arise from a main central stem. In effect, a compound raceme. See p.13.

Pedicel The stalk of a flower.

Petiole The stalk of a leaf.

Pinnate A type of compound leaf, comprising four or more leaflets in two matching rows, one on each side of a central stalk (the rachis). In *Salvia* there is also a single leaflet at the end of the rachis.

Pistil The female reproductive organs of the flower, comprising the **ovary**, **style** and **stigma**.

Procumbent Stems that are more or less prostrate on the soil surface, but do not develop roots.

Raceme A type of inflorescence characterized by a single unbranched stem, and bearing an indefinite number of stalked flowers. The flowers at the base of the stem form and open first (see also **spike**).

Rhizome A creeping stem that grows either on the soil surface or shallowly below it. Lateral stems develop from a rhizome, either along its length or at its apex.

Rosette A formation of leaves in which all arise at or very close to ground level from a single central point, and radiate outwards from it.

Rugose Leaves that have wrinkled lines and veins, which do not form a regular pattern, on their upper surfaces.

Sagittate An arrowhead-shaped leaf. The two triangular basal lobes point backwards, towards the stalk.

Sepals The organs making up the **calyx**. In *Salvia* the sepals are fused.

Serrate Saw-toothed leaf margins. Closely similar to **dentate**, but differing in that the teeth all point in the direction of the leaf tip.

Species The basic unit of classification of living organisms. All individual plants in a species share a number of features (particularly in the flower), which distinguish them from members of all other species, and are usually capable of cross-fertilization.

Specific epithet The second part of the scientific name of a plant (or animal), following the name of the genus, and applied to the species. 'Specific' in this case is the adjective derived from the word 'species'.

Spike A form of **inflorescence** sharing all the features of a **raceme** except that the flowers are stalkless (sessile).

Stamens The male reproductive organs of a flower. Each stamen consists of a stalk (the filament) and one or more anthers in which the pollen is produced. In *Salvia* each stamen has two anthers.

Stigma The outermost part of the **pistil**. This is the part that receives pollen.

Style The long, narrow part of the **pistil**, with the ovary at its basal end and the **stigma** at its tip.

Sub-species (abbrev. **subsp.**) A population of plants within a **species** that differs substantially in a number of characters from the type species as described. Sub-species occur naturally and are usually found in a separate location from the type.

Subtend In the case of **bracts**, inserted directly below a flower or a **cyme**.

Tender Susceptible to damage by exposure to temperatures below 5°C (41°F).

Tube The basal part of the **corolla**. In most salvias, narrow in relation to its length.

Type A plant that is identical, or very closely similar to, the species as originally described by its **author**; also called the 'species type' or the 'type of the species'. **Sub-species**, **varieties** and **forms** differ from the type.

Variety (abbrev. **var.**) A population occurring naturally within a species, differing in a very small number of characters from the type species as described. Unlike a **sub-species**, a variety usually shares, at least in part, the same distribution in the wild as the type species (see also **form**).

Verticillaster A unit of a whorled **inflorescence**, in *Salvia* comprising a pair of clusters of flowers. The clusters are on opposite sides of the inflorescence stem, and each is a **cyme**. See p.13.

Whorl In *Salvia*, a group of three or more flowers arranged around the same point on an **inflorescence** stem.

APPENDIX 2
SALVIAS FOR ROCK GARDENS

It is a pity that, in cool temperate countries like Britain, salvias are little seen in rock gardens. Below I have suggested a few species that perform well in the kind of growing conditions found in rock gardens – sun and excellent drainage. Those marked * are ideal for an alpine house.

SPECIES FOR ROCK GARDENS

S. *argentea* (for its foliage; remove inflorescences as they form)

S. *caespitosa**

S. *canescens**

S. *chamaedryoides*

S. *lyrata*

S. *taraxacifolia**

LOW-GROWING SHRUBBY SPECIES FOR LARGER ROCK GARDENS

S. *blancoana*

S. *juriscii*

S. *lavandulifolia*

S. *multicaulis*

S. *officinalis* 'Berggarten'

OTHER POSSIBLE ROCK GARDEN SPECIES

S. *arizonica*

S. *blepharophylla*

S. *buchananii*

S. *oppositiflora*

S. *reptans*

S. *roemeriana*

S. *sinaloensis*

APPENDIX 3
READING ABOUT SALVIAS

PUBLICATIONS SPECIFICALLY ON SALVIA

BOOKS & BOOKLETS

CLEBSCH, B. *A Book of Salvias* (Timber Press, 1997)

DAVIES, B. *Salvias* Probus Gardens Handbook No 2 (1996)

TEMPLETON, S. *Salvias in Australia* (1998) Unlimited Perennials (see Where to Buy Salvias, opposite)

YEO, C. *Salvias* (1995) & *Salvias II* (1997) Pleasant View Nursery (see Where to Buy Salvias, opposite)

JOURNALS

ALZIAR, G. Catalogue Synonymique des *Salvia* du Monde (World Catalogue of *Salvia* Synonyms) (1988–92) *Biocosme Mesogéen* Vols 5 (3–4), 6 (1–2 & 4), 7 (1–2) & 9 (2–3)

COLBORN, N. 'Hardy *Salvia*' *The Garden* Vol 122 (11, 1997)

COMPTON, J. 'Salvias from the High Sierras' *The Garden* Vol 118 (11, 1993)

COMPTON, J. 'Mexican Salvias in Cultivation' *The Plantsman* Vol 15 (4, 1994)

DUFRESNE, R. F. 'Sage Advice' *The American Nurseryman* (15 August 1995)

LLOYD, C. 'Tender *Salvia*' *The Garden* Vol 122 (4, 1997)

OTHER SOURCES OF INFORMATION

ALPINE GARDEN SOCIETY *Encyclopaedia of Alpines* (1993)

ARMITAGE, A. M. *Herbaceous Perennial Plants*, 2nd ed. (Stipes Publishing, Champaign, Illinois, USA, 1997)

BEAN, W. J. *Trees and Shrubs Hardy in the British Isles* Vol IV (1980)

BECKETT, K. *The Container Garden* (Frances Lincoln, 2nd edition, 1992)

BLOOM, A. *Hardy Perennials* (Faber & Faber, 1956)

CHATTO, B. *The Dry Garden* (Dent, 1978)

DENO, N. C. *Seed Germination Theory and Practice* (published by the author, 139 Lenor Drive, State College, Pennsylvania 16801, USA, 1994)

European Garden Flora Vol 6 (Cambridge University Press, in preparation)

GREENWOOD, P. & HALSTEAD, A. *Pests and Diseases* (Dorling Kindersley/Royal Horticultural Society, 1997)

HAY, R. K. M. and WATERMAN, P. G. *Volatile Oil Crops* (Longman, 1993)

PHILLIPS, R. & FOY, N. *Herbs* (Pan Books, 1990)

The New Royal Horticultural Society Dictionary of Gardening Vol 4 (Macmillan, 1992)

New York Botanic Gardens Encyclopaedia of Horticulture Vol 9 (1982)

The RHS Plant Finder (Dorling Kindersley, published annually)

THOMAS, G. S. *Perennial Garden Plants* (Dent and Timber Press/Sagapress, 3rd edition, 1990)

APPENDIX 4
WHERE TO BUY SALVIAS

Most of these nurseries have a garden or display area where some of the species they sell can be seen growing. Telephone nurseries before making a special journey. *The RHS Plant Finder*, published annually, is an indispensable guide to availability and sources of supply in Britain.

The Hardy Plant Society is usually able to offer to its members a considerable range of salvia species in its seed distribution service. It is contactable via the Administrator, Mrs Pam Adams, Little Orchard, Great Comberton, Pershore, Worcestershire WR10 3DP. **P**=plants, **S**=seeds.

BRITISH ISLES

Jim & Jenny Archibald (**S**)
Bryn Collen, Ffrostrasol, Llandysul, Dyfed SA44 5SB

Chiltern Seeds (**S**), Bortree Stile, Ulverston, Cumbria LA12 7PB

Four Seasons (**P**), Forncett St Mary, Norwich, Norfolk NR16 1JT

Green Farm Plants (**P**)
Bury Court, Bentley, Farnham, Surrey GU10 5LZ

The Hannays of Bath (**P**)
Sydney Wharf Nursery, Bathwick, Bath BA2 4ES

Brian Hiley (**P**), 25 Little Woodcote Estate, Wallington, Surrey SM5 4AU

Hopley's Plants Ltd (**P**)
High Street, Much Hadham, Hertfordshire SG10 6BU

Longhall Nursery (**P**), Stockton, Warminster, Wiltshire BA12 0SE

Perhill Nurseries (**P**), Worcester Rd, Great Witley, Worcester WR6 6JT

Plant World Botanic Gardens (**P & S**) 56 St. Marychurch Rd, Newton Abbot, Devon TQ12 4SE

Pleasant View Nursery (**P & S**), Two Mile Oak, Denbury, Newton Abbot, Devon TQ12 6DG

Thompson & Morgan (UK) Ltd (**S**)
Poplar Lane, Ipswich IP8 3BU

Gibberellic acid is sold by
Sigma Chemical Co, Sigma-Aldrich Co Ltd, Fancy Road, Poole, Dorset BH12 4QH.

Note: This company normally sells only to professional users or research institutes and reserves the right to decline a prospective customer.

FRANCE

B & T World Seeds (**S**), Paguignan, 34210 Olonzac

Horticulture Marie Fournier (**P**), Patrie, 32110 Magnan

Pépinière de la Foux (**P**), Chemin de la Foux, 83220 Le Pradet

Pépinière Santonine (**P**), 'Tout-y-Faut', 17260 Villars en Pons

ITALY

Vivaio Luciano Noaro (**P**)
Via Vittorio Emanuele, 151, 18033, Camporosso (IM)

AUSTRALIA

Belrose Nursery
Bundaleer Street, Belrose

Cloudehill Gardens & Nursery
89 Olinda-Monbulk Rd
Olinda, Victoria

Parker's Nursery
45 Tennyson Avenue
Turramurra, NSW

The Digger's Club
Heronswood,
105 Latrobe Parade
Dromana, Victoria

Unlimited Perennials,
369 Boomerang Drive,
Lavington, NSW 2641

NEW ZEALAND

Marshwood Gardens Ltd,
Leonard Rd, West Plains,
No 4RD, Invercargill

NORTH AMERICA

Berkeley Horticultural Nursery
1310 McGee Ave, Berkeley
California 94703

Canyon Creek Nursery
3527 Dry Creek Rd, Orville
California 95965

Logee's Greenhouses
55 North Street, Danielson
Connecticut 06239

The Sandy Mush Herb Nursery
316 Surrett Cove Road, Leicester
North Carolina 28748

Southern Perennials & Herbs
98 Bridges Road, Tylertown,
Mississippi 39667

APPENDIX 5
WHERE TO SEE SALVIAS

See also Where to Buy Salvias and National Collections.

NC=National Collection
NT= National Trust Property

BRITISH ISLES

Abbotsbury Gardens, Abbotsbury, Weymouth, Dorset DT3 4LA

Bourton House Garden, Bourton-on-the-Hill, Moreton-in-Marsh, Gloucestershire GL56 9AE

Bressingham Gardens (The Dell), Bressingham, Diss, Norfolk IP22 2BT

Cannington College, Cannington, Bridgwater, Somerset TA5 2LS

Beth Chatto Gardens Ltd, Elmstead Market, Colchester, Essex CO7 7DB

Chelsea Physic Garden, 66 Royal Hospital Road, London SW3 4HS

Coleton Fishacre Garden (**NT**), Coleton, Kingswear, Dartmouth, Devon TQ6 0EQ

Dyffryn Gardens, St Nicholas, Cardiff CF5 6SU

Kingston Maurward College Gardens (**NC**), Kingston Maurward, Dorchester, Dorset DT2 8PY

Logan Botanic Garden, Ardwell, Stranraer, Dumfries & Galloway DG9 9ND

National Botanic Garden, Glasnevin, Dublin 9, Ireland

Newby Hall and Gardens, Ripon, North Yorkshire HG4 5AE

Overbecks Garden (**NT**), Sharpitor, Salcombe, Devon TQ8 8LW

Pleasant View Nursery (**NC**) address as Appendix 4

Probus Gardens, Probus, Truro, Cornwall TR2 4HQ

Powis Castle, Welshpool, Powys SY21 8RF

Royal Horticultural Society Gardens:

    Hyde Hall, Rettendon, Chelmsford, Essex CM2 8ET

    Rosemoor, Great Torrington, Devon EX38 8PH

    Wisley, Woking, Surrey GU23 6QB

Trellisick Garden (**NT**), Feock, Truro, Cornwall TR3 6QL

CONTINENTAL EUROPE

Jardin Botanique de la Ville de Nice (**NC**), Corniche Fleurie 78, 06200 Nice, France

Horticulture Marie Fournier (**NC**), Patrie, 32110 Magnan, France

Pépinière de la Foux (**NC**), Chemin de la Foux, 83220 Le Pradet, France

Giardini Botanici Hanbury, La Mortola, Ventimiglia, Liguria, Italy

Kwekerij VOF, Roger and Linda Bastin, Trichterweg 148a, 6446 Brunssum, The Netherlands

NORTH AMERICA

Denver Botanic Gardens, 909 York St, Denver, Colorado 80206

Elizabeth F. Gamble Garden Center, 1431 Waverley St, Palo Alto, California 94301

Santa Barbara Botanic Garden 1212 Mission Canyon Rd, Santa Barbara, California 93105

Strybing Arboretum Society Ninth Avenue at Lincoln Way San Francisco, California 94117

Wave Hill Gardens, 675 W 252nd St, Bronx, New York 10471

AUSTRALIA

Cloudehill Gardens & Nursery
The Digger's Club
Unlimited Perennials

addresses as Appendix 4

NEW ZEALAND

Auckland Regional Botanic Gardens, 102 Hill Rd, Manurewa, Auckland

Marshwood Gardens Ltd address as Appendix 4

INDEX

Page numbers in *italics* refer to illustrations, those in **bold** refer to main entries

ACKNOWLEDGEMENTS

The photographs for this book were taken at Bourton House, Chelsea Physic Garden, Colegraves Seeds Ltd, Kingston Maurward College, Pershore and Hindlip College and the Worcester Garden of Tony Poulton. Material was also supplied by Terry Dagley. The cooperation of all individuals and organizations concerned is gratefully acknowledged.

Without the advice, assistance and support of a large number of people this would have been a much poorer book, and a much less gratifying one to have written.

I would like to acknowledge the help, willingly given, of the following: Terry Dagley, Peggy Heaton and Stephen Taffler of the Hardy Plant Society; Beryl Davies of Probus Gardens; Linda Jones, Diana Miller, Nick Morgan and Sylvia Williams of the Royal Horticultural Society Garden, Wisley; the staff of the libraries of Pershore & Hindlip College, the Royal Botanic Gardens, Kew and the Royal Horticultural Society; Dr Ray Harley of Kew; Ian Hedge of the Royal Botanic Gardens, Edinburgh; Sue Minter and Fiona Crumley of the Chelsea Physic Garden; Dr Pier Giorgio Campodonico and Sergio Orrao of the Giardini Botanici Hanbury at La Mortola; Michel Derbier of the Jardin Botanique de la Ville de Nice; Dr James Compton of the University of Reading; Paul Williams, head gardener of Bourton House; Howard England and Colin Sharp of Dyffryn Gardens; the Hon Mrs Peter Healing of The Priory, Kemerton; John Hubbard of Chilcombe House, David Mason and Tony Murdoch of the National Trust gardens at Coleton Fishacre and Overbecks respectively; Jimmy Hancock, formerly head gardener at Powis Castle; Chris Brickell, former director-general of the Royal Horticultural Society; Louise Sutton; Pat Vlasto of the Dorset group of the NCCPG; Graham Pattison of the NCCPG; Peter Elliman and Nigel Hewish, head gardeners at Cannington College and Kingston Maurward College respectively; Nick Dakin-Elliot and Bob Hares of Pershore & Hindlip College; Norrie Pope of Hadspen Manor Garden and Nursery; Margaret Hiley; Tim Ingram; Pierre Jourdan and Monique Cariou of the Pépinière de la Foux; Robin Bowers, principal of Kingston Maurward College; Pam Jordan of Colegraves Seeds Ltd; Ralph Cockburn of Floranova Ltd & Elite Seeds Ltd; Ian Prest of Suttons Seeds Ltd; Clare Williams of Thompson & Morgan (UK) Ltd; Anna Mumford and Ali Myer of David & Charles, and editor Jo Weeks.

Last but by no means least, my wife Deirdre, who has typed the entire script, prepared the index, made – and has had readily adopted – numerous suggestions for its improvement in content and wording, and has patiently endured much during the writing of this book from a husband vastly distracted by the genus *Salvia*.

The responsibility for any errors is, of course, my own.